# The Uses of Philosophy

# The Uses of Philosophy

Mary Warnock

BLACKWELL
Oxford UK & Cambridge USA

First Published 1992

Blackwell Publishers
108 Cowley Road
Oxford OX4 1JF
UK

Three Cambridge Center
Cambridge, Massachusetts 02142
USA

*British Library Cataloguing in Publication Data*

A CIP catalogue record for this book is available from
the British Library.

*Library of Congress Cataloging-in-Publication Data*

Warnock, Mary.
The uses of philosophy/Mary Warnock.
p.    cm.
Includes index.
ISBN 0–631–18038–9 — ISBN 0–631–18583–6
1. Philosophy.  2. Ethics.  3. Philosophy, Modern.  I. Title.
B53.W35   1992
101—dc20                              91-43916
                                          CIP

Typeset in 11 on 12½ pt Sabon
by Graphicraft Typesetters, Hong Kong
Printed in Great Britain by Billing & Sons Ltd Worcester

This book is printed on acid-free paper

# Contents

# Introduction

The papers collected together in this volume all started as lectures. They have in common also that they were all addressed to non-philosophical audiences, and that they have not, with the exception of the last, been published hitherto. I have not attempted to change their form, and thus they may seem somewhat obtrusively lecture-like, efforts to catch the flagging attention of a passive audience being ill concealed. Moreover, within the different lectures, written at different times and delivered before different audiences, there is inevitably a certain amount of repetition, a few perhaps tediously recurrent themes. Like the clergyman who, in reply to the criticism that he had preached the same sermon two years in succession on Christmas Day, said that he had had no reason to change his views on the nativity during the year, I may seem all too seldom to have changed my views. For this I can only apologize. A book of wholly non-overlapping chapters would have been a different book.

However, there may, I hope, be detected a legitimate thread running through the papers, different though their subjects are, and this is the thread of philosophy itself. All of them arose out of what could be roughly called a 'philosophical' consideration of the subject in hand, though this is more obvious in some cases than in others.

It has often been remarked how radically philosophy has changed in the last forty years or so. In the 1950s it was widely regarded (by non-philosophers) as frivolous, concerned only with words, rather than with deep questions about the nature of things, detached from values and coldly analytic. Now it has become, to use an old-fashioned word, 'committed'. It can be a practical, even an interventionist subject. There is truth in this observation, especially as regards moral and political philosophy, which, immediately after World War II, flourished largely on the belief that there was a special moral language (and perhaps a political language as well, though political philosophy was not much in vogue in universities at that time). It was to the analysis of this language and its special uses to praise and condemn that moral philosophers turned their attention and that of their pupils. It was noticed, as it could hardly fail to be, that other things were praised and condemned that had nothing to do with morality; and there were those who tried to show how morality was different, in general, from other fields of discourse. But it was nevertheless the discourse itself that was at the centre of discussion. Philosophers were not supposed to engage professionally in the consideration of what was actually right or wrong, and they became annoyed and touchy if sociologists or anthropologists claimed to show that the analysis they, the philosophers, engaged in contained a hidden set of moral values.

All this began to change in the 1960s and 1970s, partly as a result of student unrest. It became necessary, especially in the United States, for those teaching philosophy to take sides on such issues as draft-dodging and other civil disobedience. They were forced to discuss not simply the concept of justice, but whether there could be such a thing as a just war.

In fields other than morals it is perhaps less easy to point to a radical change, though here too the climate is undeniably different. Yet such is the general relation between words (or concepts) and the things they are used for that it has never been possible for philosophers, however analytic their intent, to talk about the discourse of causation or of time or pleasure and pain, for example, without, in doing so, considering at the same time what actual phenomena the terms were invented for. Our language is so crucially bound up, at various levels of generality, with the way we engage with the world that it could never have been plausible to claim to attend only to the words and not at all to what they are supposed to designate. Yet, perhaps because of the increasing 'commitment' of moral philosophy, it became gradually the fashion for philosophers to turn their minds to real-life issues only marginally, if at all, connected with values, and to involve themselves more than before with such problems as the nature of mental illness (Can there be said to be such a thing as a 'disease of the mind'?) or the relation between computer calculations and mental arithmetic. Thus there is now supposed to be a branch of philosophy called 'applied' (or 'practical') philosophy. If there is, I do not regard these papers as falling under that description for the most part. For, as I have said, they are not properly to be judged as technical or professional philosophy at all. In writing them, I have doubtless made use of philosophy, but I would not claim to have been actually practising the subject.

There is, I think, a point worth emphasizing in this connection. Philosophy is to some extent a seamless garment. It does not readily lend itself to being split up into bits. (I would make an exception, though not a whole-hearted one, for formal logic, which may reasonably be studied and made an object of research on its own, as a highly generalized and abstract form of mathematics.) I am not suggesting that every professional philosopher must know all about all branches of the subject. There are doubtless legitimate specializations, particularly in the history of ideas, in my view one of the most important branches of the subject. Nevertheless, it is best for philosophers if they can practise their trade in a setting in which the subject as a whole is all around them; and it is essential for students to be taught as broadly within the subject as possible. I therefore very much deplore the growth of specialist departments (such as departments of the philosophy of religion or of medical ethics). For such subjects, interesting and respectable enough in themselves, are essentially parasitic on the totality of philosophy, and cannot flourish in the absence of their host. I would be very much depressed if the essays in this volume were taken to license (still worse, exemplify) the dressing up of issues of the day with some fancy philosophical glad rags, detached from serious learning and research.

With the entry of philosophers into the world, perhaps even into the market-place, it is natural that they should often be expected to perform in ways alien to them; and especially that they may be expected to deliver solutions to problems which could be generally accepted as 'correct'. However, it should be made clear to, for example, civil servants or hospital administrators (who may seek a philosopher for every hospital ethics committee) that philosophy is not in the business of providing solutions to problems. If a philosopher solves a problem as part of his professional activity, it is likely to be a very minute and specialist problem that has bothered none but his professional colleagues. Generally the business of philosophy is most easily understood as that of raising questions about things which might seem to have been settled, or, more often, might never have seemed to be questionable at all. Sometimes a philosopher may contribute to a discussion by showing that the question to be addressed is different from what had been supposed. Thus, for example, a philosopher involved in a discussion of the question 'When does life begin?' may argue that this is in fact a question about the stage of embryonic development at which we should start to treat human life as worthy of protection, rather than a question (which it looks like) of fact, such that increased scientific knowledge might entitle us to answer it in a way that could be agreed on.

People who draw the kind of distinctions exemplified above are often extremely irritating to those who are not philosophers, who want to cut the cackle and get on with the action. In the 1950s, when Gilbert Ryle's exploration of so-called category mistakes was much discussed, a question was set in a final examination paper at Oxford which read: 'If I mistake a wax effigy of a police-man for a policeman, what kind of mistake have I made?' The short answer to this, of course, is 'a silly mistake'. The question was intended as a peg on which to hang a discussion of what constituted a 'category'; but the temptation, even among can-didates, to give the short answer must have been strong and hard to resist. The non-philosophical world would not have resisted it, and thus the reputation of philosophy as both trivial and given to absurd distinctions would have been confirmed.

The relevant point is that if philosophers are expected to give answers to questions in such a way that those questions need not be raised again, then they are the wrong people for the job. Their business is the very opposite of this. They may ask questions that no one else would have thought of. There was thus some dis-appointment among ministers when the Committee of Enquiry into Human Fertilization and Embryology, of which I was chair-man, did not come up with agreed, proved solutions to the problems in the new-style obstetrics and gynaecology, on which we had been asked to advise with a view to legislation (the first four or five of the papers which follow were derived more or less directly from work done on this committee). In so far as the questions addressed were questions of morality, it would have been impossible to ensure agreement. The committee took its own view (not always unanimous); the most that a philosopher chairman could do was to direct the attention of members to the nature of the questions being asked (and, as I have suggested, this was not always popular) and then to try to set out the principles which seemed to govern the answers suggested. These principles could then themselves be scrutinized, where possible taking into account the ways in which they had been deployed by philosophers in the past.

It is to be hoped that the discussions that take place in committees are helped, not hindered, by such philosophical contributions. But the outcome, the reports of the committees, will inevitably be the result of nothing except these discussions. And here I suppose there emerges a similarity (nothing more) between committees seeking solutions and philosophers working in their own professional capacity. Dialogue or discussion is not accidentally, but essentially, the proper mode of advance. Even if a philosopher works alone in his study and never speaks to anyone else (not a good way of working), he will in the end be the subject of, perhaps participator in, discussion, further questions, more attempted replies, an unending dialogue.

Philosophy, then, is a highly general kind of exploration; and it is a game for an unlimited number of players. In the papers that follow I was always, in addressing a particular question, trying to suggest to a non-philosophical audience that these general ways of looking at the matter existed for them, as well as for philosophers, and might sometimes be fruitful. To suggest this kind of thing is in my view a use to which the habit of philosophical thought may properly be put; and it can prove worthwhile in a number of areas quite different from those that have been my own concern (such as in business management or the setting of economic priorities in various fields).

To turn to the essays themselves, the first three are intended to hang together. They were delivered as the Firth Lectures in the

University of Nottingham under the general title 'A Race Apart'. The subject-matter suggested itself to me partly as a result of the work of the Committee of Enquiry into Human Fertilization and Embryology, whose report was published in 1984. They were influenced also by work I had undertaken previously as chairman of the Home Office Advisory Committee on the use of animals in laboratories and as a member of the Royal Commission on Environmental Pollution. Such committees as these give a rare chance for updating one's education, and I shall never cease to be grateful for such chances, especially valuable for someone brought up, as I was, in a virtually science-free system of education, both at school and at university.

The fourth paper was delivered in 1991 to the Eleventh International Human Genome Workshop, under the chairmanship of Sir Walter Bodmer. The fifth was the annual UNICEF lecture for 1990, delivered on the day on which the United Kingdom signed the United Nations Charter of Children's Rights; but some of the ideas, once again, arose out of the 1984 report.

Essays six and seven are set side by side because I think they reflect a shared or overlapping political interest, itself arising partly out of the work a committee (any committee) must do if it is set up to advise ministers in areas of moral controversy. I have, over the years, become increasingly interested in the question of how legislation is to be introduced in the absence of moral consensus, and how, in a climate in which we are repeatedly reminded that consensus does not exist, government is actually to be carried on. These are questions in what may roughly be described as political philosophy. The first of these two lectures was given as the Dixon Lecture at the Queen's University, Belfast, in 1989; the second at a meeting in Edinburgh in 1988.

The eighth paper was a public lecture at the University of Kent in Canterbury, delivered in 1990. In a way it follows from a lecture given there some ten years earlier, at a time when I was a member of the Independent Broadcasting Authority. In that lecture I was exclusively concerned with broadcasting and its regulation. Since that time, many of the problems associated with the regulation (or deregulation) of broadcasting have been discussed in terms of 'standards' in broadcast output. The question of 'standards' has become equally a matter of discussion in the field of education, and the present paper is intended to call attention to some of the similarities between the two sets of standards and the parallel questions of responsibility for setting and maintaining them.

Three further papers on education follow. The first of these started as a contribution to a symposium on education held at Rugby School in the mid-1980s. The second was a talk given to the Friends of the Girls' Public Day School Trust in 1980. The third was delivered at Manchester University in 1991, at a symposium on higher education.

The twelfth paper, 'Religious Imagination', was the first Colton Memorial Lecture given at the City of London School for Girls in 1989. It is a greatly expanded version of a University Sermon preached in the University Church of St Mary's in Oxford in 1984.

Papers 13 and 14 are the most nearly philosophical of the contents of the present volume. The first was a contribution to a discussion of related topics at St George's House, Windsor, in 1989, the second a lecture (the Miller Lecture) given before a meeting of the Association of Child Psychiatrists in 1984.

The final paper is, I suppose, a bit of a joke. Having recently written a magazine feature about how manufacturers seem to neglect the old section of the market, I was asked to address an annual meeting of Age Concern on the subject of choice. I thought I would try to make this talk both intelligible and philosophical. The extent to which I succeeded may be judged by readers. Age Concern published this lecture as one of their occasional papers, and I am grateful to them for permission to reproduce it here.

I would like to take the opportunity, too, to thank all the universities and other institutions mentioned above for having invited me to speak to them and for the chance this has given me to explore some of the ways in which I think philosophy may be useful when applied, albeit indirectly, to a variety of different issues.

I believe that those who study philosophy as undergraduates, as a serious part of their course, as well as those who teach them, tend to develop a way of thinking which is peculiarly philosophical and which may have a place in the consideration of many issues which also engage moralists and journalists, doctors, lawyers, and politicians. My hope is that this generally philosophical mode may in part become clear in the pieces which follow; but I suppose it is more than possible that they may reveal nothing except the style of the one continuous person who was the author of all of them. Nevertheless, despite fears of manifesting prejudice or vested interest, there remains a further paper to be written on the usefulness of the serious study of philosophy by undergraduates, especially those who are about to enter a completely different kind of activity. My hope is that the lectures collected here may lend some support to such a defence of philosophy, should it become necessary.

*Note.* Throughout the following chapters I have used the word 'man', and the related personal pronouns 'he', 'him', and 'his' as referring to the species Man. I have in no way wished to refer to men as opposed to women. In referring to the species, the notion of gender plays no part. This is the use of 'man' (the Anglo-Saxon use) that I made in my lectures when they were originally given, and I have not changed it for the purposes of publication.

# 1

# *Man and Other Animals*

In the first three chapters I propose to raise the question whether we humans ought to think of ourselves as members of a unique, out-of-the-ordinary species of animal, with principles of conduct towards one another that do not apply, or not in the same way, to our conduct towards the rest of nature, even towards other members of the animal kingdom. My conclusion will be that we are indeed, as humans, a race apart; and this, I hope to suggest, has consequences both for the way we should treat members of our own species and how we should treat the rest of the natural world.

In this first chapter, then, I want to consider man's relationship with other animals. It hardly needs saying that the Judaeo-Christian tradition places man at the top of the hierarchy, created last in the garden of Eden, in the image of God, to have dominion over all other creatures. Admittedly, in the first version of the creation myth, in Genesis 1, it seems that men were supposed to be vegetarians: 'And God said, Behold, I have given you every herb bearing seed, which is upon the face of all the earth, and every tree, in the which is the fruit of a tree yielding seed; to you it shall be for meat'. (Gen. 1 : 29).[1] But the other animals equally, in this creation story, seem destined for vegetarianism: 'And to every beast of the earth, and to every fowl of the air, and to everything that creepeth upon the earth, wherein there is life, I have given every green herb for meat: and it was so' (Gen. 1 : 30). But this state of things did not last; and after the Flood, God said to Noah, 'And the fear of you and the dread of you shall be upon every beast of the earth, and upon every fowl of the air, upon all that moveth upon the earth, and upon all the fishes of the sea; into your hand are they delivered. Every moving thing that liveth shall be meat for you; even as the green herb have I given you all things' (Gen. 9 : 2–3). Thus the mythology reflected and justified the established tradition, that men might use other animals however they pleased, harnessing them, shearing them, milking them, and eating them – that is, on the whole, the natural and common way that men have lived among the other animals.

But the morality of such a way of life has been challenged. I want now to consider some of the moral arguments as they have been expounded recently, within the framework of Western philosophy. These days, as I need not tell you, philosophy has a severely practical bent, very different from those days in the 1930s when the most pressing problem to be discussed was whether, if one went to post a letter, one's duty was to post it or only to set oneself to post it (for one might become suddenly paralysed and be unable to put the letter in the box; would one then have defaulted on one's duty?). Even in the 1950s, though we were in some ways nearer to reality, we were more concerned with the language in which moral utterances were characteristically made than with the content of those utterances. Now, in contrast, moral philosophy consists largely in the application of theory to immediate problems. The change began in the United States, where ethical questions about the Vietnam War began to preoccupy both university students and their teachers. Philosophy could not remain detached any more; and throughout the 1960s and 1970s the demand for 'relevance' dominated the universities. Gradually the mood of practicality spread, and it is now prevalent both here and in Australia, as well as in the United States.

Meanwhile, another change has come about: the vast growth and swift development within the biological sciences. Whereas in the 1950s the general public, when they thought of scientists, thought first of physicists and chemists, now they think of biologists and those working in the new fields of cell biology, biochemistry, and other related subjects. It is no surprise that philosophers are especially called upon to give their views on the problems arising within this area. For within the biological sciences questions are raised about birth and death, sickness and health, the very nature of human life. Through television and the techniques of photography we know far more about the natural world than we used to, and so it is understandable that questions should be increasingly raised about the role of humans in the world and their relationship with the rest of nature. Inevitably moral philosophers have concerned themselves not only with the treatment by human beings of one another, but also with their treatment of animals; and thousands of words have been written.

On the whole this is a welcome development. Nevertheless, as is always the case with fashionable subjects, there have been those who have eagerly jumped on the bandwagon and shed more darkness than light. There are some very bad books; and this (as well as lack of time) shall be my excuse for not taking you through all the philosophical arguments with regard to men and animals, but instead trying to give you a short account of the most important issues, from which I shall draw conclusions which cannot of course be proved.

If we are to concern ourselves with the relationship between men and other animals, then the very first question must be that of meat-eating. If there is anyone who is doubtful about the morality of man's dominion over animals, then they must, as a first step, advocate vegetarianism. For nothing is so conclusive a mark of the separation of humans from other species as that humans eat the others. No tyrant, however despotic his rule, has ever farmed his slaves, fattened them, and slaughtered them for the table. If there are those who say that to use animals for human purposes is wrong, then the first wrong and the most important is eating the animals. So I start with the moral question Ought we to be vegetarians? This is one of the questions on which philosophers have exercised their minds in recent years. I want to take as an example the work of Peter Singer, Director of the Centre for Human Bioethics at Monash University. In the prologue to a collection of articles by various hands called 'In Defence of Animals' he has set out his views, and from this I shall quote.[2]

But first it is necessary to state one obvious fact: there are many different reasons for becoming a vegetarian. There are people who dislike eating meat simply as a matter of taste; there are those who find meat too expensive or who believe that it is bad for their hearts; and there are those who are vegetarians on moral grounds, but for whom the grounds are the extravagance and waste of producing meat when so many people in the world are starving for want of land and grain. With none of these reasons for vegetarianism am I concerned. The only kind of reasons I shall discuss are those which are concerned with the status of the animals to be eaten.

I return to Professor Singer. Singer is a utilitarian. That is to say, he holds that actions of a particular kind are right if they or their consequences give rise to more pleasure than pain over all, wrong if they give rise to more pain than pleasure. But the great question is, and has always been, whose pain or pleasure is to count? Singer argues that in so far as animals other than human animals are capable of feeling pain – capable of suffering – they must be taken into account in the calculation of pains and pleasures necessary for determining whether a kind of action is wrong or right.

When Bentham and J. S. Mill first expounded the doctrine of utilitarianism (though they were not of course the first consequentialist moral philosophers), they confined the field of balanced pain and pleasure to humans. Bentham, it is true, realized that if the capacity for suffering were the criterion for counting in the felicific calculus, then other animals besides men should be included. 'The question', he said, 'is not Can they reason? nor Can they talk? but Can they suffer?'; and he wrote,

> The French have already discovered that the blackness of the skin is no reason why a human being should be abandoned without redress to the caprice of a tormentor. It may one day come to be recognised that the number of legs, the villosity of the skin, or the termination of the os sacrum are reasons equally insufficient for abandoning a sensitive creature to the same fate'.[3]

But Bentham was no philosopher. He was interested in legislation and in establishing a means for telling good law from bad. He was not prepared to follow his criterion of suffering to its conclusion. J. S. Mill, on the other hand, though he regarded the criterion of right as the balance of pleasure over pain, introduced a distinction between different kinds of pleasure, and gave superior weight to the pleasures of the civilized over those of all others. Children, savages, and animals were incapable of experiencing these pleasures, and therefore they need not be considered in their own right in the utilitarian calculus.

Singer, however, goes back to the thought which Bentham expressed. Any creature that can suffer must have its sufferings taken into account in the weighing up of right and wrong. Therefore, if animals suffer through being prepared for eating and subsequently killed, then this must outweigh the trivial pleasure that humans get from eating meat. For there is no serious deprivation, only a loss of a specific taste and variety, involved in becoming a vegetarian. This is the simplest version of his case:

> Where animals and humans have similar interests – and we might take the interest in avoiding physical pain as an example, for it is an interest that humans clearly share with other animals – those interests are to be counted equally, with no automatic discount, just because one of the beings is not human.[4]

The argument against giving humans priority is, in Singer's view, that there are no characteristics to which we can point that would mark off humans from other animals. If, following Aristotle, we define humans as 'rational animals', we get into difficulties about the meaning of 'rational'. The philosopher Locke, writing in a quite different context, was clear about this specific difference between beast and man. Men were rational and showed it in being able to think in abstract terms and go beyond what they actually sensed to form an idea of absent or nonexistent things. Moreover they could do arithmetic. Brutes, he said, do not either abstract or compound. If they think, 'it is only in particular ideas, just as they received them from the senses. They are, the best of them, tied up within those narrow bounds, and have not the faculty to enlarge them by any kind of alteration.'[5] But there are all kinds of things, even kinds of calculations, that animals do undertake, as even Locke admits, and so this kind of criterion seems useless. The more we know of the capacities of dolphins or chimpanzees, the less we can think of a total discontinuity between human and other abilities. More difficult still is the argument which in fact Singer mostly relies on. What are we to say about those humans who, while manifestly members of the species *Homo sapiens*, not only show no signs of reason, but will never be able to do so, by reason of the brain damage they have suffered. I quote Singer:

Why do we lock up chimpanzees in appalling primate research centres and use them in experiments that range from the uncomfortable to the agonising and lethal, yet would never think of doing the same to a retarded human being at a much lower mental level? The only possible answer is that the chimpanzee, no matter how bright, is not human while the retarded human is, no matter how dull he is. This is speciesism pure and simple and is as indefensible as the most blatant racism. There is no ethical basis for elevating membership of one particular species into a morally crucial characteristic. From an ethical point of view, we all stand on an equal footing whether we stand on two feet or four or none at all.

Here, then, we have the central accusation against those who want to use animals for their own purposes: the accusation of 'speciesism', or groundless prejudice; a prejudice which, like racism or sexism, overlooks the important similarities, being blinded by the trivial differences. Singer's conclusion is that the pain of other animals is as important, morally, as the pain of humans, because there is no important difference between humans and other animals. The central similarity is that we all feel pain.

But here Singer's argument takes a rather odd turn. So far we have been urged to be vegetarians because there is very good evidence that using animals for food causes them to suffer. Singer and other contributors to the collection are graphic in their descriptions of the horrors of factory farming and the methods used, for instance, to prepare veal for the market. They very plausibly argue that by every means at our disposal – legislation, boycott, and preaching – we should bring such practices as factory farming to an end. But suppose that we succeeded in our efforts and that no hens were reared except in farmyards, no eggs sold except free-range eggs, no veal consumed, no mutton except that guaranteed to come from sheep that had been humanely and painlessly slaughtered. Would we then be allowed to go back to eating meat? It seems that, according to Singer, we would. In examining Singer's arguments, in his book *Rights, Killing and Suffering*, R. G. Frey describes him as a 'conditional' vegetarian[6] – a vegetarian, that is, only until such time as animals are certain not to suffer from our eating them.

It seems to me that such arguments for vegetarianism miss the main point. It would be quite possible for someone to take the line that Singer takes and not be a vegetarian, on the grounds that boycotting food produced in a particular way would be ineffective; equally, it would be quite possible to be a vegetarian, on moral grounds, yet not especially care in what manner the animals were slaughtered or in what conditions they were kept up to the time of slaughter. There are, as everyone knows, religions which lay down that it is wrong to eat meat, without drawing any distinction between kinds of meat or ways of killing. For adherents of such religions the eating of meat is simply morally abhorrent in itself. But even if we discount (as Singer does) any religious argument or religious tradition, it would still be possible to argue that if the interests and rights to life of animals and men are to be considered as anything like equal, then it must be wrong to kill animals for the human table, no matter how humane the method of slaughter. And it is surprising that Singer does not take this view. Indeed, in a way he bypasses the question of killing altogether. He simply assumes that utilitarianism properly understood leads to the consideration of animal as well as human pain, and that this will lead us to give up meat.

The reason, I believe, why Singer does not deal directly with the question of *killing animals for food* is that he wants to show how unimportant it is to what species a creature belongs in determining how we should treat it. He is *pre*-committed, that is to say, to the wrongness of what he regards as 'speciesism'. Therefore, among all the different kinds of animals, including the human animal, he distinguishes between 'persons' and 'nonpersons', arguing that on utilitarian grounds it is more wrong to kill a 'person' than one not so designated. This is because 'persons' are capable of greater suffering; for not only are they able to feel physical pain, Singer says, but they have a kind of self-image which makes them feel the frustration of their hopes if they are killed. They have an interest in life, as well as in avoiding pain. These arguments are set out in a book published in 1979 called *Practical Ethics*.[7] Although Singer has changed some of his views since then, his main anti-speciesist position remains unchanged. In the book he concedes that it is contrary to common usage to speak of any non-humans as persons. But he is convinced that personhood must be ascribed on the basis of the possession of certain characteristics such as those I have just mentioned (roughly speaking, 'self-consciousness'), and he believes that some animals other than humans in fact possess these characteristics. He ascribes them confidently to dolphins and chimpanzees, less confidently to pigs, and not at all to flatworms, tadpoles, or human neonates. So he concludes that it does not matter very much if we kill flatworms or totally mentally incompetent humans; but it does matter if we kill creatures who take conscious pleasure in their lives and hope for their continuation. For to deprive those who are capable of experiencing it of hoped-for pleasure is wrong on the utilitarian principle.

It is not, of course, a sufficient response to a philosophical argument to say that its conclusion is contrary to common sense or ordinary usage. However, it is hard not to suspect that Singer has in the course of his argument introduced a wholly new sense of the word 'person'. For in real life and in law, where as Locke pointed out, the word has its primary use, a 'person' is a human being; and a human being is so designated if, in the light of his intelligence, self-awareness, memory, and capability of imagining the future as well as the past, he is deemed fit to take responsibility for his life. It may be that the word is sometimes extended, though rather uneasily, to include those who will one day be held responsible or to those who once were so and are so no longer. But legally and in all imaginable contexts it would be simply silly to ascribe personhood to creatures other than humans, since the word has meaning within the framework of purely human institutions such as that of property. Of course, Singer may use the word in a new sense if he chooses. But in doing so, he cannot take with the word those aspects of its meaning which make it so obviously true that persons may not be killed for the table. That aspect of the meaning remains firmly rooted in the use of the word for humans. He cannot persuade us to give up 'speciesism' by deeming some other animals also to be persons. The fact remains that we cannot morally contemplate farming, slaughtering, and eating humans; and this has nothing to do with whether or not they are persons.

It may be noted in passing that there is an incidental advantage that Singer gains from distinguishing, among non-human animals, those that are and those that are not to be deemed 'persons'. For those who claim that animals are to be treated as of equal importance to humans must answer two charges. The first is that, on their theory, they can give no reason for preferring a mentally defective human to a bright monkey. Singer answers this charge by claiming that there is indeed no reason to do so. For the monkey is a person, and the severely intellectually impaired human is not. But the second charge is that if animals are the equals of humans, have we to consider the feelings of wasps and mosquitoes and unwanted moles as much as those of humans themselves, to whom these creatures are destructive pests? To which Singer can answer no; only if someone could show that a mosquito deserved to be called a person should we be morally blameworthy for killing it.

Singer does not wish us to change our attitude towards animals or to turn vegetarian on the grounds that animals have a *right* to live; but his use of the word 'speciesism', parallel as it is with 'racism' and 'sexism', may suggest that an infringement of rights is involved, since people frequently speak of racism and sexism as offences against 'human rights'. And there is, notoriously, a strong animal rights movement, whose members base vegetarianism on the supposed rights of animals to live. Are we then infringing the rights of animals if we farm them and kill them for the table?

The concept of 'right', like that of 'person', is essentially a legal one. To take a very simple case, I cannot claim a right of way across your land simply on the ground that I want to walk across it or have an interest in doing so or even that, having an interest in it, I shall do you no harm by walking across it. I can claim a right if and only if there is in existence a law or by-law which lays down a right of way. I may believe that it would be altogether better and fairer if there were such a by-law. But in the absence of a by-law I can claim no right. I cite this simple example because the issue of rights is often confused by claims that are made about natural rights, human rights, or moral rights. Doubtless the argument in each of these cases is slightly different. But the fact remains that unless we can show that a law (of some kind or other) exists, we cannot claim a right. Thus, if we believe in a natural law, laying down, for example, that everyone should be allowed to seek food for himself and his family in order to avoid starvation, we are entitled to argue that there is an infringement of a natural right when people are forced to starve.

Human rights and moral rights make sense only against a background of a concept of a general 'human law', or what may come to the same, a 'moral law'. I do not suggest that to speak of human natural or moral rights is senseless. I suggest only that, to discover what they are supposed to be, it is necessary first to ascertain the content of that law, natural, human, or moral, under whose demands the right may be claimed. And the fact is, as we all know, there is wide divergence of opinion about the content of such laws or principles. Moreover, as soon as we recognize that what is in question here is the content of certain moral or general *principles*, it becomes clear not only that disagreement is likely, but that we have incorporated a moral dimension into the question of whether or not there exists a right. 'Is there such and such a moral right?' means 'Is there a moral principle enjoining us to permit such and such?' But this is only another way of saying 'Ought we to permit such and such?' The appeal to a right is redundant. Moreover, it has the additional drawback that it carries with it a spurious pretence to being definite, factual, and agreed. If someone says 'It is my right', this tends to produce an obedient reaction. If, on the other hand, someone says 'I think I ought to be allowed to do so-and-so', then it is obvious from the outset that this is a matter for discussion, the exchange of reasons, for justification on both sides, for explanation, and perhaps for compromise. If it is true that in the last analysis the claim to a moral right is no more than an expression of a moral belief, the belief, that is, that a law ought to exist which would secure the right, then often to claim that a right exists is positively misleading. Those who say that animals have a right to life can, at most, be understood to be saying that they believe there should be a law which would create such a right. And this is manifestly a moral judgement, not a judgement of what is the fact.

The idea that some animals, besides humans, are persons, I have argued, apart from its intrinsic oddity, can provide a ground for not eating meat only on the prior assumption that it is wrong to give preference to one species over another. The concept 'person' is extended in the light of this assumption. And it now seems that the concept of animal rights fares no better as a ground for not eating animals. For to argue that eating a chicken infringes that chicken's moral rights presupposes a moral principle that eating chickens is wrong, in the light of which principle, the chicken, or we on its behalf, may claim a right not to be eaten.

But if this is so, we ought to state the moral principle simply, and *start* with the proposition that it is wrong to eat chickens or other non-human animals. For the attempt to *derive* the wrongness either from the concept of personhood applied to chickens or from the notion of rights turns out to be circular. What we have, in each case, is a *prior* moral intuition, held on moral grounds. Such an intuition (that eating meat is wrong) cannot be *justified*, however sincerely and firmly it is held. The position for vegetarians of this intuitionist kind is little different from the position of those who are vegetarians on religious grounds. We must respect their beliefs, but not necessarily listen to their supposed arguments.

The argument from personhood and that from rights show indeed that there is, both in fact and in law, a vast gap between the attitude of most people, though not of all, towards humans and their attitude towards other animals; and that those who wish us to change things and narrow the gap must base their persuasive efforts quite openly on moral or religious grounds, and not attempt to take refuge in a redefinition of personhood or of the scope of rights. This gap in our attitudes is shown only slightly less starkly in the matter of research using laboratory animals. Indeed, there is little difference between the two cases, since after at most two laboratory procedures on an animal, that animal must, by law, be *destroyed*.

In this case, as in the case of eating animals, we must try to distinguish a moral objection to causing pain from a moral objection to using animals for research purposes and then killing them, however little pain they may have experienced in the whole process. With regard to research, it is particularly important to keep the two things distinct. For there are those who say that if research using laboratory animals is to be as useful as possible, then there must be some cases in which they will have to suffer pain. For suppose the research is concerned with the physiological nature of pain itself and how to reduce it. Is it not necessary in the interest of such research to cause quite severe pain to animals in order to examine its nature and its physiological or psychological effects? But generally, in English law, this is not permitted. Licences are issued to those who wish to use animals in their laboratories subject only to the condition that if the animal is in severe pain that is likely to endure, it will be pain-lessly destroyed, even if the project for which it was being used is not completed. Moreover, the granting of a licence is generally conditional upon an undertaking to carry out no painful proce-dures on an animal except under anaesthetic. So the law plainly recognizes the distinction between causing animals pain or suffer-ing and breeding them, using them, and killing them in the laboratory for human ends.

There is another clause in the law and in the regulations for the issuing of licences which lays down that as few animals as possible should be used in each research project. I am not certain of the logic of this. I can understand why scientists should be required to consider whether it is really necessary for them to use animals at all; but why, if they are to use them, should they use fewer rather than more? A strict utilitarian would, I suppose, argue that if pain or discomfort or even a strange life-style is to be imposed on animals in the laboratory, then these are negative things which must be weighed against the positive good to humans (or indeed to other animals) supposed to derive in the long term from the experiments. So if 500 mice are used in a project where 50 would do, there is ten times as much harm to be weighed against the probable good which is the outcome of the research, which good may not increase according to the number of mice used. But I cannot really take very seriously the idea of sum totals of pain or pleasure. Of course, if laboratory mice were a threatened species, then there would be quite different arguments in favour of using as few of them as possible. But the mice to be used are bred specially for the research, and they are in no way in danger of extinction as a species. If it is morally alright to use one mouse, it is morally alright to use 50 or 500, or so it seems to me. The pain or suffering we cause other creatures must in fact be measured individually. For each mouse feels its own pain, just as each human does.

But in the case of humans there is a difference. We do not hold of humans that one will replace another. No human is 'just as good' as one that has been killed; for each has his *own* value, both to us and to himself, and each has his own life to lead. Moreover, in the case of humans they will suffer more, each individually, if they realize that they are part of a holocaust in which other humans are being slaughtered. The same is not true of mice. Each mouse suffers and dies separately, with no side-glances at the other mice and no thought that there is injustice in the world into which it was bred and born.

However this may be, the consideration of the above examples, that of eating other animals and that of using them for experimental purposes, makes it perfectly evident that our attitudes towards humans and other animals are radically different (and we could take different examples, such as those of riding horses or keeping cats or dogs as pets or breeding animals to be especially useful for our purposes or killing animal pests). And this difference in attitude is based, as I hope to have suggested, on nothing except that these animals are of a species that is not our own. We, as humans, simply do give preference to members of our own species, just as other animals do. To argue that we have gradually extended our sympathies beyond our families and countrymen to other races and those who live at a distance from us is simply to reinforce the argument that we have gradually come to feel more sympathy for and responsibility for humanity as a whole. It says nothing about our duty to embrace on equal terms all other species of animals, or even those specially favoured animals whom we might call 'persons' along with ourselves. 'Speciesism', then, is not the name of a prejudice which we should try to wipe out; it is not a kind of injustice. It is the natural consequence of the way we and our ancestors have established the institution of life within which the concepts of right and wrong and the law have their meaning. The myth of the creation has not formed our attitudes. It is simply a story-book expression of them, as is the common case with myths.

However, as should by now be obvious, to say that we inevitably prefer our own species and their interests to others does not entitle us to be indifferent to the sufferings of the rest. On the contrary. Only humans, it would be generally agreed, are capable of a conscious, principled morality. Only they are deliberate moral agents (and this is doubtless part of the reason why we value them so highly and so differently from members of other species). But this does not entail that only humans can be *beneficiaries* of the principles which they, the humans, have devised. It is certainly not the case that, in order to benefit from a principle of morality, from the acts of a moral agent, you need yourself to be a moral agent. Indeed, this will form the theme of the next two chapters. We regard infants and the severely disabled as having moral claims on us, even though they are themselves not, or not yet, moral agents. The human species in its adult and unimpaired state has, alone among animals, the ability to conceive in the abstract that pain and suffering are *bad*; and that the world in general, of which humans alone have a concept, would be better if there were less pain in it. The point of our morality, then, is to mitigate the bad as far as we are able. Let me quote from G. J. Warnock, in *The Object of Morality*:

> Just as liability to be judged as a moral agent follows from one's general capability of alleviating by moral action the ills of the human predicament and is for that reason confined to rational human beings, so the condition of being a proper 'beneficiary' of moral action is capability of suffering the ills of the predicament. Things go badly in general if creatures suffer, better if they do not; to come within the ambit then of the ameliorative object of moral principles is not to be capable of contributing to that amelioration, but to be capable of suffering by its absence.[8]

It follows that we ought, as far as possible, to ensure that other animals do not suffer. We must avoid cruelty and the wanton causing of pain. If it were inevitable that animals suffer through being killed for the table, we ought not to eat them. If it is inevitable that they suffer pain in the laboratory, we ought not to breed them for laboratory use. But if we can use them without causing them pain, then there is no moral *reason* why we should not do so. (In chapter 3 I shall discuss some limitations to this principle). For other species, not being moral agents themselves, cannot be thought of as the equals of men. Their individual lives, though in some cases valuable, cannot be valued in the same way as the individual lives of men. And to say this is not mere arrogance. For the specifically human consciousness of having a life to lead, the understanding of the idea of one's own life, for which one is responsible, makes human life different from simply being alive. Thus, for humans, dying, or being killed, is a different matter from the mere cessation of life. Singer, in his arguments for vegetarianism, partly sees this. But, being a utilitarian, he cannot explain the *extra* value we ascribe to human life. Utilitarians, while they concentrate on pains and pleasures and on weighing up the balance of one over the other, never really face the question how *killing* the subject of pain and pleasure counts in the calculus. It is simply assumed that to be killed is the ultimate harm a man can suffer. Singer, therefore, anxious to bring at least the higher animals into the class of persons to whom utilitarian principles apply, makes the same assumption. But, as I have tried to argue, we may be morally bound to try to avoid causing animals pain while they live, without being morally bound to try to keep them in existence. This is a great part of the difference between our duties towards beasts and men. I shall explain the implications of this, and the qualifications I think we should make, in the following two chapters.

# 2

# Man's Duty to his Own Species

In the first chapter I hope to have suggested that our membership of a particular species, that of *Homo sapiens*, creates for us obligations towards other members of that species quite different from our obligations to members of other species. First, and most important, to kill a member of our own species is a different thing from killing a member of another species, and requires a quite different moral justification, which may often not be forthcoming. No one who seriously imagines himself afloat on a raft and short of food and water, debating whether to kill a human or another animal, can doubt this. Again, to use a member of our own species to subserve our own ends is now generally regarded as unjustifiable in a way that using a horse or a dog for our own purposes is not. If it is argued that our views on such matters may change in the future, just as our views have changed on the equality of all humans, whether they are white or black, whether or not they have been captured in war, I would reply that this is not possible. For to speak of the priority of the human is to articulate the framework and the boundaries of human morality. It is humans, and they alone, who are moral agents, who make choices and judge themselves to be doing well or ill, who can see that other human beings must be treated as free, choice-making creatures, since they are so themselves. We cannot admit other animals into the community of the moral, because they would be incapable of recognizing that they had been so admitted or of admitting us into their community.

However, within this moral framework, there is a strong obligation to avoid causing pain or suffering to any creature of whatever species who may be able to experience it, unless that pain can be clearly shown to be for the creature's ultimate good (even if he does not see it so). We have therefore some duties to animals. And however we use animals, and whether or not we kill them for our own ends, we must not deliberately cause them pain. Let me quote from Mary Midgley's book *Beast and Man*. She writes:

> People readily become suspicious of the suggestion that they could have any duty to animals, because they see this as likely to lay on them an infinite load of obligation, and they rightly think that an infinite obligation would be meaningless. 'Ought' implies 'can'. Indefinite guilt is paralysing. The position, however, is actually no worse than the one we are already in with regard to people. We already have the idea that we owe some sort of obligation to any human being. But it is not infinite, because what each of us ought to do is limited by what alternatives he can reach. We have to consider priorities. Conflicts of interest must be recognised, both within the human species and outside it. We have to take sides, and are entitled to put our own species first. All species do this. No creature can in fact subsist without killing some others, if only by competing with them for food. The point is not that we can hope to avoid injuring other animals or people. It is that we ought to recognise that such injury matters.[1]

Granted that injury matters and that we, alone of all creatures, can realize that it does (indeed, that we have invented the concept of 'mattering'); granted also that we should think of injuring humans as mattering more than injuring other animals, are we therefore committed to the view that all human life is of equal value? This is a central question, abstract and theoretical as it may seem, in all kinds of highly practical contexts. I want to consider three different sorts of cases where the answers we give may make a crucial difference to our behaviour.

The first is the case of new-born babies who are severely handicapped at birth or who have no chance of long-term survival.

Let us consider the notorious case of Baby Doe, born in Bloomington, Indiana, in 1982. It is a long, sad story, with important implications. The baby was found at birth to have Down's syndrome, and in addition to have a malformation of the oesophagus such that normal feeding by mouth would be impossible without immediate surgery. The surgery could not be carried out at the hospital where he was born, so the question was whether to transfer him to another hospital and operate or leave him where he was, cared for but certain to die. There was disagreement among the paediatricians concerned with the case; but when Baby Doe's parents were consulted, they decided that they did not want the operation performed, and they signed a statement to that effect.

However, the hospital administration contacted the local County court, and an immediate hearing was set up. At this hearing the judge ruled that the parents had a right to choose between two medically recommended courses of action, and that there was no case to answer. Various attempts by the hospital administration and others to get this ruling put aside by a higher court failed, and while the attempts were still being made, the baby died. Public reaction was violent, and the most remarkable outcome was a memorandum from President Reagan, ending with the words 'I support Federal laws prohibiting discrimination against the handicapped, and remain determined that such laws shall be rigorously enforced'. The immediate outcome of this memorandum was the publication of posters to be placed in the intensive care units of all federally funded hospitals, indicating that funds would be withdrawn if handicapped babies were not so treated as to keep them alive.

Paediatricians now found themselves in obvious difficulties. The so-called Baby Doe Guidelines were not guide-lines, but absolutely definite instructions. But were they really meant to apply to all babies, even if born with only fragments of a brain or with cranial haemorrhage so severe as to make it impossible that the baby could ever achieve any cognitive abilities? By means of modern technology, such babies could be kept alive for months, even years. But almost every doctor would think it right to let them die. The principle incorporated in the guide-lines and now about to be enforced by law was the principle that all human life is of equal value.

Can we actually subscribe to this principle? If we did value all human life equally, then it would be as important to preserve the life of a two-cell pre-embryo as of a fully grown adult; it would be as important to continue in life a terminally ill unconscious man of eighty as that of a young healthy child in need of surgery after an accident. In such cases we take two factors into account: first, we consider whether the creature has a life that it is leading; secondly, we take into account the quality of that life.

Some people, when faced with the realization that sometimes choices of this kind have to be made in practice, wish to draw a distinction between causing death or killing, which they would maintain is always wrong, and allowing to die, which they hold might be inevitable sometimes and hence justified. There is a considerable literature concerned with this distinction, but I have not time to explore it fully. I would argue, however, that to maintain the distinction is to make a fundamental mistake about the nature of causation. People are often inclined to hold that a cause must be some kind of 'active agent'. Thus they think the typical causal agency is that of a brick, hurled through a window, which causes the glass to shatter; or a strong man pushing a defective car off the road when its engine has failed. And it is true that the concept of pushing and pulling is deeply woven into our notion of causation. However, in real life, and especially when we are seeking to ascribe responsibility for an event to a human, as opposed to a mechanical or natural agency, we are perfectly accustomed to regarding failures to act as causes. As J. S. Mill argued in his *Logic*, if the watchmen fall asleep at their posts and fail to keep guard, thereby allowing the enemy to enter, their failure is deemed to be the cause of the disaster.[2] If I were a surgeon and for some reason refused to operate on an otherwise healthy person who had acute appendicitis, and he died, I should have caused his death through doing nothing just as certainly as if I had stabbed him. To decide not to operate on Baby Doe was to cause his death; and if killing a living human being is always wrong, then it was wrong to fail to operate. But because of the prevailing view that it is one thing to withhold treatment or withdraw it and another to give a lethal injection – that there is a difference between allowing to die, that is, and killing – Baby Doe, though condemned to die, had to die by slow, long-drawn-out stages of starvation and dehydration. It would undoubtedly have been more merciful to kill him outright once the decision was taken. But this is by the way. We have still to consider whether or not the killing was, in this case, justified.

The most familiar argument against allowing a baby to be killed in this kind of case is the so-called slippery slope argument. This argument has an astonishing power over the public imagination; but it must be distinguished from any argument based on the equal value of all human life, the principle incorporated in President Reagan's memorandum. The slippery slope argument says that if the killing of babies like Baby Doe were permitted, even if that particular killing were justifiable, then anything would become permissible. The next thing would be that parents could ask that any baby might be killed if they didn't like the look of him or if they had decided that, after all, they'd prefer not to have a baby. And from babies we could move on to other children and grown-ups. We could kill them if they were handicapped; and then, further on down the slippery slope, we could kill them if they were Jews. The only way, so it is argued, to avoid hurtling down this morally disastrous slope is never to get onto it in the first place. No killing at all should be legitimized.

Against this argument it is necessary to be quite specific about what is and what is not to be legitimized, and then to show that the full force of the law could be invoked to maintain and uphold the distinctions drawn. This kind of counter-argument is powerfully detailed in a book called *Should the Baby Live* by Helga Kuhse and Peter Singer.[3] Baby Doe was a handicapped *infant*. If he had been a handicapped child or an adult, the question would not have arisen. In any case, the motivation for the killing has to be taken into account. There is simply no analogy between the motives of the parents in the Baby Doe case and the motives of those who established the Nazi policy of wholesale destruction of the Jews. The slopes, if they exist, are not the same slopes. The decision made by Baby Doe's parents was difficult and painful, and concerned the life of one infant only. The decision to let him die could in no way be regarded even as a charter for all parents to dispose of their children, even their handicapped children. It was a decision about one child.

But of course, if all human life is equally valuable there is no need of the dubious logic of the slippery slope argument. The killing of Baby Doe was necessarily wrong, wrong in itself, whatever precedent it did or did not set. In discussing in chapter 1 the case against killing animals other than humans, I suggested that to appeal to the *rights* of animals was of no help. It merely dressed up, under an apparently factual statement that there exist certain rights for animals, the moral judgement that the laws ought to be so changed that rights were accorded to animals (rights which under the present law did not exist). The case of human infants is different. Infants are protected by law from being killed. To kill any human being who has been born is (except in case of war or self-defence) either murder or manslaughter. Therefore, legally, human infants have a right to life.

Nevertheless, this is far from solving the moral dilemma of those who are faced with the choice of whether the baby should live. We have here one of the numerous cases when human ingenuity, expressed in the development of technology, has created quite new moral problems, which need to be thought of as new, with that technology in mind. For it is now possible to keep alive, for an indefinite period, babies who in earlier times would most certainly have died within an hour or so of birth. Likewise, at the other end of life, people may be kept alive who would otherwise have died. It used to be the assumption of the medical profession, subject to the Hippocratic oath, that a doctor's duty was first and foremost to keep the patient alive. But now, that has to be called into question. It has become urgently necessary that doctors and others take into account not just life as opposed to death, but the quality of life. They must raise the question whether the life preserved by technology would actually be a life worth living.

As recently as thirty years ago, as a matter of practice, doctors used to make such decisions in the case of neonates. An experienced GP who had delivered a very severely handicapped baby, perhaps one whom he judged would not in any case live for more than a few weeks or months, would, with perhaps no more than a glance at the midwife, ensure that the baby did not continue to breathe. He would then tell the parents that the baby had been stillborn. The parents in such a case grieved; and so did the doctor for them. But they did not also have to face a criminal charge in the midst of their grief. This old-fashioned solution to the problem of severely deformed or defective babies was, in my view, the best. The responsibility lay with the doctor, who knew enough from his own experience to judge both the future possible quality of life of the infant and the effects of his living, or indeed of his instantly dying, upon the parents. It was paternalism, but a paternalism that was benign.

However, though we may regret them, we cannot go back to those days. Both the advances in technology already referred to and the rise of the abstract, theoretical pro-life groups have made it impossible to go back. For the pro-lifers are committed to the principle of the equal value of all human life, at whatever stage of development, and they are prepared to spy on doctors and nurses and report all cases where a baby has been allowed to die.

It seems to me, therefore, that we need to rethink legislation, in such a way that doctors in collaboration with parents are quite unambiguously entitled deliberately to end the life of neonates whose life-chances are one way or another seen to be very poor. Such poor life-chances should include both the near certainty of death within a few weeks or months and also the certainty of a life which, if prolonged, would entail pain, suffering, and continuous hospitalization.

Even this is not the end of the matter. We have here entered into the very dubious field of judging the quality of another person's life. But is it only the future quality of the *infant's* life that must be taken into account? Or should we be allowed to think also about the quality of life of the parents and any other children they may have?

It is hard to assess quality of life on someone else's behalf, especially when that person may never reach a stage of self-awareness or awareness of other people so as to be able to compare his life with that of peers. There is no doubt that a very severely mentally retarded person unable ever to sit up or feed himself or make any discriminations or choices in his surroundings has a life almost incredibly poor compared with the rest of us. But does he suffer? Presumably not, provided that he is not actually cold, hungry, or in physical pain. We would not like his life, any more than we would like the life of a mouse or a horse, but to say that is to suppose that, while living his life (or the life of the mouse), we would retain our own sensibilities. If we had mouse sensibilities, we'd be all right as mice. On the other hand, the kind of handicap we *can* judge is the kind which involves gradual degeneration with perhaps increasingly long spells of hospitalization, where the child not only suffers pain and sickness but can see himself gradually changing, drawing away from his peers, and facing death. This is the kind of suffering that must be real and terrible at the time for the child. And it must be the most agonizing suffering as well for the parents. Foreseeing this kind of life for their child, the parents may well choose, if they are allowed to, that the infant should die as an infant, knowing nothing.

Are they to be allowed also to consider their own future suffering and to put it in the balance in favour of their child's death in infancy? And, to go back to the case of severe mental retardation, are they to be allowed to think of their own lives and what would happen to them if they had charge of this totally dependent never-to-grow-up child? Are parents to be blamed, or, worse, prosecuted, if they choose that an infant who will grow into this kind of child and adult should die? Kuhse and Singer argue that no parent should be forced into the position of having to care for a child they had conceived in the hope that it would become part of their normal family, when they subsequently find that their whole life would be disrupted, and indeed ruined, by that care. It is wrong, they argue, that decisions should be made by those who will not have the responsibility of living with the consequences. 'We believe', they write,

> that the State is justified in intervening when parents decide for the death of their child only if two conditions are fulfilled. The first is that the child has the prospect of a worthwhile life, that is, a life sufficiently free from physical pain and psychological misery to be satisfying for the child. The second condition is that the State must be prepared to accept the responsibility of finding the child a home in which it can enjoy its life to the best of its capabilities.[4]

Of course, the second of these conditions is increasingly unlikely to be satisfied, as funding for home-helps, community care, or even mental hospitals is being decreased in real terms. Government is more and more likely to fall back on the mythology of the loving, caring family, or on the even more fictitious caring (but unfunded) community, in order to back up the moral satisfaction of condemning parents who might choose for their child not to live. It is highly paradoxical that parents are legally permitted the choice of abortion when the foetus is shown to be severely malformed or defective before birth, but that this choice should be denied them in the case of a premature baby with similar or worse handicaps, yet who may be of identical gestational age. The foetus legally aborted may even be older, dating from conception rather than birth, than the neonate born prematurely and bound to be kept alive.

To permit a decision to kill at birth, harsh though this sounds to our ears ('to allow to die' being, as I have suggested, no different in meaning, and perhaps leading to more painful practice), may in certain extreme circumstances be compatible with the general duty we have to human beings, especially to those human beings, like the parents of Baby Doe, who have worthwhile lives of their own to lead, and to whom our primary duty must be, unless we are crippled by the principle of equality of value for all lives. In a book called *Playing God in the Nursery*, the American journalist Jeff Lyons writes as follows:

> The sanctity-of-life principle derives from the same moral tradition as our concept of mercy. Is it not in the best spirit of that tradition that we temper the one with the other? We can embody these ideals best by not insisting that physicians invariably perpetuate lives that are painful and dolorous and by allowing parents the freedom to decide what is and what is not an acceptable life for their child, using the human heart as their guide.[5]

That such decisions may be agonizing is no reason for not allowing them to be taken.

I now turn to the second class of cases involving the 'equality of value' principle.

I have referred already to the fact that under certain circumstances abortion is a legitimate option for women in this country (it is as yet unclear whether the father of a child has any legal right to prevent an abortion from being carried out). The 1967 Abortion Act appeared to have behind it a mixture of principles. Recognizing that abortion cannot be prevented altogether (in that it has always existed and probably always will), the Bill nevertheless sought to regulate abortion, and as far as possible to deter women from seeking it. On the other hand, the law recognized that if women were determined to have an abortion, then their health and safety must be protected as far as possible. In 1990 the law was changed, an amendment being added to the new Embryology Bill, so that the position with regard to abortion became both clearer and more logical (Human Fertilization and Embryology Bill, clause 34). But the double motivation remains. Even today it is not particularly easy to secure an abortion. Many women, and especially many young girls, do not know how to go about it, or are too frightened to try. They may be under considerable pressure; first, because they should not have got pregnant and are afraid to admit it, and secondly because if they do consult a doctor, he may try to persuade them not to have the abortion and then fail to offer any suggestion about where to go for other advice and practical help. Moreover, it is not just one doctor, but two, who have to sign the certificate permitting the abortion to be carried out. This, then, seems to be the deterrent aspect of the law.

The health and safety aspect is that when an abortion has been agreed to, it may be carried out only in premises licensed to perform abortions and subject to inspection by the Department of Health. And if the abortion is carried out late in the pregnancy (after twenty weeks), it may be carried out only in National Health Service premises, where it is subject to even stricter surveillance. An upper limit has now been set for abortions, which was not clearly a part of the 1967 Act, and in general an abortion may be carried out only up to twenty-four weeks from the presumed date of conception. The grounds for abortion up to that time are either that the continuing of the pregnancy would threaten the health, physical or mental, of the mother or of some member of her family, or that the foetus is grossly defective. After twenty-four weeks an abortion may, exceptionally, be carried out either on that last ground or because the mother's health or life is seriously at risk.

The question we must ask is this: Within the context of the special duty to our own species for which I have argued, is abortion defensible at all? If it is, why should it be hedged about with so many restrictions? If it is not then why should it ever be permitted? The answer to these questions is complex, in that it involves the relationship between a pregnant woman and the foetus she is carrying and between morality and the law. I have suggested that we have a duty to all members of our own species greater than our duty to any other animals, and in particular that we have a duty not to kill them. The foetus is a member of our own species in so far as it is a separate being at all. There is therefore a prima facie argument against abortion. But if I was right to argue that the quality of life had to be taken into account in deciding whether to keep a handicapped neonate alive or kill it, then the same consideration will in certain circumstances determine whether to abort or not. If the foetus is grossly defective, then abortion should be (and is) permitted for this reason, if that is what the parents wish.

But does consideration of the quality of life justify what is widely described as abortion on social grounds (that is, on the first of the grounds mentioned just now)? In some cases it plainly does. It has to be remembered that we are here assuming that the present life of the foetus is perfectly satisfactory as far as it goes; it is its *future* life that is in question. Now if the foetus faces a future life in which its mother will be dead or seriously ill or insane, or if it faces a future life of acute and inescapable social destitution or risk from a destructive family, then the 'quality of life' argument will justify 'social' abortion. But supposing none of these things is true of the foetus. It is simply that the mother very strongly does not want it to be born (and the 'mental health' clause in the Abortion Act is commonly stretched so as to cover this case, provided that the abortion is not a 'late' abortion – that is, later than twenty-four weeks). Are we here justified in preferring to consider the quality of *her* life rather than that of the foetus? Is there a general duty to bring humans into the world once they have been conceived? (Of course there is no duty to bring humans into the world, whether or not they have yet been conceived; no duty absolutely in general to have as many children as possible.) Does an embryo, once fertilized, count as of equal importance, since it is indubitably human and alive, as all other live humans, whatever their stage of development? The equality of life principle demands that we believe this, and anti-abortionists do believe it. But if we do not espouse the principle that all lives are of equal value, then it seems to me that we *must* prefer the separate, independent lives of human people who have been born and who have lives to lead in the world to the life of an unborn embryo or foetus, who, though alive, has no life yet to lead. We must, that is to say, distinguish between being alive in a biological sense and having 'a life' that is to be led. It is only when someone has 'a life of his own' that we can sensibly think about the *quality* of that life. It is true that when a foetus has been diagnosed as severely malformed, we may argue for abortion on the grounds of what the quality of its life will be if it is born. But where there is no reason to think that a foetus, if born, will have a painful or hopeless life, we yet need not hold that the life of the foetus must be weighed *equally* with the life of the mother. Indeed, even in the case where an abortion is undertaken because of the malformation of the foetus, I believe that the strongest reason for aborting is in fact the suffering of the parents, not the suffering of the baby if it is born. And so, in the case of 'social' abortion, it is the suffering of the mother if this child is born that is the decisive factor. And this, I think, is consistent with the non-adoption of the principle of equal value to all lives. We value the life of the foetus, and if it is a wanted foetus, we value it very highly. But in a conflict of interests, the unborn will lose by comparison with those who have been born and are living out their lives; and this is the principle behind Abortion law in this country.

This brings us face to face with the difference between a law, which is binding on everyone, whatever their religion or moral principles, and a personal rule or principle. There are, of course, many women who, for reasons of religion or conscience, would never seek an abortion, whatever the circumstances of their own lives. And they will never be required to do so. For the law is enabling, not prescriptive. The law is not our conscience. On the whole, laws must be drawn up with an eye to the good of society and the protection of its members, whatever their morals or their religion, whether they have any or none of those commodities. So the present abortion law permits abortion in certain circumstances, and attempts to ensure that when it occurs, it occurs safely. If anything, I am more doubtful about what I have called the 'moral aspects' of the law than I am about its health and safety aspects. But perhaps the compromise we have, according to which women may seek and obtain abortions, but with difficulty, is no bad thing. It may remind the women who are considering abortion that killing a human, even a two-month-old embryo, 'matters'. It is not like killing a wasp, or even a kitten. It is the destruction of a member of the human species, albeit an embryonic one. And so the difficulties put in her path may cause the woman seriously to weigh up the relative values of the lives that are going to be affected; and this is the proper behaviour for a rational person.

In the case of abortion it is plain that whether or not we regard all human life as of equal value will make a great difference to our behaviour, or at least to our attitude to abortion law. I have left myself very little time to consider the third of my types of case, that of the status that should be accorded to the human embryo outside the uterus, the 'test-tube' embryo. But there are not many new arguments that need to be deployed in this case. As I argued in chapter 1 (though there with regard to animals), we cannot decide on the proper status of these embryos by asking whether they have rights or whether they are to be referred to as 'persons'. As far as rights go, unlike neonates, they have no legal rights whatever, at least up to fourteen days from fertilization. As for moral rights, as I argued before, to speak of such rights does not help us forward. It is only to speak of our moral principle in different words. Again, in the ordinary sense of the word 'person', there is no doubt that laboratory embryos are not persons. If we attempt to extend the use of the word so as to cover them, we are only expressing thereby our view of what is morally the right way to consider them. It does not affect what they actually are.

There is one thing that we know about these embryos. They are indisputably human and alive. Thus, for those who, like President Reagan, espouse the equality of value view of human life, there is no doubt that they should be given the full protection of the law, just as fully formed human beings are. And from this it follows inevitably that they should not be used for experimental or research purposes, should not be killed or condemned to death through not being placed in a woman's uterus, and should not be brought into existence specifically for research.

Strict utilitarians might be inclined to argue, against the equality of human life supporters, that since the immediately post-fertilization embryo is certainly incapable of feeling pain or indeed, being yet without even the beginnings of a central nervous system, incapable of experiencing anything whatever, it cannot come into the utilitarian calculus of pleasure and pain. We may have a duty to animals, at least to those that can experience pain, that we should not cause them pain; but this duty cannot extend to the early human embryo, since the question of causing pain simply does not arise. We are therefore, they would argue, exempt from the restriction that killing them or injuring them matters.

However, those who believe in the essential difference between the human species and others may feel queasy about this argument. Although there is no question of causing pain to the early embryo (at the very least up to about twenty-one days from fertilization), nevertheless, the fact that these embryos are human makes them importantly different from, say, tadpoles or the embryos of mice. In bringing them into existence and using them for research, we must at least think what we are doing, what material it is that we are using, and must be prepared to justify what we are doing by pointing to specifically human benefits.

I believe that if we can do this, we are fully justified in using these embryos for the common good. If we are prepared to accept restrictions on their use, we can plausibly argue that though the embryos are human and alive, they are not yet individual human beings. I would remind you of the distinction I drew just now between life in the biological sense and a life that is lived. There is no doubt that for living a life there must be an individual who has a life to lead. But the embryo up to fourteen days from fertilization is not such an individual. It is a plural cluster of cells not yet differentiated into those cells that will form the foetus and those that will form the placenta. Moreover, up to about fourteen days from fertilization it is not certain whether one foetus or two or none will emerge. For the last stage at which twinning can occur is fourteen days from fertilization. It is impossible, therefore, to think of an individual, with its own individual life, before this time. And our concern for the value of a life to be led is, in my view, closely connected with the individuality of each human being (I shall return to this point in the next chapter). There is no doubt that there are general benefits to the human species to be derived from research using the early human embryo. Therefore, since there is no *individual* who is being sacrificed for these benefits, it follows that to use embryos for research is justified. But restrictions on their use is necessary, to ensure that they are not used frivolously (that is, for no good end) or used when they have been kept alive to a stage at which an argument for protecting them could be based on the need to protect them as *individual human beings.*

But in any case, if we are prepared to live in a country that can justify abortion, we should be prepared at least to *consider* in a dispassionate way the benefits of the use of embryos. It is true that, in the case of abortion, we are weighing up the value of a particular foetus against the value of an existing human being, its mother; whereas in the case of embryo research, we are weighing the lives of the embryos against the lives of an indefinite set of future lives that may be improved by the research. But, in some cases and in some circumstances, we should be prepared to put *future* lives into the balance, against present lives. In this case, both the embryos and their future beneficiaries are in different ways unknown to us. The balancing is impersonal, and therefore perhaps easier. But I hope to say more about our responsibilities for the future in the next chapter.

# 3

# The Human and his World

In the first chapter, I argued that human beings, members of the species *Homo sapiens*, think of themselves as different from other animals, and must give priority, if it comes to a conflict, to members of their own species. I suggested that we do think of ourselves so and that we ought to. For the framework of morality is built around the human species, with its unique capacity for forethought and for perceiving the interests of others. This does not mean, I argued, that we are entitled to treat other animals badly; it is only that they cannot, any of them, compete with humans for priority of concern. In the second chapter, I argued that the priority of the human among animal species (in our own eyes, that is, the only eyes whose perceptions can give rise to a system of moral obligations) does not entail that we do or ought to try to value all human life equally. In our valuation of human life we should take into account the quality of that life, even though the criteria by which we judge quality are and must remain unclear.

In attempting to judge the quality of life, one fundamental distinction must be made, and that is the distinction between biological life and the lives we humans lead, plan for, and enjoy. Humans inhabit the world. That is a tautology; for everything inhabits the world. The world is the sum total of its inhabitants, including trees and rocks, as well as animal species of all kinds. What is uniquely human is not life in the world, but the ability to think about the world, increasingly to conceive it as a whole, and plan to live our lives so that we and our successors can enjoy the world we live in. Just as our human ability to think about other species gives rise to our obligation to treat these species well, in the sense of avoiding causing them to suffer, so our ability to think of the whole world gives rise to certain obligations towards this world as a whole.

So much is increasingly recognized. The growth of Green politics, the existence of such organizations as the World Wildlife Fund, the increasing anxiety felt about endangered species, and the gradual recognition that what we do now will have effects on a long-term future bear witness to the fact that we are becoming more conscious of our role as inhabitants of the world, and more conscious that we may have obligations to it. But it is extraordinarily difficult to consider with any degree of clarity what these obligations may be. For here, even more than when considering our duties to other animals, we have to beware of talking nonsense – that is, seeming to impose infinite duties on people. Yet infinite duties cannot exist. Our duty must be something we can at least attempt to carry out.

Moral philosophy has, until very recently, had little light to throw on what might constitute our world-wide obligations. The Christian rule that we should love our neighbour as ourselves very properly provoked the question Who is our neighbour? The answer, in the parable of the Good Samaritan (told in the context of a narrow sectarian Judaism), opened startlingly wide the concept of neighbourhood; our neighbour is anyone who needs us, whether he despises us or whether we despise him. And this became the Christian ideal. In the eighteenth century David Hume conceived of morality, quite rightly in my view, as a matter of expressing, and being guided by, certain feelings or sentiments of approbation and disapprobation, based on reason and justifiable by reason, but not identical with reason, requiring as well the linked human faculties of imagination and sympathy. From this sense, 'all the great lines of our duty', as he put it, derived. But he was prepared simply to accept as a fact that great distance or great numbers made it more difficult for our imagination and sympathy to encompass the proper objects of our moral judgements or moral behaviour. This failure of imagination was indeed the reason why we need moral principles, to guide us where sympathy might fail. Our sympathies are limited. A growth in moral awareness may be seen as a gradual easing and stretching of such limitation. But nearly always this stretching has been thought of as accommodating more and more humans, the extension of sympathy to cover black people as well as white being the most obvious example.

Perhaps the first opportunity to explore how we might begin to feel moral responsibility towards the whole of the natural world arose with the Romantic movement. But if so this was, on the whole, an opportunity lost. Kant, at any rate, was firmly of the opinion that humans were, because of their reason and ability to make free choices, altogether more important than the rest of nature, all bound as it was within some inexorable natural law, and that they and they alone were the proper subject of moral obligation. Our whole duty as rational humans was to treat other rational humans as free, potential choice-makers, with rational wills of their own. It was indeed, in Kant's eyes, precisely this capacity which humans share with each other to be joint members of the so-called kingdom of ends which enables them to rise above the domination of natural into that of rational law.[1] Even Wordsworth, for whom the greatest moral insights came from a sense of the mysteries and grandeurs of nature, believed that these insights would give rise to a deeper moral responsibility specifically towards humans, as they produced greater insight into the human heart itself. An openness to the sublimities of mountains, torrents, and streams led, he thought, to a strengthening of the conscience, an ability to avoid succumbing to ordinary 'selfish passions'.[2]

Blake alone of the great Romantic poets, writing at the turn of the nineteenth century, understood both what men were doing to the natural world, the consequences of their 'dark satanic mills', and the fact that men were a part of the natural whole, a part of that Chain of Being discussed and elaborated a century before by the Cambridge Platonists.

For example, in the *Book of Thel*, Blake makes Thel address a cloud thus:

> 'Without a use this shining woman lived
> Or did she only live to be at death the food of worms?'

And the cloud reproaches her:

'Then if thou art the food of worms, O Virgin of the skies,
How great thy use, how great thy blessing. Everything that lives
Lives not alone nor for itself.'

And so the worm is called to speak up, and finally the clod of clay
speaks:

'O beauty of the vales of Har, we live not for ourselves.
Thou seest me, the meanest thing, and so I am indeed.
My bosom of itself is cold and of itself is dark;
But He that loves the lowly pours His oil upon my head,
And kisses me, and binds His nuptial bands around my breast
And says: 'Thou mother of my children, I have loved thee
And I have given thee a crown that none can take away.'
But how this is, sweet maid, I know not and I cannot know;
I ponder and I cannot ponder; yet I live and love.'[3]

Blake, then, was the great prophet of the Greens. But of course
it was not until Darwin's work began to exert its enormous influence on literature and common thought that the place of man in
Nature, an animal alongside the other animals, living like other
animals on the fruits of the earth and by preying on others, came
to be seen more or less in the way that we may see it now. It is
from this relatively recently established position of man in Nature
that obligations to the natural world arise.

For obligations arise, and can arise, only within a system of
values; and gradually man had begun to see that nature as a
whole, not merely men and their creations, were to be valued, for
their own sake. Kant had proclaimed that nothing in the world
had intrinsic value except the Good Will, and, the Good Will
being identical with the rational will, only humans could possess
it. If anything in nature was valuable, it could be valued only as
an instrument for the moral goodness or the rational understanding of man, and it was out of this that the concept of human duty
could be derived.

Though our attitude towards the natural world has changed,
our moral philosophy has not entirely kept pace. There are two
main reasons for this. I do not propose to give you a complete
history of moral philosophy, and for this you may be thankful.
But I will suggest two broadly historical phenomena which may

go some way to explaining the relative conservatism of moral philosophy. The first is the extraordinarily widespread influence of Kant himself. Kant was concerned primarily, as we have seen, with the nature of those moral principles which ought to govern our behaviour and motives in such human transactions as promise-keeping, helping our neighbours, or cultivating our talents. Ever since his time, interest among moral philosophers has been largely centred on such principles and on the nature of the authority that may lie behind them. Certainly until the 1960s and 1970s, this was the chief preoccupation of moral philosophers in the English-speaking world.

The second great influence has been that of Bentham and J. S. Mill. Utilitarian ethics, which grew out of their work, was first concerned not so much with morality as with law. Bentham's view was that there should be a law restricting types of behaviour if and only if that behaviour could be shown to harm more people than it benefited and if the threat of punishment were likely to deter. Mill attempted to translate the utilitarian theory from the sphere of jurisprudence to that of morality, and he held that, for the most part, morally admirable behaviour was behaviour governed by such principles as had, over the centuries, been found to produce more benefit than harm. Thus the moral principle that one should tell the truth, though impossible to incorporate in any law of the land, would nevertheless be justified on the same grounds as those on which good law would be justified: namely, that acting in breach of it did harm, whereas adhering to it caused benefit or pleasure. Although he held that, occasionally, two well-established principles of conduct might clash (tell the truth or show mercy, for example), in most cases the established principles would be enough to guide us; and even where a decision between two principles had to be made, we would have an ultimate guide in the principle of utility itself.

As I suggested in chapter 1, classical utilitarianism never really faced the question of who is to *count* in the calculation of pleasures and pains, harms and benefits, still less *what* was to count. Which, if any, elements of the natural world should be regarded as capable of suffering harm? Only if this question had been answered would utilitarianism have been able to show what duties we have to the non-human world.

There is one major step that we may take in order to make this kind of question easier to answer. Anything can be harmed, we may agree, which is valuable; and, unlike Kant, we may be prepared to say that certain aspects of the natural world in which we live are valuable, even though they are not human. I hope that what I have said so far has suggested that this is a proper step to take. But there is more to be said. There is no such thing as value, any value, without some human to ascribe it. Imagine a totally uninhabited world; uninhabited, that is, by human animals. Of such a world there are certain things we cannot say, without surreptitiously incorporating ourselves in it as observers or as people who remember the world when we inhabited it. For example, of such a world we cannot say that some propositions are true and others false; for there are no propositions at all. It is we who divide the world up into facts; and it is by describing those facts that we introduce the possibility of truth and false-hood, accurate or inaccurate description. In such a world the waves might beat upon the shore, just as they do when a human is there to observe them; but there could be neither a true nor a false statement about such a happening. Neither could anything be good or bad without some observer so to describe it, to find it good or bad. Neither facts nor values exist in a world without humans. There are only things and happenings.

But, you may say, God could value things, high or low, even in a world without humans. We are told in the Bible that he created the world and found it good before he created man. If we are to believe in a God who is like men (or, if you prefer, in men who are in certain important respects like God), then we can believe that God values things in the world; that some are therefore absolutely valuable, some absolutely valueless. But a philosophical argument can hardly base itself on such a premise. More import-ant, perhaps, a political argument cannot either. It may be true that for those who believe that God loves all his creatures there is a plain duty of stewardship laid upon those creatures made in God's image (though the Church has not always held this). But in a secular society, to argue thus is not to provide a sufficient basis for legislation. And in some cases it is to legislation that we must look if we are interested in fulfilling our duty to the world as a whole.

So, to return to our previous point, for the human understanding, 'to be valuable' means 'to be valued by somebody'. When we speak of objects that are intrinsically valuable, we mean that they are objects which are valued by man for their own sake, not for the sake of something else. We may not be able to explain why we value highly some beautiful prospect, for example, but if we do value it highly, if we enjoy looking at it, and go out of our way to see it, then we value it not for its consequences (for it has none), nor for what it does (for it does nothing; it merely exists), but for its own sake. And if there are things that are thus intrinsically valuable, they may be destroyed or harmed. And since being intrinsically valuable means being valued highly by men, when we seek to preserve such things or save them from harm, we are seeking something that is among the essentially human values. We are seeking to save people from impoverishment or deprivation, seeking to maintain the quality of their lives. In seeking to save certain valued aspects of nature from harm, then, we are not thereby moving into a wholly different dimension from that within which we seek to preserve human beings themselves from harm. Our duties to our natural environment must be considered and weighed up alongside our other duties to humanity.

There is one further point to be made about the concept of valuing the world. Let us suppose that I value highly some plant or animal or range of mountains. I think it beautiful or admirable or wonderful. Does this entail that I have any business on these grounds to argue that it ought to be preserved? Am I not simply expressing, in my admiration, my own preferences? I do not think so. In making a proper value judgement (as distinct from deliberately expressing a personal whim), I am in some way demanding assent from others. Kant recognized this in his analysis of our judgements of the beautiful in the 'Critique of Judgement'. Though propositions such as 'This is beautiful' arise out of our own sensibility, we can and do assume that humans share sensibilities, that they all have similar capacities both for perception and for admiration. Therefore, if I regard something as marvellous or interesting or beautiful, I will be prepared to show you what it is that I see in it, on the assumption that you can, and ought, to see it too. This is the basis, obviously, for all teaching. But, more than this, it is the basis of our entitlement to speak of aspects of the shared world as valuable; fit to be valued, not simply liked or preferred by me.

With these preliminaries in mind, then, let us consider three different and specific examples. The first is that of oil pollution. I take the case of oil, rather than chemical pollution of other kinds, because of the kind of effect that oil pollution has. On the whole, it is a fairly benign form of pollution, yet a form about which feelings run high. The direct effect of a vessel's clearing out its sludge too near the coast may be fouled beaches. Now beaches covered in oil are disagreeable and smelly; and even if the worst of the black contamination is cleared away, for years people may find themselves walking or sitting in patches of oil. This will not hurt them or make them ill, but it will spoil their pleasure. A clean beach is an object that we value; but the effects of oil on a beach are very different from the effects of raw sewage, which are positively dangerous, as well as immediately disagreeable. But of course the effects of oil are not confined to humans. Fish are not especially affected; indeed, there is some evidence that they flourish in oily waters. But in the Shetland Islands sheep have been affected badly, because they eat seaweed on the shore (there and there alone as far as I know). Farmers can protect sheep from this damage by fencing off the shore. That would be a nuisance, and fairly expensive, but not impossible. But, notoriously, the creatures worst affected are sea-birds, especially those such as guillemots which ride on the tops of the waves and become hopelessly damaged by oil on their feathers. Puffins are also badly affected. Once a bird has its feathers oiled, there is really no hope for it at all. Individual birds may be treated, but they seldom survive. My question, therefore, is how much do we, and should we, value the life of sea-birds? And what measures are we justified in taking to protect them from the hazard of oil pollution?

There is an argument, which we may think of as the hard-headed argument, which goes as follows. Oil in the sea, even in the case of a serious accidental oil-slick, does not at present turn guillemots or puffins into endangered species. They are not liable to disappear off the face of the earth. They will just take to a different habitat. They will go further north, towards the Arctic, where the waters are cleaner. We shall lose the puffins from Sumburgh Head, but we shall not lose them altogether. Therefore it is not worth enormous expenditure on policing the waters and prosecuting the offenders, in order to keep the seas off the Shetlands (or any other specific bit of the British Isles) clean.

I find it hard to assess this argument. I fully concede that if the bird species were genuinely endangered by oil, then we ought to try hard to conserve them (and, as a matter of fact, I would suggest that we cannot know that they are not endangered; but I shall return to the argument from ignorance later). But should we try to conserve them where they are? There is no doubt that the inhabitants of the Shetland Islands, and more especially perhaps their visitors, greatly enjoy the presence of the puffins. For many of us the variety of species of birds on and around the Shetlands is something very highly valued indeed. But it is, after all, like beaches free from oil; what the economists rather bleakly refer to as an 'amenity'. How should the conservation of amenities rate among human duties? The very word 'amenity', like the word 'leisure', with which it is often closely linked, fills me with gloom, a gloom which I have not fully analysed, and do not altogether want to. For I believe that lurking behind my distaste there is a kind of snobbishness, a desire that, though I want some parts of the countryside conserved for me, the pleasures of people in general should not be considered. If my favourite, secret parts of Wiltshire become a leisure amenity, I shall no longer care whether they are preserved or not. But if I am to be consistent, I must argue that what is generally valued has some claim to be preserved on those grounds alone. And if we (I and many others) value highly the presence of puffins and clean beaches on the Shetlands, then there is a prima facie duty not to allow these things, whether we call them amenities or not, to be destroyed.

My second example is somewhat similar. It is the example of the seals. Seals off the coasts of Norway and Great Britain were recently under threat of extinction. They were afflicted with a virus which destroys their immune system and makes them prey to infections of all kinds. Their death was frequently the result of pneumonia. Humans have always felt an affinity with seals, reflected in folk-songs and stories long before this century. Although seals are in some areas a threat to man's livelihood (when they take too much fish), there is always a great outcry at the culling that goes on, especially in Canada. Seals are mammals, and have strangely human expressions. We cannot resist them. Therefore the danger that they may become extinct seems a genuine tragedy. According, once again, to my principle that if something is generally valued, it is valuable and must if possible be preserved, it is right that we should proceed energetically with research into the virus that is the cause of the epidemic and do our best to save the seals from extinction. Even if there is something irrational in our preference for seals over other animals, there is no doubt that almost everyone would agree that the world would be a worse place, would have suffered a great loss, if there were no more seals. But, of course, if it came to the point when we could carry out research either on Aids or on the seal virus, then there is no doubt which would have priority. Fortunately, such a stark choice is never likely to be necessary. Rather, we have to try, through the various different institutions that exist, to finance research into both viruses. But it is necessary to remember that in principle we might have to choose.

Does our duty to save the seals become greater if it is shown, as at present seems unlikely, that their deaths are caused or hastened by pollution, which humans have caused? I do not think that it does. We know we have made bad decisions in the past about pollution – bad from our point of view – harming ourselves directly as well as through the harm to our environment. We can acknowledge this and urge the government to make us do better, through legislation. But our duty to the rest of nature would not come to an end even if we changed our habits and in no way contributed to the harm and damage that the environment suffered. And of course, though this does not affect the nature of our duty, once again we have to remember our ignorance. We do not actually know what the long-term effects of the disappearance of seals or any other animals from our shores would be.

The question of ignorance brings me to my final example, which is far more difficult and complicated than the first two, for in it, the ignorance factor is multiplied almost to infinity. It is a matter of great urgency at the present time to raise the question what our duties are, not to existing human beings and their existing environment, but to future unborn human beings, not yet even conceived, and the world they will inhabit. I have time to do no more than touch on the fringes of this topic, and I shall do so by considering the problem of the disposal of nuclear waste.

There are, however, some puzzling philosophical problems to be mentioned in a preliminary way. It could be argued that we can have no duties to people, or indeed other animals, who do not exist. We have no specific duties to people long dead; why should we give more consideration to those not yet born, when we do not even know whether they will be born? There is no one there to consider. The present must be the field in which we practise morality, well or ill. But, though such an argument might be advanced, nobody genuinely holds this view; nor have they ever done so. For one thing, quite apart from those who believe that somehow their ancestors live on, there are many poets, historians, and educationalists who believe that there is a kind of duty to preserve and do justice to the past. Secondly, to take an extreme example, the great landscape gardeners of the eighteenth century would have been out of work if their patrons had not been prepared to look at least 200 years ahead to how the gardens at Rousham or Stourhead would look when the trees were grown, the prospects to be seen as they had been conceived in the imagination of Kent or Capability Brown. But you may say that such wealthy gardeners were thinking of their own descendants, their own flesh and blood, who, as they thought, would still be living in their great houses and cultivating their great gardens into the unending future. We can have no such security (and indeed, theirs was misplaced). Is it possible for me to feel this kind of connection with possible persons in no way related to myself?

Derek Parfit, one of the few philosophers seriously to address the question of our wider duties, to the environment and to the future, has argued that we need a wholly new concept of personal identity if we are to have reasons for taking the future into account in our decisions about what it is right or wrong to do. We tend to think of personal identity as belonging to a specific, individual human being, born on a particular date to particular parents and existing continuously until the day he dies, whatever changes and vicissitudes he undergoes. Instead, Parfit believes, we should think of identity as the linkage between different phases of a human being's life *and* between different human beings. Thus, if

I am able to remember nothing of my infancy, I should disown it. That infant was not me. But I may, on the other hand, have to admit identity with my student, with whom I have shared all my ideas and who outlives me. Parfit holds that to identify myself, the person I am, with a single member of the human species is metaphysically naïve and morally wrong; and he seeks to prove this by an elaborate parable of my brain being transplanted and shared equally between two other humans, who now become identifiable with me, myself having been dispersed between them. I shall not follow him into this fantasy, for I am by no means convinced of the usefulness of such arguments. But he makes the moral, as distinct from the metaphysical, point differently.

Because of our member-of-the species-centred view of personal identity, we are inclined, he says, to limit our responsibility for the consequences of our acts to those cases where, singly and separately, we caused something to happen. Thus I may feel a guilty responsibility if I knowingly set fire to some papers and left them to burn, and this caused a whole forest to ignite. But there are many cases where what I, individually, do makes no difference to the future. I cannot harm the ecology if I go out one night and catch a fish. But the society of which I am a member may be guilty of over-fishing, and thus of gross environmental harm; and I ought to identify myself with this society, to which I am connected by membership. I must not confine my ascription of guilty responsibility to myself as an individual agent.

This 'depersonalization' has another consequence. It shows that we need not know to whom we have a duty in order to have it. The utilitarian calculus has always rested on the supposition that, more or less, we could count heads, and estimate how many individuals would be harmed by a particular policy, how many would benefit, with perhaps a half-glance at the future, and the supposition that what harms people now will continue to do so, and similarly with benefits. But we know now that such a calculation is inadequate, and we are to be blamed if we continue to make it. I may benefit if I tip my rubbish into the sea, but what about the future? I may, as an individual policy-maker, avoid harming people if I store nuclear waste on the site of a power station, but what about those who will be harmed when the short-term safety of the waste comes to an end? Of course, if people do not exist, they cannot be harmed. But if we can depersonalize our way of thinking, we can come to believe that our actions make things better or worse, harmful or beneficial, without there necessarily being any *specific* people whom we can put into the calculus of pleasures or pains.

If we are prepared to say that some aspects of the environment are valuable – although, as I have argued already, this is a human-related statement – in that the value of the world is to be understood to mean 'value to some human', we need not know *which* humans, *how many* humans, or indeed, whether *any* humans will exist in order to make the judgement of value in the future. We can make it now on their behalf. If any humans exist at all, then it is worse for them if, for example, they are born affected by radiation from their environment. Therefore we have a duty to protect them.

But for how long? Parfit argues that there should be no more limit on the time span of our sense of responsibility than there is, these days, on our space span. If I know I am responsible for somebody's death or starvation, it should make no difference whether this person is in Outer Mongolia or on my doorstep. So, he believes, if I am responsible for a death in a thousand years, it should be no different from my being responsible for someone dying tomorrow. It is only my limited notion of myself, tied to a single human body with a beginning and an end, that limits my vision. He calls our normal view, namely, that we are less responsible, the further distant the future, the 'social discount theory'. And he says:

> Suppose we are considering how to dispose safely of nuclear waste. If we believe in the social discount theory we shall be concerned with safety only in the nearer future. We shall not be troubled by the fact that some nuclear waste will be radio-active for thousands of years. At a discount rate of 5 per cent, one death next year counts for more than a billion deaths in 500 years. On this view, catastrophe in the future can be regarded as morally trivial.[4]

But, as he thinks that this example shows, the social discount theory, though it is a theory presupposed by most welfare economists, is morally indefensible. Such is his argument.

I believe that Parfit is unrealistic. For we have to reckon with the factor of ignorance. However great our scientific expertise, we cannot know the future for certain. The further ahead we gaze, the more unpredictable the course of events becomes. There are too many complexities, too many interrelated changes (including the wholly unpredictable effects of human invent- iveness and ingenuity). It is impossible for us to feel as closely connected with the distant as with the immediate future. When so vast a number of events will have intervened, how can we tell which is most properly designated a cause? If I strike a cricket ball too exuberantly and it hits the conservatory, I know it is I who am responsible for the resultant damage. We are bound to take this kind of case as the starting-point and model for causal connection, and thus for responsibility. We move outwards and away from this central point. This has always been, and I suspect must remain, the basis of our ascriptions of responsibility. If there are too many of what the law calls a '*novus actus interveniens*', then we cease to blame ourselves.

Nor do I believe that it is possible for us to adopt Parfit's recipe for a greater sense of responsibility: namely, that we should cease to think of our own agency as bounded, more or less, by our own individual lives. We are the lives we know ourselves to be leading, which will end in death. Despite all science-fiction examples, we are too much our own bodies, which are born and die, to allow for that collapse of individuality that Parfit asks us to embrace.

So, how far are we bound to have regard for generations not our own and yet unborn? My answer is, I fear, not dramatic. I believe that we must learn to take seriously our special status on earth as human beings. This does not entail giving up our sense of our individuality. Far from it. It is partly our ability to see ourselves as individuals, living our lives in a natural environment, that leads us to conceive of a duty of care. We must understand that our special status within that environment derives from our nature as *human* individuals, with the capacity to make moral decisions. In the course of the last three chapters, I hope to have made clear that it is our special status that places us under an obligation not merely to our own species, but to members of other species and to our natural habitat. We must make use of all the knowledge that we alone among animals possess, in order to fulfil these obligations. We know that we have (so far) undisposed of nuclear waste that will still be radioactive in 1,000 years' time and will still be highly dangerous in 500 years' time. We do not know what new factors may be operative all those years ahead, or whether there will be any people or none who may suffer from the effects of the waste. But we do know enough to show us the absolute moral necessity of finding a solution which we think will be less damaging than others. And we need nothing except the consciousness of our own humanity to bring out the starkness of this duty.

My final conclusion is this. I have argued for the uniqueness of man, for humanity as a race apart. And I have argued that from this derive the values that we ascribe to the world and the duties that go with these values. First among these duties is that of educating our children to see themselves in the light of custodians (as God's creatures, if we so like to think of it), with a steward-ship to carry on. Whatever the core or foundation curriculum in schools is to be, this curriculum must be central to lessons both in the sciences and the humanities; we live in a man-centred universe, and we must teach the responsibility entailed by this awesome fact.

# 4

# *The Human Genome Project: Ethics and the Law*

The human genome project is one of the largest, most adventurous co-operative scientific undertakings in the history of science. No one doubts that it generates ethical problems; and I cannot tell you much that you have not already heard many times about what these may be. One problem, more political perhaps than moral, is the vast expense of the project. How are we to be assured that we are going to get value for money? It is extraordinarily difficult to imagine an answer to this question when we have as yet so little idea what the outcome of the completed 'map' is going to be. However, we should perhaps bear in mind that while the interest and excitement that surround the project may be purely scientific, the ultimate purpose of it is medical. By enabling us to know more, it will also enable us to use the new knowledge for therapeutic or preventive ends. Thus, ultimately we should be able to survey the medical scene, and say 'Has it been worth it?' But this will not be for a good many years yet.

I must say a word first about the two words 'ethical' and 'moral'. I do not believe that there is any great difference in their meaning, but I marginally prefer to use 'moral' for the kind of issues I am going to discuss. On the whole, I believe that 'ethical' suggests that there may be a code of conduct (as in 'professional ethics') by adhering to which we can be sure that we have done right, behaved reasonably well. 'Moral' suggests to me the possibility of profounder disagreement, more thorny problems, and the need for more thought. Others may not share my understanding of the two terms; but I will stick to 'moral problems' simply on the ground of their manifest complexity. I shall go on to argue, in addition, that, in the case of some of them, they will in turn generate legal problems. For we are dealing here with an area in which it is certain that regulation will be demanded, and it is most likely that regulation will have to be through the creation of new or amended laws.

Most of the moral problems we face are concerned with the uses to which the new understanding of genetics, through the gradual completion of the 'map', will be put. But it is perhaps worth raising the preliminary question of whether the new knowledge in itself, however used, will pose any problems. Will it, that is to say, so radically change our view of human nature that we shall find all our thinking, especially our moral thinking, undermined? The thought that this may be so is a thought about determinism. It suggests that the possibility of producing a map of the genetic links within an individual may show us how that individual is bound to be, not only with regard to his physical health (Will he die of heart disease, for example? Will he develop Huntington's Chorea?), but also in respect of his mental attributes and his character, his aggression or passivity, his intelligence or stupidity. If such a degree of prediction is possible in the case of an individual, shall we not have to give up holding him responsible for his actions, good or bad? Shall we not simply have to watch him act out his destiny, according him neither credit nor discredit? And how will such determinism by genes affect our thoughts about ourselves? How will we feel when we have to decide something, whether what clothes to wear to the opera or what career to take up or whether to pass information to the enemy for money? A thoroughgoing belief in determinism seems extremely difficult to reconcile with the structures of the language in which we talk about ourselves and others. Quite apart from words of praise and blame, specifically moral words, our whole vocabulary is full of active verbs, by which we refer to things we do, as opposed to things that happen to us; and we feel convinced that we and others could have acted otherwise than we did, at least in a vast number of cases.

The first thing to notice here is that the problem is by no means new. The freedom of the will (or its apparent freedom) has constituted a philosophical difficulty for centuries, even if the power supposed to control or determine human conduct has changed from time to time. There has, of course, been theological determinism

(God ordains and knows all that I will do); but, more potently, there has been a kind of determinism by Nature since the time of Aristotle.

To render determinism harmless, I believe that we need only to deploy the concept of ignorance. Even if it is true that, theoretically, and if humans lived in laboratory conditions, all their choices would be predictable, in the real world there are so many unknown and accidental factors which may move them one way or another, so many thoughts they have about the future derived from a complex past, that it would be impossible ever totally to predict or even explain how one individual made his choices. Spinoza regarded freedom as 'ignorance of necessity'. This may be as far as we can go. Our language of free choice is grounded in such ignorance, and will remain so (since we cannot possibly know everything about our environment) despite any knowledge we may acquire about our own, or other people's, genetic map.

The fear that determinism has evoked, the sense of dis-orientation, has always arisen from the thought that if our actions and reactions are predictable, they can no longer be prop-erly ascribed to us in the way we want them to be. But our ignor-ance of the factors that influence our choices, the things stored, for example, in our memories, derived from the chance cir-cumstances of the past, is a permanent and ineradicable feature of our lives and of our self-identity. Even if we become more able to talk in terms of the probability of someone's acting in this way or that, we can never aspire to certainty of prediction. As for our-selves, from within, we have our own consciousness of the factors we want to take into account. We know the difference between situations in which we are driven by irrational impulses and situations in which we weigh things up and consciously decide, for example, to wear this rather than that. A combination of consciousness and ignorance is quite enough to account for the internal sense of freedom that we have, as well as to protect us against the possibility of having all our choices anticipated in utmost detail. Given this background, I do not think we need fear that the whole language of action, choice, and responsibility will be demolished by our new genetic knowledge, however extended that may become.

If the mere existence of new knowledge poses no moral problems, then, we may say that there is nothing against its pursuit. Indeed, one could argue that since humans, and they alone, have the capability of approaching an understanding of the universe, including themselves, by scientific methods, they have a duty to do so. There is nothing whatever to be said for attempting to halt the pursuit of knowledge at any one point, even if that were possible.

However, the difference between past and present debates about freedom is that in the past we could do nothing to change the obstacles that seemed to stand in the way of free will. Nothing could change the will of God if he had destined you for ruin. Nature could not be made to break its own laws. But now the very words 'genetic manipulation' or 'genetic engineering' seem to pose a threat. The information that we shall receive will, it seems, be precise; and we know what alterations have already been achieved by genetic engineering in plants and in animals other than humans. There is thus a belief that not only are our actions, thoughts, and feelings programmed to be as they are, but that the programme can be rewritten. And so the real moral questions arise when we turn to consider not the existence of knowledge, but its use. There is a widespread fear among non-scientists that the new knowledge derived from the genome map may be abused.

Scientists sometimes speak as if their task in this connection were one of reassuring the public. This is not necessarily a good way to put the matter. There *are*, of course, irrational fears. If a child is afraid to go upstairs by himself or to walk past a certain gate in a field, I may reassure him by going with him and showing him that there are no bogeys. I may turn on the light and leave it on; I may in dozens of different ways make him feel confident that, after all, there is nothing to fear. I may be able to explain to him how he came to think of as frightening what was not in reality a threat. When we allay these irrational fears, it is good. But the general, non-scientific public are not children. They may be subject to fears which result from ignorance or from the sensationalism of the media (media-persons understandably love to excite their readers or viewers with shocking new possibilities). But some of their fears may be rational; and in this case, mere reassurance is not what is required. Discussion, explanation, and dialogue are needed, within the context of which people can see what moral issues are at stake.

It is not, however, an easy task to begin such debate and dialogue with the public. There are two obstacles in the way, and the first is public scepticism. People are simply unwilling to believe what they are told by experts, whether scientific or governmental. Their scepticism is particularly deep if they suspect that they are being told something to keep them quiet or to pull the wool over their eyes (this is the drawback of too manifestly attempting to set fears at rest). Their reaction is either that most maddening of insults 'I hear what you say,' meaning 'I hear, but do not believe,' or, equally irritating, 'You would say that, wouldn't you?' In the case we have in mind, that means: 'You tell me that there is no reason to fear the new genetic knowledge because you want to go on with your research, perhaps for financial gain. I will believe only those who are disinterested, and that does not include you.' This creates a particular difficulty for the open discussion of scientific or technical issues, for it tends to mean that anyone will be believed except the person who knows what he is talking about.

Somehow such scepticism must be overcome, otherwise no dialogue between scientists and the rest of the population can begin; and without it there is no possibility of reaching the kind of moral consensus we are going to need for settling our new moral problems. And if these cannot be settled, scientists and practising doctors will be unable to do what they genuinely want to do, which is to continue work for the general good.

The second difficulty is perhaps more philosophical, though it has practical consequences. When we are discussing advances in technology and in human knowledge, we may find ourselves asking how far ahead we are supposed to look. Should we concentrate on what is possible now? Or should we try to look, say, a decade ahead? Or should we allow our imaginations to carry us into an indefinite future, where all kinds of things, at present absolutely impossible though just about conceivable, may offer themselves to our attention? Suppose someone says, 'If X were possible, it would be wrong,' is it enough to say, 'Well, it isn't possible, or not yet'? At the Ciba Foundation conference held in Switzerland in 1989 this question was raised and discussed at some length. Professor Bernard Williams, the Oxford philosopher, suggested that such an easy answer could not count as a moralist's answer. He said, 'It is a requirement on moral argument that it shouldn't simply stop at mere technical fact, and say that the question does not yet arise; but it is not a requirement on a moral argument, in my view, that it should be able to cope with any *conceivable* possibility.'[1] He went on to say that scientists would not achieve the result they want (that is, to counterbalance the exaggerated view people hold of the dangers of genetic intervention) simply by insisting on present practical impossibilities. They are obliged to go somewhat further than that, and philosophers may help them, up to a point, by suggesting to them how much further it is reasonable to go.

Philosophy, including moral philosophy, is well accustomed to dealing with wholly hypothetical examples. For example, a philosopher interested in personal identity might say, 'If it were possible to perform a total brain transplant, would the patient who received the brain be in some way identical with the donor?' To discuss this question would then be expected to throw some light on how we now, and in ordinary circumstances, think about personal identity. Again, a moral philosopher might ask, 'If you were in possession of the ring of Gyges which rendered its wearer invisible, would you do things which you do not now do?' and the ensuing discussion would be expected to reveal something about the possibility of a sense of right and wrong independent of public opinion. And so, in the case we are interested in, we may ask, 'If it were possible to ensure by genetic manipulation that your child had certain characteristics of your choice, would it be right to choose what sort of person he would be?'

The answers to such questions may be illuminating, for they may bring to light principles of a general kind, themselves a proper subject for debate. For example, someone might want to defend the principle that it is morally wrong to treat our children as the mere vehicles for the satisfaction of our own aspirations. Or someone might want to argue that, in choosing characteristics for our children, we would be entering an area where we are profoundly ignorant of what other changes we might be bringing about at the same time, and that this alone should inhibit interventionism. Such principles or insights might well inform any further discussion about more realistic problems. To some extent, then, hypothetical or impossible examples may be helpful.

Nevertheless, I do not believe that we should be too bound by the conclusions we may come to about these 'matters of principle' (and if philosophers encourage us to be so bound, they are doing the progress of research a disservice). There are two different reasons why such examples may be less than helpful, at least in the particular case we are discussing. On the one hand, those who regard all genetic intervention as wrong have no need of such examples. For they see the wrongness in the very things that are *now* possible. On the other hand, if we argue from the wrongness, as we see it, in the hypothetical case to a potential wrongness, or wrongness in principle, in the things that can now be done, we are relying on one of two dubious arguments. The first is the so-called slippery slope. We are suggesting that if we proceed with the interventions that are now possible, we shall inevitably be led to something worse. Alternatively, we are suggesting that, because there is a principle involved, though what we can do now and are planning for the immediate future may not *look* bad, it must somehow *be* bad because it falls under the same principle. Both these arguments are, it seems to me, suspect.

But it is time, more than time, to move on to the nature of the moral problems themselves. These seem to me to fall into two groups. The first group centres on social issues concerned with privacy. The knowledge locked up in the human genome map will be available for use only if individuals are subjected to genetic screening. Screening will show the individual genetic map for each, and when this map is read, not only will it afford a partial explanation of, as it were, what that person is like; it will also reveal what tendencies he has, even what disorders he already has which have as yet produced no symptoms. And so the first moral question is whether screening should always be voluntary or whether some people should be compulsorily screened, and whether parents should be obliged to have their children screened or whether they may refuse to do so. It is easy to reply to this question by a defence of freedom and privacy. But in the long run, though economic considerations may well dictate how elaborate and widespread screening should be, it seems to me inevitable that everyone will have to submit to at least some compulsory screening.

It may seem immediately morally abhorrent that there should exist a genetic file on everyone, so that in principle everything could be known about the genetic status of everyone in the world. Yet there are those, especially insurance companies, who may claim a legitimate interest in the data. At present the convention, in seeking insurance, is that of maximum honesty. And it is difficult to see how insurance could continue as an institution if this were not the case. Insurance companies will therefore demand a genetic print-out just as now they demand a medical examination, and the result will be that people and their families may be compelled to discover things they would have preferred not to know. Similarly, where potential employers now demand a medical check, they too may demand a genetic screening and print-out, as may those admitting people to universities or the armed forces. There is no doubt that such invasion of privacy will be seen as morally objectionable, according to some ideal of respect for autonomy and independence. Yet it may be demanded by society.

It seems plain that we have here a problem which, though it is fundamentally moral, must nevertheless be tackled by public regulation, to limit as far as possible the evils of such widely disseminated information about individuals. In order to get such regulation in place, we need discussions between lawyers, members of trade unions, insurance brokers, civil servants, and those already expert in matters of data protection. It is not too early to start such discussions, so as to have plans for regulation in place, ready for the time when the issues are not simply *likely* to face us, but already do so. It is better in such cases to be prepared, rather than to have to take cases to court one by one as they arise, where someone is complaining of a breach of confidentiality. (Incidentally, the whole issue of confidentiality between doctor and patient will have to be rethought as a matter of urgency; and no doubt such organizations as the British Medical Association are already engaged in rethinking them.)

Apart from the moral (and perhaps social and political) problems that will arise from the dissemination of knowledge and the invasion of personal privacy, there is another group of problems concerned with what is threateningly known as 'genetic engineering'.

We must distinguish first between genetic diagnosis and what is sometimes called 'gene therapy'. Genetic diagnosis was first carried out in the case of pregnancies where there was a high risk of the foetus's being affected by a monogenetic disease. The screening was carried out in the second trimester of pregnancy, and an abortion was offered to the mother if the foetus was affected. The development of chorionic villus sampling dramatically affected the time in the pregnancy when the screening could be carried out. The danger to the foetus was less at this time, and the abortion, if decided on, was less traumatic. To avoid abortion altogether, the logical next step is pre-implantation, rather than pre-natal, diagnosis, where a number of embryos are fertilized *in vitro* and only those found to be healthy are implanted. The drawback to this practice, of course, is the relatively low success rate of *in vitro* fertilization. An alternative, not involving *in vitro* fertilization, would be the flushing out of blastocysts from the uterus and the reimplantation of those unaffected by the genetic defect. The avoidance of abortion in both these techniques is a very desirable feature for a couple who want a healthy baby.

I cannot myself see any possible moral objections to such procedures. To attempt to secure the birth of a healthy baby seems a morally admirable aim, and one wholly compatible with the general aims of medicine. There is, however, one argument put forward against such procedures which must be considered, because it could be used as an argument against any kind of genetic intervention. Those who regard any such intervention as morally abhorrent often accuse those who advocate it, and therefore wish research to continue, of 'playing God'.

It is not clear exactly what this accusation amounts to. It may be another way of expressing a conviction that some things are 'natural' and others 'unnatural', a distinction in itself notoriously unclear. (Is it, for instance, 'natural' to have one's life saved by an emergency removal of one's appendix? Is birth by caesarian section to be disallowed on the grounds that the surgeon here would be 'playing God'?) Sometimes, however, people who make such accusations may go on to adduce the consideration that if crippling monogenetic diseases are eliminated through selective destruction of embryos, those people who have been born with such a disease or who suffer other kinds of handicapping conditions, inherited or indeed acquired, will have been somehow downgraded. They will feel that society would prefer them never to have been born. Such arguments should perhaps be examined further, because they are so often put. The 'Handicap Lobby' is increasing in size and strength, both in the United States and in Europe.

The arguments are sometimes put forward by or on behalf of those who suffer a relatively mild form of handicap, physical or mental. We are always shown shining examples of people with handicaps who have marvellously adapted to them and are leading happy and useful lives. It has to be emphasized, however, that intervention of a preventive nature is aimed at the abolition not of just any handicap, but of certain disastrous diseases, whose outcome is fatal or which constitute a crushing and intolerable burden to the sufferers and their families. To try to prevent the birth of children with such diseases as these is to imply nothing about people with less radical handicaps, many of whom undoubtedly live quite tolerable lives, which could be made even better if we tried harder. The same is simply not true of children born with, say, Tay–Sachs or Lesch–Nyhan disease. The mildly handicapped lobby has no right to speak on behalf of children who suffer from these conditions or on behalf of their parents.

There is, in any case, a confusion in the argument which needs to be unravelled. The purpose of genetic intervention is to ensure that instead of a child who might have been born with an incurable disease, another child is born who will be healthy (or who at least won't suffer from that particular disease). There is no identity between the child who *is* born and that other child who *might have been* born and was not. We are not saying of two otherwise equal children, 'I prefer one to the other.' For there was no other. All that a parent who has allowed a selected embryo to be placed in her uterus has done is to assert, absolutely in general, that she prefers a healthy to an ill baby. And with this few would quarrel. We must distinguish between talking of the existent and the non-existent, and not pretend that they can be compared with each other, on equal terms.

Again, when a child has been born handicapped, we must distinguish between saying of this existent child, 'It would have been better if this handicapped child had not been born' (and there are some cases where people do say that) and saying, on the other hand, 'It would be better if this child had not been born handicapped.' The latter in no way writes the child off; it just expresses regret that he is ill. It is a hopeful thing to say, if there is some remedy for his illness. And, of course, one day there may be a cure, through gene replacement.

So we move from diagnostic (and preventive) genetic interventions to gene therapy, properly so-called. Here the distinction between somatic cell therapy and germ cell therapy is generally taken to be all-important. In somatic cell therapy, the aim is to introduce non-defective genes into particular cells of patients born with a monogenetic defect, to replace those which carry the disease. The complexities of such procedures are enormous. Doubtless, the more we know of the human genetic system as a whole, the more numerous the possibilities of therapy will become, including, perhaps, the cure of some common polygenic disorders such as diabetes. For with continued research, probes for such disorders may be developed. But in whatever way the difficulties are overcome, there is widespread agreement (except of course among those who, for the reasons I have tried to explain, believe that all genetic intervention is wrong) that such therapy is not open to moral objection. As long ago as 1982, the US Presidential Commission whose report was entitled *The Splicing of Life* held that the incorporation of a gene to treat a disease in an individual was in principle no different from the repeated administration of the product of that gene, and that any additional risks could be justified by the severity of the illness of the patient. Research on gene replacement will proceed, I presume, in parallel with the development of pre-natal and pre-implantation diagnosis and the identification of genetic defects in general.

Unlike somatic cell therapy, germline therapy could in principle be carried out by altering cells in early embryos or in the fertilized egg. Indeed, transgenic mammals produced by these means are already used for research purposes, and the same techniques could be applied to humans. This form of gene manipulation reaches all the cells of the organism, and the genes thus altered are themselves heritable. It has to be noticed that the new genes do not replace, but add to, the defective genes, which might therefore recur at some stage. But it is not so far possible to predict when they might recur. Indeed, the main reason for the general rejection of germline cell therapy is its unpredictable outcome. For its consequences seem to extend for ever.

It is in general the case that when the consequences of our acts become so widely diffused, so vague that we cannot quite tell where they begin and end, we tend to let ourselves off feeling responsible for them. But in the case of germline therapy it is possible that the consequences of intervention may be able to be charted; and however far distant the effects, it may be hard not to ascribe the unwanted consequences to 'playing God' some time in the past. Nevertheless, there might be some circumstances in which, if we knew more, we might be justified in pursuing germline therapy. For example, if it became possible, as indeed it might, to eradicate for ever immune deficiency diseases, in particular Aids, through germline therapy, the present or immediate future advantage might seem sufficient to outweigh the argument from ignorance, however keenly felt. I would not therefore wish to rule out for ever the legitimacy of germline genetic manipulation at the embryonic stage.

The real reason for the general assumption throughout Europe that germline intervention will be prohibited is the fear of the power others may have over us and our descendants. We are used to being in the power of doctors when we or our children are ill (though *we* may feel the power of doctors over us more than *they* either feel it or in reality exercise it). However, we do not like the idea that someone unknown, but certainly not we ourselves, will be able to exercise power over not only us but our children, by choosing, albeit a bit blindly, how we should be. For we all fear, and not without reason, that one day such power might be exercised not by benevolent doctors, but by political tyrants who would use us for their own ends.

So here we come back to the slippery slope argument: the argument that relies on the fear that if something is possible, we will inevitably do it, whether it is good or bad, right or wrong. This argument has an immense influence on the human imagination, and was certainly the argument most frequently invoked, both in and out of Parliament, in the debate about the permissibility of research using human embryos. I predict that in a short time, when the debate about the use of our new genetic knowledge enters the public arena, the slippery slope argument will once again dominate the headlines, and not only the headlines. The argument is that though what is being immediately proposed may be all right, it will inevitably lead to worse, until at the bottom of the slope there lie unknown horrors (and indeed some known horrors, like the use of humans for research before consigning them to the incinerator). I have already suggested that too much weight should not be given to this kind of argument. The reason is that we can, if we will, block this slope at any stage we decide to, by legislation.

The passage through Parliament of the Embryology Bill was an example of how a majority of both houses, anxious and often suspicious though they were, in the end were persuaded of the power of the law to block a slippery slope. Legislation was introduced to make it a criminal offence to use embryos for research after fourteen days from fertilization *in vitro*. The block on the slope was thus the criminal law. If someone some time wanted to change the limit of research time from fourteen days to some later stage in the development of the embryo, then that person would have to go through the whole process of arguing this through Parliament, with the risk that he might lose even the ground so far occupied by those in favour of research. It is a daunting task, and not one that will be lightly undertaken. In effect, the slippery slope has been blocked, in this instance, for many years to come; and if the matter is reconsidered in the future, the barrier may be erected even higher up the slope.

With this model in mind, we may ask how, in the case of gene therapy, the slope is to be blocked. There is pretty general agreement on this, not just in this country, but in Europe and Australia and the United States as well. There must be a list of conditions, all of them capable of being described as diseases, which shall be the subject of research and shall be the target of gene therapy, whether somatic or germline. The list may change from time to time, no doubt, but only through an Act of Parliament or through a statutory body answerable to Parliament. To block the slope, I have no doubt that legislation will be required. Self-regulation will not be enough, if only because the possibility of making vast sums of money out of genetic engineering is so manifest, and the temptations may therefore be such that the usual sanctions of peer disapproval may not be strong enough to counterbalance the tendency to greed or self-aggrandizement. In establishing the fields within which research and treatment may be permitted, I believe that the law *must* be invoked.

And so, finally, we come to what is probably the most intractable moral problem of all, but one by no means unique to the field of our enquiry. The question is not so much *what* is right and what is wrong, as *how* such distinctions are to be made in the public domain, and with a view to legislation. If we lived in a theocratic society, in which certain priests, elders, or ayatollahs were supposed to have direct access to divine commands, the problem would be easy to solve. The question of intervention at the cell stage would have only to be put to these experts, and they could be relied on to come up with an answer acceptable to everyone. For the *authority* to make such decisions would be theirs. But in a mixed, democratic society with a mixed, hybrid system of morals and no recognizable moral experts on the scene (instead, if anything, a Protestant belief in the sovereignty of the individual conscience), things are very different.

At the present time, research using human embryos (subject to strict limitation) is permitted by law; the rights and wrongs of this need no longer be a subject of public debate, even though there are, and will remain, a number of people who are opposed to any such research. There is still the question, however, of the purposes for which such research should be undertaken. There is no longer any question of its being solely for the relief of infertility; too many other possibilities have become manifest. To alleviate which conditions, then, should embryos be used in research? Is it tolerable to society that public money should be spent on alleviating just any conditions? It seems clear from the foregoing argument that a barrier must be erected so that we do not slide down into what many regard as the frightening place where people can choose for themselves or, worse, have chosen for them what sort of people there should be. We therefore need, as I have suggested, a list of conditions, research into which should be encouraged. Such a list need not be as restrictive and bureaucratic as it might sound. For obviously research into one medical condition may spill over into others; and the list of conditions to be funded would fluctuate all the time. We will have to bear in mind, first, the overriding *medical* impetus behind the human genome project; secondly, that interest in various items on the supposed list will vary from time to time; thirdly, and not least, that there will always be questions about whether current research is actually paying off. Does it give value for money? All such questions, in their different ways, are value questions. They must be settled by a method that will command general respect and agreement.

There are inevitable differences between moral judgements (or value judgements) made in the private and the public domain. In private someone may adopt a moral principle and decide to stick to it though the heavens fall; he may martyr himself for a moral cause, and be admired for doing so, even by those who do not share his moral convictions. In the public domain, on the other hand, moral judgements must almost necessarily be made by committees of enquiry, or ethics committees. I have no doubt that, sooner or later, such a committee will come into being to consider the questions we are now thinking of. It will have as its task to decide what will be, on the whole, for the best, or for the common good; what will not outrage too many people, and what will have a chance of getting through Parliament if statutory regulations and statutory powers are to be proposed. These considerations form a method for settling moral issues; but they are of their nature mundane and non-heroic. A committee of enquiry or an ethics committee cannot martyr itself. Nor will it be persuasive and do what it was appointed to do if it is too visionary, too future-orientated, too idealistic. Matters of public policy must in the end be settled by Parliament. But before Parliament is ready to discuss them, someone – and that means some committee – must debate them, openly, and present their conclusions to the appropriate minister. Such issues as these should be subject to control, but not the control of any one person.

So *who* shall decide how the control is to be exercised? If, as I believe, there must be legislation to regulate the use of the new knowledge we shall acquire from the human genome map, and if, as I also believe, such legislation cannot be introduced without a fair degree of moral consensus, how is such consensus to be achieved? Part of the moral issue we face is, as I have suggested, not what is right and what wrong, but *how an agreement is to be reached on* what is right and what wrong.

There exists a common assumption that moral questions can be solved by hard and clear thought, and that moral conclusions based such thought can then be incorporated into regulations, by Parliament or by professional bodies. These assumptions are mistaken. No select band of moral philosophers, however hard they think, can ever come up with a single *correct* solution to problems such as those posed by the genome map, since of their very nature moral problems do not admit of such solutions. For morality rests not on calculation, or not on that alone, but much more on a sentiment of right and wrong, based on tradition, feelings, taught scruples, and perhaps a genetically inherited reluctance to do certain things.

It is difficult to make a start towards consensus when the tradition-based feelings people have, which constitute their morality, are so diverse. Nevertheless, it is within a committee that such differences may best be explored, and conclusions that are moderately satisfactory best be reached, in the eye of the public, and slowly. This is, I believe, the only way to address the issues and in some, probably ramshackle, way to reach a consensus to bring before Parliament. It is perhaps comforting that, although the issues are unlike any we have faced before and may seem alarming, the major moral problems that arise from them are familiar. They are to do with who should exercise power over whom, who should be required to make decisions about right and wrong that will issue in legislation, and how it is possible to educate people to base their moral sentiments on understanding rather than ignorance. None of these questions is easily answered. But at least they are not mind-bogglingly novel.

# 5

# *The Good of the Child*

There is, as I need hardly tell you, a huge literature of rights, concerning both rights in general and the specific rights of those who are in no position to claim them for themselves, such as children and other animals. Some of this literature is simply theoretical, some more practical and polemical in style. I will skip any kind of overview of all the arguments, but try instead to work out how the concept of children's rights may fit in with two other familiar concepts, the needs of children and the good of the child.

But first a preliminary word about the pitfalls. When people talk about rights, whether the rights of humans or of other animals, they are making claims for what *ought* to be accorded to the supposed bearer of the right, whether that is food or freedom or the absence of pain. If someone says 'I have a right,' the implication is that if he is not accorded that which he claims, then someone else is at fault. Lying behind such claims and justifying them (for we cannot claim just anything we want as a right), there must exist a law or a by-law or a strong convention establishing the right. And, if possible, such a law should carry sanctions, to be used against those who act in breach of it. The simplified model is of a right of way. If you claim that a right of way exists through my land, then I am bound to let you through, even to mark the path (though, admittedly, nowadays subject to there being no overriding agricultural or other need to block this path). But it is of no use for you to claim a right unless you can prove that such a right has been assigned to you as a member of the public. If it has, then, in principle at least, you could sue me if I refused to let you cross my land.

Now I fully admit that this is a simple, and indeed a simplified, example. But it is important none the less. For you cannot claim a right of way on the grounds that it would be convenient for you to cross my land, or even on the grounds that it is essential to your well-being that you should cross it. If you have no right but *need*, for some reason, to cross my land, then there are two things you can say. First, you can say that though there is no by-law permitting you access, there ought to be, and that the by-laws should be amended. Or secondly, you can say that though there is and can be no by-law, yet out of human charity I ought to let you go across my land. In either case you will be appealing to your need, and the way to satisfy your need will be either through a change in the law or through an appeal to my good feelings and moral sense. What you cannot do, in the absence of any by-law, is to continue to claim that you *have* a right. Let us suppose that you are confined to a wheelchair, and crossing my land is the only way that you can get from your house to the railway station in your chair. There is no recognized right of way across my land, but you may properly say that you need access to it, in order to catch your train to work each day. It is not certain, in my view, whether your need would be enough to activate a change in the local by-laws. It is certain that if I am a decent sort of person, the consideration of your need will cause me to let you go through my land. But my kindness to you in this respect does not, I believe, go any way towards giving you a right; and if I sell my property to someone else, you would have to appeal to them all over again, though you might cite the precedent that I have set; and he may feel terrible if he thinks of refusing your request.

I think we ought to bear this simple example in mind when we consider the relation between needs and rights; and even between the good of the child and the rights of the child. For the important thing about rights is that they are necessarily contained and defined by a law (or at least a convention) and that they are therefore universal. Anyone who is governed by the law is given the right under that law. And the claim to a right must be capable of being proved (or disproved). Whether or not you are being deprived of something rightfully yours should be capable of being settled, if necessary, in court.

But, you may say, I am being too legalistic, I am talking about legal or quasi-legal rights. What about moral rights? Surely I would not deny the existence of rights outside the narrow confines of the law itself? I certainly agree that we may, and do, talk about moral rights. But if the very existence of a justified claim to a right depends on the existence of a law, then the claim to a *moral* right equally depends on the existence of a *moral* law or principle under which the right may be claimed. Let us suppose a society like our own in which there is a general, though by no means always observed, principle that one should be truthful. If I ask you the way to the station and you deliberately mislead me, telling me to turn right when I need to turn left, then I may indignantly claim that I had a right to be told the truth. This claim and the moral rule lying behind it are general as far as they go. But they are subject to all kinds of limitations. If I enquire into your private life, having no reason to do so, and motivated only by curiosity, you may well argue that I have no right to be told the truth, or indeed to be told anything at all. Most people would agree with this moral principle as well. But suppose you are my doctor and I ask you the prognosis of my condition and you tell me a lie, there is here, I suspect, no agreed moral principle. I may believe, as my condition deteriorates, that I had a right to be told the truth; I may think that this claim is supported by the morally binding contract between doctor and patient. You, my doctor, may, on the other hand, hold that the relation between doctor and patient rests on another moral principle: namely, that the doctor must decide whether or not to tell his patient the truth in accordance with his judgement of the best interests of the patient. Each party to this non-legal contract may interpret the rights and duties that flow from it in a different, but perfectly honest and sincere, way. In arguing with you that, as your patient, I had a right to be told the truth, I am setting out my view of what you ought to have done. I am telling you what moral principle should be a guide to your conduct. In such a case, there is actually no need to talk about rights at all. I can come straight to the point and say, 'You should have told me.' You can reply, 'Not so. It was better for you not to know.' We are here plainly and openly disagreeing about a matter of morality. To introduce the intermediary concept of my right or yours simply obscures the issue.

But if I do not think much of moral rights, surely, it may be said, I must take more seriously the concept of a *natural* right. For these are rights that belong to all creatures, or all creatures of a specific kind, in virtue of their nature. Such rights are, like full-blown legal rights, general; and it should be possible to discover what such rights are. Moreover, it can be argued that, like narrowly legal rights, they are backed up and justified by the existence of a law – namely, natural law. I need not remind you of the thousands of words that have been written and spoken over the centuries on the subject of natural law and natural rights. Often the concept has been used as a grander and more permanent-sounding alternative to that of moral rights. For we all know that ideas of morality are, as Aristotle said, capable of only so much exactitude and definiteness, and no more; they are subject to change, and are affected both by geography and by history. But nature remains the same; and if a man's rights are derived from his nature, then these rights will remain the same for all men and for all time. It should be possible, then, to claim a right simply on the basis of being human; and the point of the Convention on Children's Rights[1] is to call attention to the undoubted fact that human children have certain additional characteristics, and that therefore being a human child entails certain additional rights, deriving from the nature of childhood itself. For the nature of humans and of the human child contains within itself certain needs; and if there are any natural rights, then, as Professor Hart argued forty years ago,[2] the strongest candidate is the right to be regarded equally, in respect of these needs. It is an infringement of human rights, or of human children's rights, to be disregarded when it comes to the satisfaction of basic needs common to all. This is the natural law which justifies the claim to a natural or inalienable right: that, being human, *all* of us must have basic needs satisfied. The convention makes a special case for human children, calling attention to special needs. I personally regard this natural law as itself a moral principle, though a fundamental one. And, if so, then the fundamental right is a *moral* right, rather than a natural right. But perhaps the name does not matter. Both the law and the right derived from it are absolutely general.

The principle of *equality of consideration*, then, in Hart's view the only natural right, entails that all children must have their basic needs satisfied; and if a society does not satisfy them, then that society is failing in its duty, for the children are being deprived of what is theirs by right.

So far, so good. But the pitfalls remain. For who decides what are the basic needs of a child? Article 6 of the Convention lays down that 'every child has the inherent right to life'. But do we have to take 'every' absolutely literally? Food, water, and health care could probably be agreed as essential to life. But must *all* children be supplied even with these? What about those very tiny new-born babies born after only twenty weeks or so of pregnancy, with slim chances of long-term survival or of survival without an intolerable burden of handicap (babies born, for instance, with only fragments of a brain)? These babies are children, and they are human. Have they the right to be kept alive as long as it is possible to keep them alive? Are they deprived of a right if they are allowed to die? I do not think so. But to say this is to reduce the comfortable *universality* of rights, even when they are derived from basic needs. Again, how basic must a need be if its satisfaction is to count as a right? If we look at the words of the Convention, we find that children must be brought up as far as possible in their families; that they must not work; that they must be educated, and educated in a particular way 'to understand human rights'; and that they must have the opportunity to play and to exercise their imaginations in the arts and in free speech. All this is excellent, no doubt, but we should be clear that we are here putting forward an ideal concept of childhood, an ideal embraced, on the whole, by prosperous countries of the West. It is a childhood which is, relatively speaking, prolonged. The prospects of death are low; the need for begging or earning money is minimal; education is provided, free, for all; and there is leisure for play and the pursuit of the arts. The disabled are given special help. This has not always been even the ideal of childhood; and it is, of course, completely beyond the powers, or even the desires, of a large number of countries.

This would not be denied by those who subscribe to the Convention. For their aim is avowedly moral and improving: to provide 'agreed international standards by which nations can in future be judged'.

But, as Angela Neustatter wrote in *Children First*, the Convention goes further even than this. It not only supplies criteria by which the performance of different countries can be judged, 'It recognises that many nations may be willing to ratify the Convention but that they may not have the resources to fully implement it. Enshrined in the Convention then is a global responsibility to help.'[3] The Convention is supposed, in fact, to supply not only an ideal and a means of assessing the success or lack of success that countries have in attaining that ideal; it is also to contain an absolute imperative to aid in the attainment of the ideal. Not only is a particular ideal of childhood set up, but it seems that, necessarily, we all have an obligation to ensure that, as far as possible, the ideal is achieved. I do not believe that the attempt to attain an ideal, whether on one's own behalf or on behalf of someone else, can ever be properly described in terms of rights; and the further we move from the basic needs of human children, the nearer to the notion of an ideal of childhood we get, and the further from what could possibly be called the 'rights' of the child. I do not decry the ideal as set up by the Convention. Far from it. In particular, I believe that there is much to be said for a long, irresponsible, protected childhood. But I believe we ought to recognize that such a childhood has always been a function of affluence or relative affluence, and that to think of it as a right is no more realistic than to think of non-poverty as a right. It is something that we may work towards, but not something that it is even intelligible to *claim*.

Nevertheless, there is much in the Convention that is of the greatest importance, and it is absolutely right that we in the United Kingdom should subscribe to it. Perhaps most important of all is Article 3, which lays down that 'In all actions concerning children, whether undertaken by public or private welfare institutions, courts of law, administrative authorities or legislative bodies, the *best interests of the child* shall be a primary consideration.' While the concept of rights itself seems to stem most naturally and easily from the concept of need, and especially, as I hope to have suggested, from the concept of *basic* need, Article 3 seems to go further. It suggests a notion of the good of the child which is altogether more complex than the mere supplying of food, water, air, and clothing in order that the child may survive. For the 'interests of the child' must be taken to refer to a long-term good, something that the child would aim for if he could, and that good parents would aim for on behalf of their children. And this concept is, I suppose, identical with that of the good of the child. So we are now told, by the Convention, that the child has a right that his good should be a primary consideration. And this is indeed a moral right, based on a moral principle worth defending.

I believe that, as a matter of fact, the expression 'the interests of the child' is a better one than 'the good of the child' which I have chosen for my title. For to speak of someone as having an 'interest' suggests that he is a separate creature with wishes and preferences, as well as needs, of his own. When we act in our own interest, we consult these wishes and preferences, as well as our needs.

An animal or even a plant may have needs; and so we may give our dog an injection for his own good and in so doing satisfy his health needs; or we may move our rose-bush to a more sheltered position so that it may flourish out of the wind. Yet we would not, except as a joke, speak of this move as being 'in the interests of the rose-bush'. In moving it, we consult not its interests, for it has none, but our own. To lay down, therefore, that a child must, as of right, have its interests consulted is to make the assumption that the child is an individual, with his own desires and preferences, a person in his own right, not the property or possession of someone else. And this of course comes near to the fundamental natural right suggested as the unique natural right by Professor Hart – the right of each existing human to be considered, his interests not put on one side or disregarded.

Why, then, if the interests of the child are what we ought to consider, have I chosen instead to entitle my lecture 'The Good of the Child'? The reason is simply that this is the phrase most used by the courts in this country, and by the medical profession and the social services. All these administrators and professionals claim to hold that 'The good of the child is paramount.' This is the concept most frequently deployed in talking, for example, of settlements in divorce cases, in adoption, in disputes arising in cases of surrogacy, in the removal of children from home to a safe place. The phrase is used so automatically, with such aplomb and confidence, in such cases that it might be supposed by the unwary that the good of the child is something readily determined – that we actually know or can find out what the good of the child is. And all the time there is the hidden supposition, too, that the child himself has no say in what his good may be – just as our rose-bush, which has no *interests*, has no say in what is for its good.

However, a failure to consult the child, to find out what he wants or prefers in the manner implied by the notion of acting in his interests, is not altogether blameworthy where the child in question is an infant. And it is in the case of actual infants, who cannot express or even perhaps feel their wishes in any coherent way, that the concept of the good of the child is very often employed. Nor can we be blamed if we sometimes seem ignorant or uncertain about what the good of the child may be. For evidence is extremely difficult to come by in such fields; and we are all to a greater or less extent governed by prejudices or beliefs not much better than old wives' tales about what will or will not, in general, turn out to be good for children.

I shall say something about some of these difficult cases in a moment. For the time being I want to put in another word of warning. Adopting the Convention on the Rights of the Child ought not to make us feel self-satisfied. In adopting it, we must look at our own practices, as well as those of countries which, for economic or cultural reasons, seem not to have gone far along the road towards ensuring for their children the kind of childhood enshrined in the Convention. Even if most people in Britain would say that they endorsed such an ideal of childhood, yet there is no doubt that the British do not actually *like* children very much. We may grant that a child, once born, has a right to life and a right to health care and education. But there are many children in this country who, though not bought and sold or forced to go out to work, are nevertheless not only hungry but, still more frequently, oppressed, neglected, and abused. You have only to listen to parents talking to or shouting at their children in supermarkets; you have only to see them often totally ignoring the distress of a child, to recognize the truth of the charge that we, many of us, do not care much for children, even if we are members of a supposedly 'caring' society and support, albeit in a somewhat niggardly way, the so-called caring professions. And it may be that this lack of warmth, characteristic of the British (but not of, say, the Italians or the Chinese) is reflected in our notions of the good of the child. Too often we do not think of the child as actually or potentially a separate human being, but as a creature who is the possession of his parents, the responsibility of the State, whose good may be determined by principles rather like the principles of animal husbandry or horticulture.

Bearing in mind, then, that we are by no means above reproach in our own attitudes to children, I want to consider briefly some cases in which it is extremely difficult to determine what may be for the good of the child. And here we come upon an apparent paradox. Though it may be true that the British are not very good at liking children, yet they tend to be passionately anxious to have them. Those who find themselves to be infertile are often prepared to go to enormous lengths and great expense to have a family of some kind.

Some of the methods available to help the infertile, especially *in vitro* fertilization, carry no implications for the welfare of any children who may be born, as far as we can see. But wherever people other than the couple who want the child are involved, as in adoption, artificial insemination by a donor (AID), or surrogacy, the good of the child has to be considered from the beginning of the transaction.

Adoption is fairly easily dealt with. On the whole, we manage adoption quite well. We forbid adoption in exchange for money. We give the biological mother of the child time after the birth in which she may change her mind; and we take into account that we are dealing with existing children who will almost certainly be better off being adopted than spending their life in institutions, provided that we ensure as far as possible that their adoptive parents will be able to look after them and thoroughly understand their commitment. All the long processes of adoption are motivated by the consideration of the good of the child.

But the cases of AID and surrogacy are very different from that of adoption, and from one another. And it is with regard to such cases that, though we may use the phrase 'the good of the child', we are really so extremely ignorant of the outcomes that we must be, to a large extent, guessing. AID has been practised for a long time, and it has become a more or less accepted method of starting a so-called artificial family. But the numerous committees and commissions that have considered it since the 1950s, notably the Feversham Committee in 1960 and the Peel Committee of the British Medical Association twelve years later, have been less than happy about it, and have often expressed their anxieties in terms of the probable good of the child born as a result of this process. In their book *The Artificial Family*, the sociologists Drs Snowden and Mitchell expressed some fears about the effects on the marriage partners where there has been a birth by AID (and, presumably, would have thought the effects of surrogacy even more unlikely to be good for a marriage), but their main dissatisfaction with such families is on account of the children of the marriage.[4] The centre of their objection is the secrecy normally involved in AID. And I want to say a little about this, in the context of the good of the child.

Some would argue that, at least provided the marriage is stable, no harm can be done by allowing everyone, including the child himself, to believe that his social father is also his biological father. Provided the doctor, if one is involved, and the mother can be trusted to keep their secret, no one need ever know. In some Asian families, even the father is deceived. Since infertility is widely believed to be a female disorder, and since childlessness is a ground for divorce among some Muslims, it is fairly common for women to seek AID without letting their husbands know.

Though the medical profession would not advocate the deception of the male partner, they have not in the past had anything to say against the deception of the child. Indeed, advice on AID has been given on the assumption that secrecy will be preserved, as part of professional confidentiality. Care has always been taken as far as possible to match the donor with the social father (sperm being labelled 'blue eyes', 'six foot', etc.), and sometimes couples have been advised to have sexual intercourse at the time of insemination so that they might really at least pretend not to know that the child who was born was not the child of his social father (even though the doctors involved might have ascertained that there was virtually no chance of normal conception). As late as 1979 the Royal College of Obstetricians and Gynaecologists published a leaflet saying that whether or not to tell a child that he was born through AID was a matter for individual decision.

'Unless you tell your child, there is no reason for him ever to know.' And women are often told to go home from the clinic and 'forget all about it'. But my question is whether it can possibly be for the good of the child or in his best interests to be brought up to believe something that is not true: namely, that he is the genetic offspring of his mother's husband. I know well that there are many children who are brought up with such deception, whether the deception concerns AID or an adulterous relationship. But it seems to me that in such cases the parents are not consulting the interests of the child, but their own. The child is being used as a means to the parents' ends: namely, to seem to have a 'normal' family. And using one person as a means to another's ends can never be right unless the person has consented to be so used (and not always then). As an AID child who is deceived about his parentage grows towards adulthood, more and more he is being treated as less than human and rational, less than equal with his parents, but rather as their tool. I cannot argue (for I could never prove) that AID children who are told their origins are better off or happier in any measurable way than they would have been had they not been told. Indeed, they may well be less happy (provided the deception was thoroughly kept up). Nevertheless, I believe that if they are not told, then they are being wrongly treated. They have been deprived of the basic human or moral or natural right to be considered as an equal, of equal importance with other people. And this cannot be in accordance with Article 3 of the Convention.

There is a different question I would raise about the artificial family, one likely to arise especially acutely in the case of the use of surrogates. This is the question of the legal disputes likely to arise where some sort of contract has been entered into, sometimes thought of as a pre-birth adoption contract. There are moral problems that may be raised about the status of the surrogate mother in such arrangements, and about her receiving money or gifts in kind in exchange for undertaking a pregnancy. But these do not concern me at present. I am concerned only to raise a question about the good of a child who may be born to a surrogate and may then become an object of dispute, either if he is found to be defective and the commissioning parents are therefore unwilling to accept him (and such a case has been recorded), or if the surrogate mother, having given birth to the baby, finds that she does not want to hand him over to the commissioning parents, or if she changes her mind before she has given birth. There have been notorious cases of both the latter kinds. It seems to me that, however carefully a surrogacy contract is drawn up, and however much the parties to the contract are advised beforehand of their rights and obligations in the matter, there will always remain a real risk of dispute in such cases. Where a case comes to court, the judge is always prepared to come to a decision with the good of the child as the most important consideration before him in making his judgment. Both in this country and in the United States, the contract itself has no legal validity, and will be set aside as void in the case of dispute. The judge, therefore, must, and does genuinely, try to find a solution that is in the best interests of the child, whatever was contained in the contract. There is a strong presumption in law that in cases of dispute the mother of the baby will have custody of it; and 'mother' in the eyes of the law means 'the woman who gave birth' (this understanding was confirmed by legislation in the 1990 Embryology Act). It is sometimes argued on the other side that the good of the child must demand that he be given to the commissioning parents. For they wanted a child so desperately that they were prepared to pay sometimes vast sums to procure the services of a surrogate. But this argument does not seem to me to be very powerful. First, it may not be altogether for the good of a child to be probably the only child of parents who have spent years longing for a child and have finally spent perhaps more money than they can well afford in order to have one. The burden of mixed guilt and responsibility on such a child may be too heavy as he grows to maturity. Secondly, what the commissioning parents wanted was *a child*. They may not be the best people to judge whether they are acting in the best interests of the particular child they have got, especially as he ceases to be a child.

But however the case is decided on each separate occasion, it seems to me that it cannot be for the good of the child that he should start life as a subject of legal dispute, possession of him being claimed by two warring parties. Once again, it would be very hard to prove that this is damaging in any specific way. But at least we can say with certainty that to be a subject of dispute in this way is to be treated as an object like any other; it is not to be treated as a person with the future possibility of having interests and rights of one's own. As in the former case, I believe that we should regard it as a failure to adhere to the spirit of Article 3 of the Convention – and I hope that in future we may see it this way.

I have taken these two very difficult cases in order to suggest that though we are surely morally obliged to adopt the Convention on the rights of children, and especially to argue for Article 3, and though under the Convention we shall have further obliged ourselves to consider the good of the child as paramount, we are by no means in the clear when it comes to discussing what the good of the child is, still less what are his interests. We are too liable to suppose that what is in our own interests is in the child's. The case of the artificial family is a particularly serious indication of this. For there can be no doubt that what people who want children want is their own satisfaction, not that more elevated thing 'the good of the child'. They may come to want that when they have a child; they may not. But the fact that they want a child does not by any means entail that they will in future consult his interests, and certainly it could not entail that they consulted those interests before he was born. For then he had no interests and no rights.

Those of us who have children are liable to treat those children as our property, parts of our effects, to dispose of as we like. This again is contrary to the spirit of the Convention. If we are to take the interests of children seriously, we need to think again, as the authors of the Convention did, about what childhood is and what it should be; and about the sense in which we may properly speak of 'our' children, increasingly, as they grow up, separate individuals such that they *can* be the bearers of rights for themselves. But they must also be loved and liked. This cannot be wholly a matter of rights.

It seems to me to be a fundamental moral principle that we ought to love and cherish our children as beings separate from ourselves and with their own distinct characteristics. But this is hardly the sort of moral principle to generate a right that could be claimed. For long after a child's rights to have his basic needs supplied have been satisfied, there are still many moral offences we can commit against him. No ascription of rights will ever be enough, by itself, for the good of the child; for that, we need moral and practical understanding.

I will end by reading two short quotations, both from the periodical *Children First*.[5] Dr Alan Gilmour, Director of the NSPCC, is there quoted as saying this: 'It's time society started changing their attitude to children and began to look at the world from their eyes.' And Dr David Pithers, psychologist at the National Children's Home, having told a terrible story of parental pressure and withdrawal of love, said this: 'Parents need to look carefully at what they do to their children.' We can do better if we exercise imagination and truly think about our children, seeing things through their eyes. I believe that adopting the Convention, though it will not mend all ills, will perhaps be a start on rethinking and a beginning to a change in our own attitudes.

# 6

# Towards a Moral Consensus

The problem I want to explore in this chapter is a general one: How is government to be carried on, if, lying behind it, there is no consensus morality? If there is, as we are often told now, no general shared sense of what is right and what is wrong, how are laws to be enacted? How will they ever get through Parliament? And, if enacted, how are they to be enforced? That there exists a close relationship between law and morality would be universally agreed. But whereas there must be one clear set of laws, albeit changing gradually over time, and one established system of justice in any one society, our society is pluralistic, and this means that there exist within it a variety of different cultures and, going with them, different concepts of the good. I want to spend a bit of time considering what a consensus morality is, and to what extent it is true that we have to live these days without one. If we have to, then the relation between morality and the law must be newly thought out, and to do this will be part of the business of philosophy. We may have to look forward to a situation in which the law, being consistent and unifying, may have to guide, rather than reflect, moral thought.

I would like to start by going back more than a quarter of a century. My excuse is that philosophical problems do not, on the whole, get solved. They arise over and over again, in different circumstances and with different degrees of urgency, and it always repays us if we look at them anew, with the eyes of the present time.

In 1959, the report of the Committee of Enquiry on Homosexual Offences and Prostitution, chaired by Lord Wolfenden, was published.[1] This report recommended, among other things, the removal of criminal sanctions against homosexual practices between consenting adult males, on the ground that even if such practices were generally believed to be immoral, there needs to be more reason than that for the criminal law to be invoked. The control of conduct, even if agreed on accepted standards to be immoral, is not necessarily the business of the law.

In the same year, Lord Devlin, then a Lord of Appeal in Ordinary, delivered the Maccabean Lecture to the British Academy, entitled 'The Enforcement of Morals'.[2] In this lecture, he argued that a shared morality was as necessary to a society as a recognized system of government. Indeed, it was, he said, essential to the very existence of a society. Now the law must be invoked in order to preserve whatever is essential to a society's existence. The infringement of a society's shared moral code was thus, Lord Devlin argued, analogous to treason, in that both, if allowed, would destroy the society within which they took place. So the suppression of immorality was as much the law's business as the suppression of treason or other subversive activities.

On this argument, then, to act in a manner contrary to consensus morality is to subvert. Arguing against Lord Devlin, H. L. A. Hart, at that time Professor of Jurisprudence in the University of Oxford, in his Harry Camp Lectures delivered at the University of Stanford in 1960,[3] drew a distinction between 'positive' and 'critical' morality. The positive morality of a society was that which was generally shared within that society. It could be regarded as 'conventional' morality. Critical morality steps back from this conventional morality, and raises a variety of different questions about it. One question may be whether adherence to such conventional morality is on the whole beneficial or actually harmful; but another question, more relevant to Lord Devlin's argument, is this: If such morality is enforced by law, would the consequences of such law's existence be harmful or otherwise? For example, suppose it is part of conventional, or positive, morality that adultery is wrong, would a law enforcing fidelity in marriage and criminalizing infidelity do more good than harm? The harms that we could envisage from such a law would be loss of individual freedom, an extreme intrusiveness in the matter of seeking evidence and prosecuting, and great difficulty in actual enforcement, so great in fact, that the law itself might be discredited, with harmful consequences of a general nature. In this case it would be agreed, in many societies, that even if adultery is morally wrong, to criminalize adultery would be more morally wrong still.

According to this sort of argument, then, which is Hart's and Wolfenden's, that something is agreed to be morally wrong is not by itself sufficient to justify its being made illegal. Before criminalizing an offence, it is necessary to show in addition that leaving people free to commit the moral offence if they choose has genuinely harmful consequences, more harmful than the restrictions of freedom and other harms that might flow from legislation.

There are two points to be noticed about this old dispute. The first is that it is specifically concerned not with the nature of morality but with the relation between morality and the law. The second is that, whatever Hart may have thought of Devlin's analogy between the breach of a shared conventional morality and an act of treason (and it is doubtful whether he thought much of it), he never denied that there existed within society a shared or conventional morality, a consensus as to what is right and what is wrong. The question was simply what the relation should be between the criminal law and such a shared morality. Neither Hart nor Devlin raised the question what the status or role of the law should be if there were no shared morality. Indeed, for Devlin, it appears that such a question would be meaningless. For if a shared morality is, as he held, the cement which binds a society together, and if society will collapse when such a morality is weakened, then, if there were no such morality, there would in some sense be no society and, therefore, of course, no law. A society without consensus would be a contradictory concept.

Thirty years later, however, we are in the position of doubting the existence of a moral consensus. There is no doubt that society exists; we live in it. But its common, shared morality seems to have disappeared. There is nothing of which we can be sure that the man on the Clapham omnibus would say 'It's wrong'; nothing about which we could be certain that he and all his neighbours would feel 'intolerance, indignation and disgust'. The criterion for agreed immorality upon which Lord Justice Devlin relied thirty years ago seems to have disappeared. How could we agree with Devlin that the law must enforce morality, if there is no common notion of what is morally wrong?

Hart did not, as I have said, deny the existence of a common morality. However, his distinction between positive and critical morality, between first-order questions and second-order questions, seems to open a way to determine, by some agreed standard, what the law ought to do, where it ought and where it ought not to intervene whether there is an agreed morality or not. And this agreed, objective standard might be thought itself to be sufficient to point the way to a genuine consensus about what is morally tolerable and what is not. Even if, at first sight, there seems to be no consensus of approval or disapproval at the first-order or positive level, the second-order or critical level might supply a criterion in accordance with which we could say 'This would be a bad law', or 'This would be a good law.' For, if it is possible to say, 'Bad though such and such behaviour may be, it would be worse to criminalize it', then there must be a standard of 'bad' and 'worse' that is generally acceptable, if the argument is to be in the least persuasive.

The relation, then, between the positive and the critical must rely ultimately on an agreed test of the better and the worse. And according to Hart's argument, this test is in terms of harm and benefit. If a law would do harm because of the loss of freedom it brought with it, because of its intrusiveness, or the difficulty of its enforcement, then that law would be 'worse', by agreed standards, than the evil it was designed to stamp out. The absolute and proper balance of good and bad, better and worse, on this argument is to be calculated in terms of the harms and benefits of the alternatives. Here, then, we have an example of consequentialism, in the particular form of a kind of utilitarianism.

Utilitarianism lays down that the criterion by which we judge a kind of action to be good or bad is whether it brings about more pleasure than pain over all, and this 'pleasure' and 'pain' can be translated into terms of benefit and harm. If a type of action, such as theft, harms more than it benefits; if a kind of measure such as introducing fluoride into the water system diminishes tooth decay while having no harmful side-effects; if a law permitting the use of animals for experimental purposes, though it offends some, yet substantially benefits many; then all these acts or measures must be morally approved. If the reverse, then they must be condemned. The principle of utility is offered both as the principle by which alone moral judgements can be made and as the principle according to which alone legislation can be morally defensible. It is, in fact, both an explanation of the phenomenon of morality and a justification of the system of legislation. It is also that which offers a criterion according to which proposals for new legislation must be judged.

As propounded by Jeremy Bentham, in *An Introduction to the Principles of Morals and Legislation*,[4] the principle of utility was first and foremost a doctrine to distinguish between good laws and bad. It was later explicitly extended by John Stuart Mill to cover morality as well as law. But its jurisprudential origins are worth bearing in mind. Hart, a true follower of Bentham in this respect, was prepared to argue, as we have seen, that whether or not there was moral consensus condemning a particular practice, any measure that sought to outlaw that practice must itself be judged on utilitarian grounds. The question must be whether such a restrictive measure would itself produce more harm than benefit, more pain than pleasure; and if it could be shown to be harmful on balance, then the next question must be whether that harm would outweigh the benefit supposed to result from prohibiting the practice at issue.

To be consistent, a utilitarian must argue that not only laws, but moral rules themselves, must be judged by these same consequentialist criteria. For otherwise we would have to allow two quite different meanings to the words 'good' and 'bad', 'right' and 'wrong'. And this no one would wish to do, or so the utilitarians claim. For, they would say, there can be only one interpretation of the concepts 'good' and 'bad', 'right' and 'wrong'. A multiplicity of interpretations would make the use of such terms unintelligible. We could not make the comparisons of harms and benefits we are being asked to make. And so they face us with the question whether our moral beliefs themselves are in fact derived from the principle of utility.

It would be extremely convenient to believe that the principle of utility underpins both the law and morality. For the calculus of harms and benefits must surely be capable of being precisely worked out. The balance ought to be capable of demonstration.

So, if, looking round the society in which we live, we find it hard to identify any moral consensus, utilitarianism might seem a lifeline to hold on to. For here, surely is something that might produce agreement if all the facts were honestly examined.

It might once have seemed, as an alternative to utilitarianism, that Christianity could provide an agreed morality, and people sometimes speak optimistically as if it still could. Yet not only has Christian doctrine sometimes given inconsistent answers; but we must obviously now recognize that not all of our society is Christian. I do not mean that many have lapsed, though this may be true, but that many are, for example, Muslims or Jews, with their own strongly rooted moral beliefs. Yet none form a majority in society. A sensible secular moral code, capable of being agreed upon, seems a very attractive prospect. For example, it might seem desirable to teach such a code to children at school. Indeed, many people who write about moral education take it for granted that the way to teach children to think morally is to teach them to calculate the harms and benefits that will flow from what they do or what other people may do. They are, in short, to be taught utilitarianism.

In the 1950s, there was a popular philosophical distinction drawn between statements of fact and statements of value. It was widely held that these two kinds of statements were readily distinguishable one from the other, and that, whereas there could be no agreement about values, or only accidentally, there could and must be agreement about facts. For facts were simply there to be observed. They were parts of the furniture of the world, existing quite independently of people. If you denied something that I asserted as a matter of fact, the difference between us could be settled one way or the other. Either you were right or I was. Values, on the other hand, were matters of taste or 'attitude'. You might like something that I disliked, and when such a difference arose, though we might try to influence each other by fair means or foul, in the end we might have to agree to differ.

However, if what is right and what is wrong could be shown to turn on the question of which produced in people as a whole more pleasure than pain, then this should be capable of being settled by asking people or counting heads. We could do a survey, conduct a poll. If you thought something wrong which turned out to give the majority of people pleasure or to benefit them, then you could be shown this result, and would necessarily change your view. For, on the original utilitarian theory, the words 'right' and 'wrong' simply mean 'pleasurable or painful, beneficial or harmful to the majority'. And so, if morality were really a matter of such calculation, we could in the end agree. Even the word 'consensus' would be misleading within such a theory of morality. We do not speak of 'consensus' where a fact is manifest to everyone. The TV ratings, for instance, are not a question of consensus. We can know as a matter of fact that more people now watch *Eastenders* than watch *Coronation Street*. In strictly Benthamist, utilitarian terms, then, we know that *Eastenders* is better. If all this were true, we could, given time, reach not just consensus, but absolute agreement. Those who refused to accept the facts with regard to the balance of pleasure over pain would be as unarguably eccentric as continuing flat-earthers in the twentieth century. We could disregard them. Why can we not, then, accept utilitarianism, and move by easy stages, by education and science, towards an agreed common morality?

However, there are great difficulties in accepting simple utilitarianism as the basis of morality. As Bentham and Mill saw, a law must, on the whole, be justified, a Bill got through Parliament, on the basis of broadly utilitarian arguments. Will its provisions do more good than harm, be productive of more happiness than unhappiness in society as a whole? A law is applicable to everyone in a given society. The desires and aspirations of everyone must therefore be, as far as possible, taken into account. For, in the end, the laws of a society determine for everyone what it is like to live in that society, whether it is tolerable or the reverse. Compromise and pragmatism are essential to the law. On the other hand, morality itself cannot be wholly deduced from such principles. And if morality, unlike law, demands something more than a simple utilitarian justification (or foundation), then there will always remain a question about the relation of the law to morality. If their basis is not identical, which is to have priority? In society as it is, there exists, as we have said, an ineradicable diversity and plurality in the justifications offered for moral as opposed to legal decisions, whether these decisions are taken by individuals in their private or in their public capacity. Let us briefly consider, then, the difficulties in the way of adopting utilitarianism as the sole basis for moral judgements.

In the first place, there is a whole cluster of difficulties centred on the concepts of pleasure and happiness, the concepts upon which utilitarianism appears to depend. The pursuit of happiness is not a straightforward idea. Happiness is elusive, and is likely to creep up unawares upon people who are pursuing something else; while those who think that happiness and pleasure are identical, and deliberately pursue pleasure itself, often fail to get what they want. Literature and life seem equally full of examples of such paradoxes.

It has often been argued that, even if we cannot easily tell what will bring happiness, we can be sure what constitutes unhappiness. The goal of the utilitarian, then, may be rather to do nothing to cause unhappiness in ourselves or others and, more positively, to act always so as to remove causes of misery. Thus, if poverty and sickness are prime causes of misery, our main duty may be to work for the elimination of such conditions. The great philanthropists of the nineteenth century were largely motivated by such considerations. Politically, at least, this line of thought has generally led, in broadly utilitarian and socialist ideology, to the substitution of some such concept as 'welfare' for that of happiness.

In the sphere of personal morality, however, such a concept seems largely irrelevant. If I am tempted to break my promise to visit a boring relative in hospital by the inducement of a fascinating dinner party (where let us say, I would not only enjoy myself, but also perhaps further my own career), considerations of the welfare of people at large play no part at all, it seems, in my moral struggle. If I keep my promise, it will be because it was a promise, and breaking it would not only bring disappointment to the bedridden bore, but would be, in my eyes, intrinsically wrong. It could not in this case be justified by any calculation of consequential pleasure or advantage. My conscience would not allow me to go to the dinner party in the circumstances.

In such a case, where we are accustomed to invoke the notion of conscience or the largely equivalent notion of shame, even if not in so many words, we seem to appeal to two related ideas.

First, our own personal satisfaction or gain must not be given priority in a moral decision; indeed, it ought, as far as possible, to be left on one side. Secondly, and related to the first idea, we feel that we ought to act in obedience to some sort of general rule (in our example, the rule that, once made, promises must be kept). Our conscience would prick us if we abandoned the rule; in other words, we would feel ashamed to do so, in pursuit of our own ends.

Immanuel Kant[5] was famous for his theory that morality consists wholly in obedience to the categorical imperative; to self-imposed rules, obedience to which constitutes an end in itself. As soon as considerations of happiness or welfare enter into our motives in acting, Kant argued, our actions cease to have any moral value, but are simply parts of the general course of nature, within which all animals seek their own comfort or survival. Morality is uniquely human, because only humans can make rules for themselves and keep them. Kant's categorical imperative, like the Protestant Christian idea of individual conscience, is a hard master, perhaps unacceptably hard. And there is another assumption that lies behind the doctrine of the categorical imperative which we may find just as difficult to accept. It is assumed that, if people honestly and sincerely obey their own consciences, there will be no conflict. In the end, there can be no dispute about what is morally right and what wrong. Everyone, individually, will come up with what will turn out to be the same answer.

This, alas, is the weakness of the theory. We have to admit, today, that moral disagreement is a fundamental, not an accidental or temporary feature of morality. Nevertheless, the idea of a moral principle, to be followed though the heavens fall, is, it seems, essential to morality. And so far Kant was right. But he faces us with a dilemma. How can we reconcile the notion of the absolute authority of the individual conscience with the ideal of an agreed or consensus morality?

J. S. Mill, though he thought himself a thoroughgoing utilitarian, was not unaware of the importance of principle to personal morality. He agreed with Kant that morally good people act not as a result of a calculation of the consequences of what they are about to do, but in obedience to their principles. But he held that these principles themselves had at one time or another been adopted, perhaps by our remote ancestors, only because obedience to them had been found to lead to the greatest happiness of the greatest number. What we now believe to be a matter of principle, not expediency, may turn out on examination to be a matter of long-term or general expediency proved successful over the years. Thus it has been discovered over the centuries that it is useful – indeed, necessary to society – to have a system of trust, in accordance with which promises can be relied upon. So we now adopt the principle of promise-keeping and regard it as binding, without having to take future consequences into account.[6]

I doubt if many people would deny that there is truth in such a view. You may feel an immediate reluctance to betray a friend or steal an apple from a fruit stall and you may explain your reluctance in terms of conscience or obedience to a principle, whether of loyalty or of honesty. Yet it may also be shown to be true that the adoption of such principles is generally beneficial to society and that their non-adoption would be harmful. I would not deny this; nor would I deny the very general proposition that the existence of morality within a society is beneficial to that society or that its absence would be harmful.

Nevertheless, it is of the essence of morality that it should be felt, and that it should be capable of being felt, with passion, whatever the advantages or disadvantages, benefits or the opposite, that may flow either from moral principles in general or from obedience to this principle *now*. Of course, in everyday life we often embark on a calculation of the probable outcome of our decisions in terms of pleasure or pain, benefit or harm, whether we are trying to decide where to go for a holiday, how much money to let our children have, which job, if any, to put in for, or when to retire. Very often such decisions as these have no apparent moral dimension at all. But the stronger the moral element in our decisions, the less we are likely to be guided entirely by calculated benefits. When we spontaneously use a vocabulary proper to morality, a vocabulary that contains besides 'right' and 'wrong' such words as 'cruel', 'dishonest', disloyal', 'cowardly', and so on, as well as the word 'ashamed', then we are talking in a manner that cannot be dispassionate. We are expressing in these words our specifically moral *sentiments*; and if we had no such sentiments, we should have no morality.

People sometimes speak as though it were somehow disreputable to be guided, in decision-making or in moral judgement, by feelings. For example, when the Committee of Enquiry into Human Fertilization and Embryology was in existence, I was often told that these were highly 'emotive' issues, and the suggestion was that if the committee did its duty, it would manage to eliminate emotion and consider all the problems of remedying infertility, of the new techniques and of the related research, in a totally rational manner, without reference to 'mere feelings'. This was a mistake. Since at least some of the issues with which the committee was concerned were moral issues, it was not only impossible to eliminate feelings; it would have been a contradiction to try to do so, and still fulfil our obligation to examine the moral problems generated by the new techniques.

David Hume, though a wholly rational man and an extraordinarily clear-headed philosopher, argued that morality was 'more properly felt than judg'd of.[7] This is, perhaps, a misleading way of putting it. I would say instead that when morality is judged of, it is in terms of feeling. And if this were not so, as Hume himself clearly saw, we would never act in accordance with a moral principle, against our own immediate or even long-term interest. If morality were a matter of calculated benefits, not only would our own advantage have to be weighed as equal to the advantage of others (and this is something that, in real life, morality forbids; we have to try to be unselfish and put our own interests on one side); but also the difference between the moral and the expedient would disappear. And this it obstinately refuses to do. The vocabulary of morals and the 'feel' expressed in that vocabulary are simply different.

To say that morality is a matter of sentiment does not entail, as is sometimes supposed, that we are not in control of what our moral feelings are. It is a mistake to think that we cannot change or discipline our feelings. Jane Austen, a strict moralist, knew this. Her most severe condemnation of her characters, through the voice of the most morally upright, is that they do not 'feel as they ought'.[8] The implication is that they could feel differently. We are not simply a prey to our feelings, moral or otherwise. Our feelings may be manifest in our attitude; and we are capable of changing our attitudes.

Yet some of our moral sentiments may be of fundamental importance to us, and we may be unable or unwilling to give them up. The concept of a good man cannot be separated from the concept of a man of integrity, one who will have an ideal and pursue it though the heavens fall, perhaps even to self-destruction. Such a man will not, or not always, think about the consequences of his actions: rather, if he thinks of consequences, these are of less importance than the ideal, especially if the consequences will adversely affect only himself. I am not suggesting that all morally good people are fanatics or martyrs. Yet, if there were not the possibility of sacrifice for the sake of the good, there would be no morality. There would be no moral ideal to try to live up to.

If, then, there exists no moral consensus within our society, this is to say that there exist no universally shared moral ideals. Unless we are to argue, like Kant, that in the end all moral principles somehow miraculously harmonize with each other, we are faced with the bleak thought that moral conflict is inevitable. Even within the class of principles held by one person, there is no presumption of harmony. One of my principles may well be, in certain circumstances, incompatible with another. All my ideals may not be capable of being fulfilled together.

Such is the view of a contemporary philosopher, Stuart Hampshire.[9] He holds that utilitarianism is insufficient to account for or justify our moral beliefs. He holds further that within every society there are certain barriers which it is morally impossible to cross. At what point these barriers are fixed, what the particular moral principles involved are, will depend on the culture and history of the members of a particular society. What counts as a barrier is a matter of profound feeling, not reason; but the feeling will have grown up as part of the cultural history of the society or of the individual whose morality is in question. Where diverse cultural histories are involved, there will be conflict. It is therefore part of Hampshire's view that conflict is an inevitable element in morality. We cannot hope to eliminate it; indeed, if we did, if we found that moral consensus was becoming easy to achieve within society, we might reasonably take this to be a sign of moral decay. True morality must be felt in the bones. It will not be wholly susceptible to reason. It will be incorporated in an ideal which may lead the idealist into conflict with reason and also with those whose ideals are different.

To take an example: even within our own society, there are those who believe it to be a paramount duty, if they are doctors prescribing for their patients, to prescribe nothing that is not proved to be as safe as possible. To determine the safety of a drug, it is necessary to test it, and to test it may involve the use of animals. There are others within the same society who hold that any sentient creature, of whatever species, deserves to be treated with total respect, not used as a means to a further end. To prefer humans to other animals, in the sense of justifying the use of other animals by reference to the benefits to humans, is, in the eyes of these people, as untenable a prejudice as is the preference for white humans over black. Here we have an example of two conflicting moral ideals, and two ideals that conflict in a peculiarly intractable way. One party holds that human health and welfare must, morally, be the paramount consideration. The other party holds that the sufferings of other animals are exactly as important as the suffering of humans. Neither must be sacrificed to the other.

This is, of course, one among many possible real-life examples of moral conflict. And in Hampshire's view, since the issues would be generally agreed to be moral issues, conflict is inevitable (hence the title of the essay in which he first put forward these views: 'Morality and Pessimism'). To suppose that a convergence of views could be somehow fixed up would be to misunderstand the nature of morality.

If the arguments so far have been valid, if Hampshire is right, and if morality is a matter as much of sentiment or feeling as of rational calculations of harm and benefit, then it is people's feelings and attitudes that have to be changed if we want to approach once again a moral consensus. To present people with reasonably calculated balance sheets of benefits and harms cannot by itself be enough.

Yet perhaps to try too hard to change people's attitudes is itself immoral. We none of us like propaganda, and some of us feel a bit squeamish about the techniques of advertising, often deployed to bring about just such a change. It might be thought especially dubious to attempt to change feelings which, in the nature of the case, are grounded in religion and traditional culture.

Nevertheless, we should not despair. For one thing, we should not exaggerate the size of the problem. Let us ask ourselves, what are the practical difficulties in governing a country against a background of moral diversity, or absence of consensus? There are, it seems to me, two different kinds of problem.

First, there is a problem at the coal-face. There is the problem of policing, of controlling behaviour such as mugging, rioting, theft, or fraud, and of sentencing those who are convicted of such offences. If there is no general feeling against this kind of behaviour among the public at large, then the police, attempting to control it, will be widely regarded as enemies; and judges, in uttering sentences, will also be regarded as unjustified, as biased, or unduly interventionist. But in such cases, if police and judges act in accordance with accepted conventions, they are not universally condemned. On the contrary, victims or potential victims of the criminals will on the whole support police and judicial action. We have to remember that what is at issue here is not, typically, two conflicting concepts of what is right and what wrong, not two conflicting moralities or ideals, but, on the one hand, a notion of morality and, on the other hand, none. The conflict is a conflict between a sense of morality and justice, lined up against quite different passions: greed, racial or sectarian hatred, or lust. Such passions exist, and have always existed in human nature. They have to be subject to external control, since individuals are not always ready even to try to control them for themselves. And if they are not controlled, society could not survive. They will not wither away by themselves. This need for control has always been the philosophical explanation of the establishment of society itself, and within society of law. It is the Hobbesian view, that without the control of law, man's life would be intolerable and also, as everyone knows, brutish and short. Morality and the law here seem to go hand in hand – indeed, to be identical. We not only think it morally outrageous to assault an old man and steal his savings, but we also have confidence in the belief that the perpetrators of the outrage may be caught and brought to trial and to punishment in accordance with the law.

Our own sense of justice, and the justice institutionalized in the system of police and lawcourt, cannot here be distinguished. The law is morality institutionalized.

Here, if anywhere, Lord Devlin's metaphor of the cement binding society together has force. If there is no moral consensus in such an area, it is because there are many people who do not actually care about morality; they simply do not think about what is right or wrong. Against them, other people must be protected by law. The law constitutes a consensus morality, fitted out, it's true, with powers of enforcement, but a morality none the less, without which there would be no society. Here is a limited part of the criminal law, but a crucially important one, where laws, based on utilitarianism, may serve as a substitute for morality for those who have no moral sense, and a means of enforcing morality for those who do. The only moral problems arise if the policing force is itself suspect and open to charges of bias and corruption.

The second kind of practical problems is different. These are the problems of getting new legislation through Parliament. Here, where there is a dispute, it is one that arises, as like as not, out of genuine moral disagreement. Let me take two recent cases: in the so-called Gillick case, Mrs Gillick genuinely believed that it was morally wrong for a doctor to give contraceptive advice and issue contraceptives to an under-age girl who came to him, without informing the girl's parents and taking them into consultation. Her proposed law would have criminalized any doctor found to have done that. Many people, including many doctors, thought that such a law would itself be morally wrong. It would jeopardize the essential relation of trust between doctor and patient, and would make the obstacles in the way of girls seeking contraceptive advice far greater. Those on both sides of the dispute were perfectly sincere in their views, and none had any apparent personal interest which might make their views suspect. It was, as far as could be judged, a pure case of moral non-consensus. There was no possibility of agreement, nor even of compromise. When such a case arises in Parliament, the majority view must prevail. There is no other way. And not everyone will be satisfied; that is the nature of the cases.

Another recent case was the proposed legislation which would have permitted schoolteachers to continue to use corporal punishment against their pupils, unless these pupils had been excused such punishment by their parents. This was a case somewhat confused both by European law, which made the use of corporal punishment in schools an offence, and by the sheer administrative absurdity of having, in any one school, some 'beatable' and some 'non-beatable' children. So there may have been some who argued against the Bill on practical grounds, others on European grounds. Nevertheless, it provided a good example of a genuine dispute about what is right and what is wrong, and many people based their arguments on moral grounds. It is a useful example in another way. In Parliament, as well as in the debates in the press or on television which habitually surround such issues, it is absolutely necessary to look at the matter from, in Hume's words, 'a steady and general point of view'. One must consider the implications of ruling for or against a particular practice, not from the standpoint of a vested interest, not even from the standpoint of a particular religious or family conviction, shared by only a few of one's compatriots. Since legislation is in question, legislation that would affect everyone in a society, no matter what their personal convictions, the general and wide implications of a measure have to be considered. All the relevant facts, as well as the different value judgements, must, as far as possible, be taken into account in this general view. Now those who advocated the continuing use of corporal punishment in schools seemed either to be thinking back to a past in which they themselves beat or were beaten ('Six of the best never did me any harm'); or they were listening to the voice of those few schools where beating was thought to be uniquely effective as a deterrent. What they failed to notice was the accumulating body of evidence showing that the most successful schools, those with the lowest truancy rates, and the greatest pupil and parent satisfaction, were schools in which no violence, whether verbal or physical, was practised against pupils. This evidence was purely consequentialist, and was separate from the feelings of those parents who thought it a moral outrage that their children should be beaten or of those who felt that beating would 'teach the child a lesson'.

In the end, when the anti-corporal punishment clause was included in the Bill by the House of Lords, it was a mixture of

European and consequentialist arguments that prevailed. It is not extravagant, I believe, to suppose that the informed and, on the whole, non-hysterical debate on the issue might well have done something to influence public attitudes for the future. Yet if, after all, corporal punishment had been retained in schools as a general recourse, if Parliament had permitted it, what would we have to say? Parliament must have the last word in matters of legislation. So what happens if Parliament seems to have gone wrong? When this happens, it is crucial to hold on to the benefits of democracy and freedom of speech.

Sometimes a law is passed, like the recent abortion clause in the 1990 Embryology Bill, which seems to some people to be too permissive. Such people argue that abortion will be too easy to obtain, that it will be more or less granted on demand, and that the alleged rights of the unborn child have been overlooked. I believe that such people are wrong, and that not only did the decision of Parliament represent a majority opinion, but that if the laws are properly kept, the safeguards observed, something like a moral consensus may well in the end emerge. Until that time, those who are morally offended by the Bill have two differ-ent options. On the one hand, they may accept the fact that people are legally permitted to do things they personally would regard as morally wrong and would therefore never do. In the case of abortion this need present no problems unless they are doctors. And even if they are doctors, they may always hand over applicants for abortion to others, if their own moral convictions will not allow them to have anything to do with it. On the other hand, they may embark on a campaign to get the law changed, so as to forbid others to do what they would not do themselves on moral grounds. Here the question must be raised, as we have seen, as to whether the existence of a restrictive law would have worse consequences than its non-existence. We may be certain that in the absence of general moral consensus there will always exist moral pressure groups, and, as long as freedom of speech exists, such groups can be powerful. This is a necessary feature of democratic life (and, as I have argued, if morality were not in part a matter of deeply held feelings such as emerge in pressure groups, it would not exist at all). As long as such feelings can be publicly expressed, there is always the possibility of a change of heart on the part of Parliament. For example, if it were not for the persistence of what was probably once an eccentric minority, there would probably now be no coherent laws governing the use of animals in laboratories. There would certainly be no legislation making compulsory the education of severely mentally handicapped children. A minority view passionately held and based on proper information may in the course of time become the accepted moral presumption of society, and may ultimately be reflected in legislation. But equally – and this I would like to stress – if legislation itself is the outcome of public and well-informed debate, it may serve to educate people to a new and better-founded set of moral convictions.

I conclude, then, that the absence of a general moral consensus in society, though it causes difficulties in government, is no reason for a total breakdown of law and order, provided that there remains a respect for the law itself. Nor is it a bar to the passage of good laws. But we have to be patient. Consensus may, given time, develop out of the apparently beneficial operation of a law. But everything possible must be done to ensure that the law itself, in each particular case, is seen to be harmless overall in its administration, and beneficial in its general outcome. And so it may come to be accepted. If either of these conditions is not satisfied, the existence of a law may prove a positive obstacle to moral consensus.

The most important thing we can do – and, indeed, the most we can do about our moral differences – is to keep talking, not in the hope of ironing them out, but in the hope that we can create a kind of society within which differences can be accommodated as far as possible within the law. The law must be seen as a framework within which people can, if they wish, impose on themselves more stringent or different obligations and within which they can, if they choose, campaign for their own views to be more widely accepted. Philosophy may have something to contribute to this perpetual dialogue. But so has Parliament itself, which in the publicity of the debates surrounding legislation has a crucially educative as well as legislative role.

# 7

# *Honesty and Cynicism*

As so often, I find that I have chosen the wrong title for this chapter: I should not have called it 'Honesty and Cynicism', but 'Candour and Cynicism'. I hope to make clear the point of that correction as I go along. As to the other word in the title, I shall not attempt a definition. I can promise you that I am not going to treat you to a discourse on the original cynics and their place in ancient philosophy. Rather, I shall simply assume that we all recognize cynicism when we see it, and that we mostly dislike it. Again, I hope that the reason for this dislike will emerge. Broadly, my thesis is that we are a better-educated nation than we used to be, but that this runs the danger of turning us into a nation of cynics. And this, I shall argue, would be dangerous.

That we are better educated than before is, I think, indisputable. Indeed, it would be extraordinary if it were not so. More people receive a formal education than ever before; they stay at school longer; and more, if still only a small percentage of the population, go on to further or higher education. Illiteracy, therefore, though it still exists here and there, is very rare. Most obviously, people are exposed to a vast amount of information, and to education in a very wide sense through radio and television. They could hardly help being less ignorant than their grandparents.

Though in general it is true, then, that people are better educated than they were, in the ways I have suggested, and certainly in terms of being acquainted with far more facts and having available to them vastly more data, yet there are respects in which such a statement needs to be qualified; although many people are less ignorant than they used to be, there are factors in contemporary life which may make it more difficult for them to *learn*. First, since education is, fortunately, increasingly available to everyone, the old distinction between the educated class and the class of the uneducated has largely disappeared. This means that there is not commonly found that kind of respect for the educated which made it natural to accept their pronouncements or follow their leadership. The democratization of education has made the role of disciple, even of pupil, quite difficult to accept. Secondly, among those who are educated, it is probably true that there is less reading than there used to be. Certainly the idea of the self-educated man, for whom the public libraries were such a boon when they began, who read voraciously, and learned discrimination as he went along, is almost dead. And I believe (though it would be impossible to prove it) that it is through reading that one learns to distinguish different tones of voice, different styles of discourse, so that one can tell the frivolous from the serious, the sensible from the silly, the true from the false – in the sense that coins may be true or false (and the opposite of the 'true', in this sense of the word, is not so much 'false' as 'phoney'). A want of such discriminatory skill, not instinctive but learned, may lead to a direct consequence: the belief that everything is false, that there is no touchstone or discoverable criterion of the true or the genuine. There is a *third* factor which is even more difficult to pin down, the malign influence of which is still harder to prove. The roughly-speaking sociological and educational theories of the 1950s and 1960s made it unfashionable for teachers to claim the authority that derives from knowing more than their pupils, and this in turn led to a denial that any sharp distinction can be drawn between the true and the false. The pupil's ignorance came to be thought of as just as 'valid' as the teacher's knowledge; and the concept of 'your' truth and 'my' truth or, for example, 'male' history and 'women's' history made all truth appear dependent on a particular point of view. It began to seem futile, or actually retrograde, to look for 'the' truth. Relativism became a powerful ingredient in almost everyone's thought, and to some extent it remains so to this day.

Perhaps the worst effect of such creeping relativism is that, in order to avoid it, people may be tempted into a wild and dogmatic absolutism, especially with regard to moral questions. And nothing is more inimical to learning than dogma. So there are obstacles in the path of educational progress. Nevertheless, the very fact that there is a lot of information available, a lot of potential knowledge in, and on, the air, makes it inevitable that people in general know more; and in addition, the kind of technological skills that are now increasingly widely disseminated require a standard of education and a level of understanding unthought of even fifty years ago.

Yet professionals of one kind and another – doctors, lawyers, teachers, broadcasters, clergy, and most especially politicians – have found it extraordinarily difficult to adapt to this new level of education. They, we, the professionals, still tend to treat people like children. We forget that, though other people are often tiresome, obstinate, or prejudiced, slow to do what we would like them to do, yet they are in a position to know a lot, and they have the moral right to be treated as just as rational as we are, capable of grasping the truth when they see it, and not to be fobbed off with myths, fairy-tales, lies, or evasions. Indeed, despite the countervailing factors I have mentioned, the very fact that there is a lot of information available makes people in some ways hanker for the truth. They would like what they are told to be true; and when it turns out not to be, when what they are promised is not delivered, then naturally they turn cynical. They become extravagantly cautious. They cannot accept anything they are told, whatever the evidence, and they refuse to believe that there exists anyone among their rulers, advisers, or teachers who is prepared disinterestedly to seek out and present the truth. Whatever anyone says, the presumption is that he says it only in order to gain something to his own advantage; and if he backs up his statement with evidence, then that evidence will have been cooked.

As we all know, and are frequently told, there are lies, damned lies, and statistics. If I, for example, living and working in a university, seek to analyse the function of the universities or their present state, I am assumed to be an interested party, and therefore incapable of sound judgement. It is taken for granted, without question, that I am not honest. The depressing cliché is trotted out yet again: 'Well, she would say that, wouldn't she?' It often seems that the people most likely to be believed on any topic whatever are those who know least about it. They, at any rate, cannot be thought to be trying to preserve some vested interest.

Now we do not want people to grow up gullible. We cannot, and certainly ought not, to reintroduce an age of credulity. I have already suggested that dogmatism is a serious obstacle to education, and I believe there is a real hazard here. There is a tendency, long noticeable in the United States, but increasingly in this country as well, to try to escape from cynicism by the road of religious fundamentalism. The chief characteristic of any fundamentalist religion, whether Christian, Jewish, or Muslim, is that it relies upon a text, which is meant to function as the basis for education and truth. Knowledge is therefore finite, and it is essentially unhistorical. The only new understanding that is possible must be new interpretation of the given text, which, as it is supposed to contain truths that have been revealed once and for all, is not a fit subject for critical or historical scrutiny.

Such fundamentalism is, an invitation, or rather an exhortation, to accept uncritically what are held to be the central teachings of the faith (and these not only on matters such as the creation of the world, but on such twentieth-century subjects as genetic engineering or the proper status of the immediately post-fertilization embryo). Negatively, therefore, fundamentalism acts as a brake on scientific research and on the pursuit of historical evidence. The fundamentalist does not believe that it is desirable to pursue knowledge wherever that pursuit may lead. Knowledge itself is not considered a proper goal. The message is that we should believe what we are told by our religious teachers and not meddle in matters best left hidden. Yet the fact is that we cannot unlearn what has once been discovered. We should not hope to return to a pre-Copernican, pre-Cartesian time. We could not, if we tried, believe that what Aristotle and Aquinas said was the sum of all possible knowledge. It is therefore wrong to try to escape from the pervading scepticism by this route.

Instead, it seems to me, there is a positive duty, which falls especially on schools, but on other institutions as well, to teach people to distinguish what can from what cannot be believed. So-called media studies are widely regarded as a rather eccentric, if not downright frivolous, ingredient in the school curriculum, certainly no part of either the 'core' or the 'foundation'. Yet, whether under this name or another, it seems to me absolutely essential that children should be taught to notice the devices that are used to persuade them, whether in newspapers or the broadcasting media.

I am not suggesting that such persuasive devices should not be used. Of course they should and will always be used; for to persuade is a central aim of human discourse. But there are distinctions to be drawn, and we ought to educate people to be aware of them. I want to try to separate three different concepts, all relevant to the critical attitude which, as I contend, children should be taught to adopt. These are the concepts of rhetoric, advertisement, and propaganda.

First, rhetoric. In the Middle Ages, rhetoric was one of the seven liberal arts studied in the universities, and, along with grammar and logic, formed the trivium, or foundation curriculum. Whereas logic, even as late as the nineteenth century, was supposed to set out the rules of thought, rhetoric was concerned with the rules according to which thoughts might be communicated to others. But it was equally closely connected not to logic but to eloquence, its aim not merely to inform, or even to persuade, but (like the BBC and the IBA) also to entertain. Eloquent speech, like poetry, is an art-form, a source of pleasure, to be heard at least partly for its own sake.

Because of this association with eloquence, the words 'rhetoric' and 'rhetorical' are often used in a derogatory sense. 'Empty' is the adjective most often used to qualify 'rhetoric'; and the 'rhetorical question' is the epitome of pointlessness, no answer being required, or even allowed, its purpose wholly to add effect. 'Need I mention?' I ask, and then proceed to mention, in true Ciceronian style, all the same. Rhetoric is thus a concept to be understood in the context of *style*. What is said, whether true or false, new or old, is not really its concern. It may be the case that, as orators have always hoped, we are to be persuaded by an elegant or impressive, rather than an uncouth, style. But if so, we should understand as far as possible how to separate the truth value, as the logicians say, from the manner of the utterance. This is not always easy; and it is, as I have suggested, part of the function of English lessons at school, both reading and writing, to train children to be able to recognize and also to use rhetorical devices.

The second of my divisions is advertising. Advertisement, in the commonest contemporary sense of the term, is a branch of rhet-

oric. Its aim is not only to inform and persuade, but also to entertain. A bare statement that there exists a kind of chocolates called
Black Magic, a bank called the Bank of Scotland, even with the
added bit of advice that you should buy some or use its services,
would not do. The advertisement must be memorable; and
increasingly it is understood that one good way to achieve
memorability is through wit and elegance. Like all rhetorical
devices, advertisements must be judged by their effectiveness; but
this does not mean that we judge them by strict causal criteria.
We can say of an advertisement, as we can of a sermon, that it
was effective, without knowing in the least whether anyone's
behaviour was changed by it. Of course, if an advertising
*campaign* is to be described as effective, it must be known that
sales of the product or use of the service have increased. But
a single advertisement can be judged effective if it gives pleasure. And this shows that advertisements (and sermons) are art-
forms.

Advertisements, then, are essentially attempts to persuade
which are easily recognized as such and are judged largely by
stylistic criteria. It is an important part of the current notion
of advertising that the advertiser announces himself and his
intentions quite clearly: he intends that you should buy his product, and he knows that you know this. It is true that advertisements may have some undesirable effects. For example, we are
often told that they cause people to want things they would not
otherwise have wanted or to yearn for things they cannot have.
But this kind of side-effect is inseparable from many art-forms. If
I had never read the novels of Dorothy Sayers as a child, I would
never have hankered, as I did, for an aristocratic, rich, clever,
sensitive, musically talented husband. If I had never listened to
*Die Winterreise* in adolescence, I might never have imagined
myself totally and cosmically disconsolate. All works of art may
feed or help to form our fantasies, for good or ill. But this does
not alter the central fact, which is that advertisements announce
themselves as attempts to persuade us to buy. They promise that
the product is good. If we are persuaded, and it turns out that the
product is not good, this has no effect on our *general* belief in the
reliability of promises or in the truth of what we are told. Very
properly, we reflect of the advertiser, 'Well, he would say that,

wouldn't he?' We know that his motive for saying it was self-interest. He as good as told us so. We knew it as soon as we learned what an advertisement was. If we are fooled, we have no one but ourselves to blame. Within reason, it's a case of *caveat emptor*.

The case of propaganda (my third division) is utterly different. In the original sense of the word 'propaganda', like 'advertising', meant something open. A propagandist would have announced himself as such. For what was to be propagated was the true faith, and no one would have been ashamed of such a mission; the more zealous the propagandist, the more overt the message, no doubt the better. But the sense of the word has changed since 1622 when the *Congregatio de propaganda fide* was first established. *Now* propaganda does not announce itself. It is, of its very nature, hidden. It is a secret weapon used not to persuade but to manipulate. If it aims to please, it does so not, like rhetoric, by means of its style, but by means of its content. For instance, it may be used to lull people's fears, to give them a sense of security beyond that which the true facts warrant.

In World War II there existed a distinction between 'propaganda' and 'black propaganda'. The former, though designed to lower the morale of the enemy and to raise that of people at home was, by convention, supposed to have some basis in truth. It was a selective version of the truth; much was suppressed, but what was released as news was more or less accurate. Black propaganda, on the other hand, was wholly fictional. It was not served up to people at home, but only to the enemy. For instance, broadcasts would be made purporting to be relayed from inside Germany (though in fact emanating from London); it was alleged that there were underground groups infiltrating the country, and absolutely fictitious stories were invented, to discredit German leaders. It was not until after the war that the existence of black propaganda became widely known. If it had been known at the time, it might have seemed disgraceful, and it might have undermined faith in the news bulletins heard by those at home. Even the 'white propaganda' available in England was not so described at the time. We all talked about German propaganda, but not British propaganda, though we all knew it existed; but when, as often happened, there was scepticism about the content of news bulletins, *then* bulletins were described as 'propaganda'. Thus it was clear during the war that 'propaganda' was equivalent, if not to lies, then at least to something that couldn't claim belief; and if we were loyal, it was easier to ascribe it to the enemy than to ourselves. But, because of its secrecy, it had a creeping tendency to undermine our trust. Could we believe any of the news stories we heard?

Now, more than forty years later, things have not changed very much. The commonest form of propaganda is the selective truth-telling which avoids actual lying, but lets only the good news be known. Let me take just two examples. The first is a particular case. As everyone knows, this has been the first year when in England and Wales, the GCSE examination was taken in secondary schools. All those involved have been anxious about the examinations, and it is fairly well known that there were difficulties in finding enough examiners, as well as in other aspects of the new system. In April the following story appeared in *The Times* and other newspapers:

> According to the [leaked] minutes of the latest meeting of the GCSE publicity committee, Ministers, examining groups and the Department's publicity machine will be mobilised in an effort to promote the 'good news' about the new examination. It says, 'examining groups will continue to give reassurances, for instance that there are enough examiners'. During June [incidentally, before most of the papers would have been marked] 'positive noises' should be made about the standard of the examination papers.[1]

Here is white propaganda in its most naked form. The concept of 'positive noises' is a complete revelation of an attempt to manipulate. Even if nothing said was an actual lie, 'positive noises' represents the attempt to manipulate by emphasizing the good, what people want to hear, whatever the real facts. The very use of that Civil Service expression 'noises' is derogatory: it suggests that people don't need content or meaning, only sounds. They can be fobbed off with less than real language.

My second example is more general. It concerns the way in which government and industry respond to those who express anxiety about the use of nuclear power for the supply of energy.

Now it so happens that I personally believe that nuclear power must continue to be used, and that it is incumbent on the Central Electricity Generating Board, subject to strict Government regulation, to ensure that nuclear power stations are safe and that there is a safe and proper means of disposal of nuclear waste – safe, that is, for the next two or three hundred years or longer. But though I think this is what ought to be ensured for the future, I am less than convinced that, at present, we can have any such confidence. Moreover, I take seriously the arguments of those who want to abandon the use of nuclear power altogether. But neither those who, like me, are in favour of the use of nuclear power nor those who are against it can be satisfied with the kinds of reassurance offered by government and industry. Well might their arguments be described as 'positive noises'.

We are told that there is a smaller risk, on average, of dying in a nuclear accident than in a railway accident (as if 'average' rates of death were in the least relevant in this context). We are told that the incidence of leukaemia among those living in the immediate vicinity of nuclear power stations falls within the statistical average (but if no one lived in close proximity to a power station, perhaps the average would be lower). Above all, we are told that Government plans are worked out in accordance with the so-called BPEO (Best Practical Environmental Option), as if this were some separately ascertainable standard. In fact, it is no more than a rough guide to what seems to the Government acceptable and likely to be within a reasonable and pre-arranged budget. There is no magic in the BPEO; it is nothing more than a name for that which government thinks it can afford. Thus, even for those who want nuclear power to be used and its safety improved, there is no satisfaction. All of us, the pros and the antis alike, become disillusioned.

It is on the basis of cases such as these, and many more, that we all begin to believe that propaganda is everywhere; that all official statements are propaganda. The 'good news' simply ceases to convince. So what is to be done? It is difficult to undo the harm, to break the habit of suspicion or heal the damage to confidence engendered by propaganda. The obvious solution is a policy of openness, a policy that is prepared to face suspicion and distrust, but to prove its own worth. This, however, is much easier said than done.

In the first place it has to be acknowledged that there are areas in which openness is not an option. If a country is contemplating the necessity of devaluing its currency, for example, and someone asks a minister of that country whether this is his intention, it would be impossible for him to say 'Yes', or even that he was thinking about it. His only possible answer would be 'No'. Certain information, again, which might radically affect the stock-market if known ahead of a deal, must necessarily be kept hidden. Commercial companies cannot be expected to publicize openly their own plans or innovations for the benefit of their rivals. Thus we live, and must continue to live, in a world where there exist some matters which cannot be openly discussed, where prior knowledge and free discussion would destroy the point of the enterprise.

However, it should be possible to separate these commercial or market cases from those of a more purely moral or political nature, where policies of wide scope must be adopted such as to affect the public at large in important aspects of their lives. Even if such policies will, in the end, have a commercial dimension (as is the case with the use of nuclear power stations), yet the interest of the public in them is so clear that commercial considerations may have to be given second place. I do not suggest that an absolutely hard and fast distinction can be made between the 'commercial' and the 'public', the 'confidential' and the 'open'; but I believe that habits of openness should be seen to differ radically, at least at the extreme ends of this spectrum.

But even if such a broad distinction can be drawn, difficulties remain. What is meant by 'openness'? In July 1988 there was a notorious case in which a Dr Bewick told the press about what he thought was progress in the transplanting of animal organs to humans so that they would not be rejected. In particular, he was enthusiastic about the possibility, in the future, of using pigs' kidneys for transplant in the case of human kidney failure. His colleagues were displeased with him for speaking to the press, rather than publishing his (and their) findings in the learned medical and scientific journals, where they would be subjected to proper peer criticism and scrutiny. So Dr Bewick resigned.[2] Of course, what happened was that the popular press took up the dramatic aspects of the story, omitting in their reporting any of the caution which, doubtless, Dr Bewick expressed. They overlooked the fact that research on such transplants had been going on for more than twenty years; they left out any reference to possible future research programmes. Instead, they started again a vast debate about the use of animals in medical research, the ethics of organ transplant, the concept of brain death, and the relation between a recipient and the donor whose organ he receives. And at least some newspapers, in addition, took a highly self-righteous line about the *people's right to know* about the horrors going on behind laboratory doors. We know that in the past there have been people who objected to the organs of black donors being transplanted to white recipients; now we have the MP Sir Michael McNair Wilson, a possible case for a kidney transplant, saying, 'I would never have a pig's kidney inside me. I want to go to my grave a human being, not half-human, half-pig.'[3] And Bernard Levin was just as definite, and apparently just as ill-informed. If openness entails the handing out of half-prepared information to an ignorant and scandal-seeking press, then it is understandable that the medical profession may seem to be against it.

But the opposite of openness, the selecting of information pre-packaged so as to be fit for the ears and eyes of the child-public seems equally, or more, undesirable. Once again we are faced with the need that people should *learn* to distinguish the true from the false or exaggerated; that they should be given some means of picking through the rhetoric to whatever is, or may be, true within it. And so they must learn to distinguish honesty from deceit.

But now I come to the point where I have to say that perhaps honesty is not enough; for it is not identical with the openness which people hanker for and which they deserve. Honesty may be thought of as a policy of not actually lying. To be caught out in a lie is still a disgrace, even in an age of advertising and propaganda. As I have said, 'black propaganda' was always a matter for some shame, justified only, and dubiously, by the demands of total war. So 'Honesty is the best policy'; it will keep you from such disgrace. But, notoriously, the principle of not lying may not seem much of a principle, for the truth may be hidden or disguised in a variety of ways short of the 'lie direct'. In an educated democracy people demand, and deserve, more than this from those whom they have elected, who, being in positions of power and influence, are held to be accountable to the public at large. A different kind of openness is required in the public domain.

When Lord (then Sir Robert) Armstrong said that he had been 'economical with the truth' in the Spycatcher case, he was, of course, using a phrase well known in Roman Catholic education. You are economical with the truth if you choose what true things you say to whom, how far you may properly disseminate what is true. This is a common-sense policy which we nearly all fall in with in our private lives. Honesty does not demand that we tell everything to everyone. If someone asks whether a friend is ill, we may say 'Yes', and even go on to say that he is in hospital, without feeling that, in the name of honesty, we are obliged to go on to say that he is recovering from his attempted suicide or is undergoing a cure for alcoholism. If we would say these things to some people, but not to others, then we are being economical with the truth; we are managing it discreetly.

But in public affairs this is not enough. We are not any longer willing simply to submit to our rulers or those who by reason of their position exercise power over us, and accept what they say. We insist on their *accountability*; and this means that we insist on their telling us what we *need* to know. Thus, subject, as I have said, to the proviso that there are some areas where to reveal things in advance would be to nullify them, render them impossible or not worth doing, in general what we demand is a principle of *candour* in high places. For candour goes beyond honesty. It is an absence of reserve which carries its openness and genuineness on its face. It is a readiness to tell the truth without bias, to speak disinterestedly, to admit, if necessary, that things have gone wrong, that one's opponents may have points in their favour.

Candour is extremely rare in politicians (the last example I can think of is Lord Carr when he was Home Secretary; and it is a quality he still possesses, so that his speeches demand to be listened to, shining out as they do with the whiteness of innocence, concepts from which the very word 'candid' derives). It is so rare that it is not an ideal that can be adopted in a hurry, for at first people will not recognize it for what it is. A candid politician will seem, at first, unsure of himself, prevaricating, lacking in the qualities of leadership. The currently accepted rhetoric of leadership is like that of advertising; honesty may be the best policy, but candour is not demanded. A leader must speak in a manner which suggests no doubts, which allows of no mistakes, no hesitations, no hint of possible good on the other side. Thus leadership is judged by the criterion of victory in the shouting match. There is little or no place for candour in Prime Minister's Question Time.

Yet I believe that it is only if candour is adopted as the ideal in public life and only if people are gradually brought to value it and to distinguish the sincere from the insincere, the true from the phoney, that the grip of universal cynicism can be loosened. A genuinely candid man will in the end disarm the most confirmed sceptic. His openness, his readiness with information and explanation, will ultimately be manifest and self-announced. Faced with such a person, as politician or teacher, only a paranoiac could continue to believe that there is a plot afoot. Candour generates trust.

But you may ask why it matters. What is wrong with cynicism? Have I not myself made out a case for scepticism rather than gullibility? Isn't it the inevitable consequence of better education that we shouldn't believe everything we are told? I concede that the educated person will not, and should not, believe *everything* he is told. But he should believe that which is based on good evidence; and he should allow that some evidence *is* good. He should be able to trust some sources of evidence, so that he will sometimes be able to be persuaded. As long as he is sceptical about the sources of evidence; as long as he suspects that parts of the truth are being concealed from him, that the arguments adduced are motivated by a desire for profit or political gain, then he will never be persuaded. But if there is no hope of persuasion, there is no hope of consensus either; and without consensus the only way to govern is by force.

Of course I exaggerate; but there is some truth in my contention. To return for a moment to the example of nuclear power: if it were admitted, by government or industry, that people are rightly frightened of accidents in nuclear power stations, that the dangers they fear are different in kind from dangers encountered on the roads or in the air; if it were conceded that people are not unreasonable in being alarmed by an apparently higher than average incidence of leukaemia among those living close to these sources of radiation, then solutions might be sought jointly. More stringent safety measures could be properly explained. In some cases it might be genuinely possible to reassure people, because they might come to believe in the fairness of the evidence presented. In other cases, even if they were not reassured, they might be prepared to accept the risks for the sake of the advantages they could gain, and to see at least that this was a matter for rational choice. The advantages of this kind of dialogue would be a general improvement in health and safety. Explanation is a necessary preliminary for government decisions about the future of nuclear power and the disposal of waste. But explanation is useless if it is not believed; and the only way to establish trust is to provide yet more information, to pursue a policy of manifest openness, subject to public scrutiny. A step in this direction has already been taken by the industry itself in opening the power-stations to the public. But more needs to be done.

What is true of the electricity generating industry is true of all industries and all issues that affect the environment. The better informed about environmental pollution the public is, the more still it needs to be told. Here, above all, past mistakes should be candidly admitted, and new policies properly set out. Once the atmosphere of suspicion has been dispersed, real discussion can begin. It is not always possible to reach consensus. But the aim should always be to try; there can be no true consensus of opinion without equal access to the facts.

So I am advocating a great initiative. What is needed is a new way of disseminating the truth so that it can be believed. Professional people of all kinds, as well as politicians, should learn, like good teachers, a *style* of presentation which commands belief. But this style must not be mere rhetoric. Politicians and the rest of us, perhaps especially journalists and those concerned with broadcasting, should remember that we are not advertisers, still less are we propagandists. Nor are the public children. The more we press for higher educational standards, the more urgent this realization becomes. A good system of education ought to produce a nation of critics. But it must not be allowed to produce a nation of cynics. The remedy is in our own hands.

# 8

# *Who Sets the Standards?*

When I last lectured at Canterbury, in 1980, it was on the subject of education in broadcasting. I was then concerned not with educational broadcasting, but, as I recall, with the educative in a wider sense, and I attempted to show the extent to which good broadcasting, both radio and television, could educate people by stealth.

Behind such a thesis lay certain presuppositions. The first was that though many people, and especially young radio listeners, would object to the idea of education if so named, yet they *could* be educated if imaginative and creative programmes were offered them. The second presupposition was that it was a good thing to educate people in this way, to give them what they didn't know they wanted; to give them what would open their eyes and ears to wider and different objects and would offer them opportunities to pursue interests they didn't even know they had. The second of these presuppositions, that it is good to educate was, of course, made easier to adopt – indeed, was inevitable – since the statute of the BBC and in those days the Bill that gave its functions to the IBA incorporated the trio of obligations: to inform, to *educate*, and to entertain. We all had to be thought to educate if we were in the broadcasting business, whether we liked it or not.

But, looking back, I can see that such presuppositions were, in a very obvious sense, élitist. Why should the broadcasting authorities adopt such a *de haut en bas* attitude? Why should it be assumed that doing good to people was part of the remit of the broadcasters? It would have been perfectly possible to regard the so-called authorities in a different light – simply as agencies to distribute the then limited and sought-after frequencies. Instead, we and Parliament adhered to the Reithian philosophy of the BBC. Broadcasters on Capital Radio might not put on dinner-jackets to read the news from IRN, but the spirit of the original broadcasters was still in the air. We knew what people ought to have, and we were obliged, by Parliament, to try to give it to them.

I must say at once that I do not immediately dismiss from consideration anything that can be described as 'elitist'. It depends, as philosophers are supposed to say, what you mean by 'elitist'; but in any case, elitism aside, it is important to notice two facts. First, what has replaced the broadcasting philosophy of do-gooding is the philosophy of the market. According to this philosophy, people know what they want, and will pay for it. What they do not want will wither away, because it will not be paid for. The presupposition on which the old philosophy rested, that people do not always know what they want, let alone what they need, has gone. Secondly, it is perhaps worth noticing that it is a Conservative Government which has insisted that the market should take over from the Reithian know-all, the superior being who, by virtue of his status or his class, could dictate to the multitude. Conservatives have turned out to be radically egalitarian in this field.

Ten years on, I want to widen the scope of my observations. For it is not only in the matter of educative broadcasting, but in the heart of education itself, that market forces are now supposed to prevail. In schools, polytechnics, and universities, equally, people are supposed to be given what they will pay for, and only that. Just as people become more discriminating and more demanding in choosing hi-fi equipment or cat food, and so, through competition for sales, quality rises and eventually prices may be likely to decline, so with education. The public is supposed to make greater and greater demands on education, and so what they want will gradually be provided, and at a price they can afford.

In the case of most 'consumer goods', it is public demand which triggers inventiveness; and newly marketed goods can generally be seen to fill some newly identified need. A gap in the market will generally produce a new technology; and if the gap was, after all, illusory, if no one wanted a mechanism for toasting six bits of bread at a time or for removing dead flies from the window sill without sweeping them up, then the technology is not developed, the product not actually put on the shelves. It may be tested in Reading (the characteristic middle-of-the-market town), but it will not get as far as Canterbury or Penrith. The question I want to address is whether this analogy can hold in the case either of broadcasting or of education. As far as Government thinking goes, I should say there is not an analogy here, but an actual identity. Broadcasting and education, both, are parts of the consumer world. They must be thought of not simply as *like* commodities sold in the high street, but as actual commodities to be so sold.

So where do 'standards' come in? Well, in the case of consumer goods, there may be a presumption that standards will rise as competition increases. If I manufacture cat food, I want, of course, to make a profit. And that might lead me to put into the cat food only the cheapest ingredients and sell it at as high a price as I can get away with. But there is a need, even with cat food, that I comply with health and safety regulations. I can't risk poisoning pussy. Moreover, there are visual and olfactory qualities to be considered. My product can't offend the eye or nose of the purchaser too badly. And there is a snob element as well. Not only may pussy prefer a better quality product, but, mysteriously, pussy's owner may actually prefer to pay more, believing, rightly or wrongly, that this will ensure quality. All these things, within reason, make for increased quality as my rivals and I compete with each other for the market. The market in clothes is another very good example of the way quality and price may rise through competition. Moreover, the advertisers are on our side. They know how to sell the stuff, and we know that we mustn't stray too far from what they claim on our behalf.

So the standard of the product geniunely has a chance of rising as both cats and humans become more sophisticated and more discriminating. Increasingly, too, purchasers rely on consumer groups and on publications like *Which*, whose purpose is to compare quality, safety, and value for money within groups of rival products. Consumerism and better informed opinion are forces to be taken account of in the developing market, not just in respect of prices, but of health and environmental factors as well. In this sense too, standards may rise.

There is much discussion of standards both in broadcasting and in the world of education. It is worth pausing to ask the question, in both these areas, 'standards of *what?*' Let us start with broadcasting. A high standard of broadcast output ought to mean no more and no less than that output is of high quality, just as standards in cat food manufacture would ensure that the cat food was of good quality, nourishing and hygienic, as cat food should be. But at once we find a difficulty. There is in existence, as I need not remind you, a body called the Broadcasting Standards Council, set up under Home Office auspices, though independent, and having, as its first Chairman, Lord Rees-Mogg. You might think that the Council would have been charged with the task of ensuring that broadcasting was of high quality and that it would fulfil the functions of a consumers' association. But it is not so. On the contrary, the Council is concerned only with the question of whether broadcasting output, including advertising, does or does not offend against standards of taste and decency. Whether the output is in the ordinary sense good, whether it is enjoyable, funny, informative, imaginative, original, thoroughly researched – none of these questions is of any interest to Rees-Mogg and his men. It is as if the Good Food Guide contained nothing except a list of those restaurants which could be guaranteed not actually to poison the customer. Once this was ensured, the food could be as disgusting as anyone pleased, or as boring or unimaginative. Or it is as if the universities, instead of having any positive duties towards educating their students, were held to have fulfilled their function if they had laid down rules to protect their undergraduates from coming to positive harm while *in statu pupillari*. They might invent rules against the taking or supplying of drugs, against smoking or drinking to excess, procedures to ensure that landladies did not rip off their lodgers or motorists knock down cyclists. In this imagined university, so long as the rules were enforced, what else happened would be a matter of indifference. So the Broadcasting Standards Council seems to have nothing to do with the old trio of information, education, and entertainment. It has merely the role of protecting the viewer or listener. And the only evils the consumer is to be protected against are bad taste and the corruption supposed to derive from too much sex and violence.

I am not against such protection. Far from it. Personally, my threshold of tolerance for shock and offensiveness is exceedingly low. I once had to resign from membership of a team appointed to check films for their fitness for television when I found that I didn't think any of them fit. I would be the first to complain if standards of taste and decency were seen sharply to decline. However, I greatly object to the use of the word 'standards' to mean nothing but such standards of decency. It is like using the word 'morality' to refer only to sexual morals. By thus purloining the word to cover only part of its proper meaning, the government seems to me to have perpetrated a fraud on the public. 'Broadcasting Standards' ought to include what we naturally think of as standards of excellence or, less pretentiously, standards of good broadcasting output, such as have, over the years, made it a cliché (but one containing a good deal of truth) that British broadcasting is the best in the world.

Commercially, as I have argued, the existence of different products to choose from is generally supposed to elevate standards (that is, standards of goodness) in the things that are chosen. People on the look-out for 'value for money' will not refuse to pay more for something they deem genuinely better. They take the idea of 'value' seriously. They recognize the better when they see it, taste it, or use it, and choose accordingly. The new Broadcasting Bill offers us more choice, more channels on conventional TV, more satellite broadcasting and cable, more local and community radio stations, and new independent national radio. And so the question is whether, in the field of broadcasting, more choice will entail better products, and if not, why not.

Ten years ago, Asa Briggs wrote thus: 'Whatever else competition in broadcasting is like, it is not like competition in commodities. Questions of content, presentation appeal and quality *sometimes arise there*, as well as questions of price, but they *always* arise when we assess broadcasting output.'[1] In my view, Asa Briggs exaggerated the difference between broadcasting and, say, cat food. 'Content, presentation, appeal and quality' are important elements in probably all competitive manufactured goods to be sold commercially. And no doubt, as I have said, competition and the forces of the market improve products as a general rule. However, grave doubts have been repeatedly expressed about whether broadcasting is not importantly different from other commercial products. What we are offered in the Bill is competition as the mechanism for the improvement of broadcasting. The question is whether this can work. Is the market capable of setting and maintaining high standards of broadcasting? And if not the market, then who or what else? High standards are not easy to maintain. Competition is certainly one way to improve standards. But, in broadcasting, can it be allowed to operate by itself?

Ten years ago, when Asa Briggs uttered the words I have just quoted, what was supposed to ensure that quality was maintained in British broadcasting was regulation, exercised by both the BBC and the IBA. The new way forward is deregulation and control, if any, of the very lightest; the snaffle, not the curb. Regulation was something easy to accept by people brought up on the BBC. In the 1950s, when commercial television came on the scene, there were dire warnings from all sides about the inevitable degeneration of standards, once commercial forces came into play. What essentially prevented this from happening was that the IBA was established by government with the same regulatory powers as the BBC. The doom-prophets were proved wrong; competition between BBC and the independent companies proved nothing but beneficial to both sides – but only because both sides were subject to regulation, and the old imperatives were still in place: to inform, educate, and entertain. Those people who, this time round, have tried to appeal to the 1950s as an analogy with the present Bill, who have said, 'See how gloomy people were then, and all for nothing', have missed the essential difference between then and now – the difference of the *removal of regulatory powers*.

It may be argued that the BBC can still provide 'public service broadcasting' subject to regulation, leaving the provision of what people actually want to the market, through the commercial channels. But this is a very short-sighted argument. In the first place, if the BBC is designated the uniquely 'public service' channel (or set of channels), it will immediately have a different role, and will probably lose a great many of its audience. Also, in the field of 'public service', there will be no competition, and there will be enormously powerful reasons for the BBC itself to produce programmes which are as cheap as possible. After all, it is now only a few years before the licence comes up for review. If the BBC cannot prove itself popular, then the one thing it must prove is that it is cheap. Only so can it hope to get the present arrangements, or something like them, continued. (Already in 1991, the demands on the BBC to economize are such as have to be obeyed; the licence fee is already being held down, below the rate of inflation.) Before the early 1950s, when the BBC had an almost total monopoly, the need for economy showed its dire results in the absence of competition. However, when the independent companies came into existence, they were, under the then Broadcasting Act, committed to the same values as the BBC, and were subject to regulation just as strict; and so competition had its good results, and both BBC and ITV advanced together to the position of providing 'the best television in the world'. But without regulation on both sides, there will be no real competition between BBC and the independent companies. It is inevitable that quality will, on both sides, decline, if for different reasons.

My question is why it seems so obvious that this will happen. Whey can we not trust the 'great British public' to see to it that quality remains high in broadcasting, while we do more or less trust them to ensure that the quality of cat food not only is maintained, but in all probability is improved by the operation of the market?

This seems to me a deep question. For, on the whole, I would be prepared to argue very strongly that people are in general treated too much like children. It is not so much that they are subjected to too much regulation, but that they are told too little of what they need to know if they are to make sensible choices. Government, and perhaps especially civil servants, have not caught up with the fact that most people are better educated than they used to be (largely as a result of documentaries and current affairs programmes on television). People are not prone, as they perhaps once were, to accept what 'they' say.

Democracy no longer means simply that all adults have the vote; it also means that all adults (and all children) should be told enough to enable them to understand the issues on which they are voting. It is not right to try to pull the wool over their eyes in such matters as changes in the organization of the National Health Service or environmental pollution. And, increasingly, it is not possible to deceive people. On the whole, people are cynical about what they are supposed to believe, and hardly believe any of it. So why is it that I, for one, believe that broadcasting should still be subject to regulation, and not left to the operation of the free democatic market? Will people not voluntarily choose those news, documentary, and current affairs programmes, to say nothing of drama and music programmes, from which they have learned so much in the last fifty years?

The answer is complex. In the first place it is a financial matter. Leaving on one side the probably temporary position of the BBC, finance for programme-making must, albeit indirectly, come substantially from advertising revenue. Advertisers want to buy time only in association with what *they* regard as popular programmes. They will not buy if their advertisements would be shown during what they think are over-informative or educational programmes (apart from prime-time news). Not only is it difficult to persuade advertisers to buy time when that time is to be surrounded by documentaries or other supposedly minority programmes, but such programmes (including high-standard drama and adaptations of novels such as *Brideshead* or *The Raj Quartet*) are intrinsically expensive, and take a very long time to plan and make. The new companies will have had to bid high to get their franchise. Somehow, they will also have to get that money back quickly for the sake of their shareholders. It will simply not be possible to resist the temptation to make cheap programmes with a short planning time to fill most of their schedules. Quiz shows, bought-in American films, run of the mill soap operas, these will be the kinds of programmes that will please advertisers and satisfy shareholders, if the shareholders regard their investment as just a good prospect like any other.

The only way to ensure that there are high-quality programmes among the cheap ones is for regulation to demand that there should be. In other words, it is not possible to maintain standards in commercial broadcasting without protecting certain key areas, not just news and current affairs (which are already protected in the Bill), but documentaries and other expensive programmes which need to be planned far ahead. Without such protection, the latter will not, and cannot, be made. And of course, if they are not made for commercial television, they will gradually disappear from the BBC screens as well. It will seem a wanton extravagance for the BBC to make all the expensive programmes. As it looks towards 1996 and the review of the licence system, the BBC must attempt to show that its programmes are just as popular as those of the independent companies, and no more expensive.

What I am suggesting is that the transaction of producing television programmes is not really a transaction between the producer (or company) and the audience, but between the company and first, the advertisers and then, the shareholders. I do not suggest that there is corruption here or that programmes are biased or geared to the interests of either group. It is only that they *must* be such as to make quick money. The public, then, the viewers, have little involvement in, or chance of changing the nature of what they see. They will be given plenty of choice, but it is likely to be choice between various cheap, supposedly 'mass-appeal' programmes.

But, it will be said, if these programmes really are mass-appeal, if they are indeed what people like and want, what does it matter if they are cheap? Surely the advertisers must be right. After all, they do research. They are in a position to *know* that it is worth their while to advertise in the breaks in a quiz show, rather than in a documentary about China. Who are *we* to say that the documentary is better, or of a higher standard? Why can't we trust people to set their own standards? Regulation, as I have already conceded, is essentially elitist. If I am so keen on a new, educated democracy, then I should be arguing in favour of trusting people's taste, and that of the advertisers, who have found out what that taste is.

My reply to this objection takes us on to education, and indeed to the nature of education itself. What is missing in the Bill is any obligation (any general obligation, that is) to use broadcasting to educate. It is true that franchises are not, as was at first proposed, to go *simply* to the highest bidder (who would be the most likely to overbid, and therefore probably have the greatest need to make or buy in cheap programmes once the franchise was his). As the Bill stands, there is a kind of quality hurdle to be got over by the applicant companies, consisting presumably in promises to make a certain number of 'quality' programmes. But it is not clear that any of these programmes will have to be shown at prime time; nor is it clear that, if a company is in financial trouble, that company will not be allowed permanently to postpone the redeeming of such promises. That people actually like and enjoy high-quality programmes when they get them is not, unfortunately, enough to make them count, for advertisers, as popular; and as they are also intrinsically expensive, the expense of making them may well remain too high.

The essential nature of the kind of educative programme I am talking about is that it is imaginative, original, the outcome of a creative mind at work, and therefore essentially unpredictable. People could not know in advance that they were going to want such a programme, because in advance they would not know what it was going to be. Being thus unpredictable, such a programme would not appeal to advertisers. It would not have been made according to any formula; it would open new horizons to those who watched it, making them feel, as all works of imagination do, that this was not trivial, that it was infinite in its possibilities, that there was more in it than met the casual eye. This kind of programme, whether drama or documentary, whether about the natural or the urban world, is what I mean by educative television.

A good teacher makes his pupils understand more than they knew they wanted to understand, more than they knew existed to be understood; similarly with the kind of television (and radio) that I am talking about. People will receive them, be educated by them, enjoy them, *unexpectedly*. If the programmes had come labelled 'educational', they would not have been watched. As they do not (but as drama or fiction or documentary), then they are watched, and they have their effect. Following what advertisers, and indeed audiences themselves, *think* they want is essentially conservative. No one will venture on the new, and television will become formula-dominated, more of the same, with minor variation, as much American soap opera is. It is possible originality that needs to be protected by regulation. And the standard of the original and the imaginative cannot be set by you and me, nor by the majority of the audience, nor by the advertisers. It must be set by broadcasters themselves, those who are creative and devoted to their art, determined to make high-quality programmes, in whom the companies (or the BBC) put their faith, and with whom they entrust their money, but always subject to regulation. For regulation was, precisely, a *protection* for imaginative broadcasting.

There is more than an analogy here with education. We hear as much about educational standards as we do about standards of broadcasting. And though there is nothing quite so absurd in the world of education as the Broadcasting Standards Council, yet in education, too, the concept of standards has been to a certain extent hijacked, and co-opted to serve a theory of education and its purpose which is of almost unbelievable narrowness. For education of a high standard is now seen as education geared to industry and commerce, to preparing people for jobs, a process to be got through as intensively, quickly, and cheaply as possible. Quite deliberately, the language in which education is now discussed has been brutalized. We are asked to produce 'performance indicators' by which standards may be judged, and these indicators are expressed in numerical (and therefore readily comparable) terms. How many students are taught for how many weeks by how many staff? What is the level of wastage? What is the ratio of different examination grades or classes of degree? What proportion of students after leaving remain in a job for more than three months? What is the overall cost per unit? How is the outcome to be measured in terms of value added to the input? And so on.

Such terminology is applied to secondary, as well as tertiary, education. The overall aim is that education at every level should be cost-effective. Schools and universities can offer a diversity of courses provided that the market will bear them. The only ingredient missing from the scene is the advertisers, who do not yet pay for the courses on offer (though even here it is to be noticed that some maintained schools in Kent accept advertisements to be displayed in the school hall in exchange for money; and it might be that such advertising could soon begin to have an effect on the curriculum).

The problem in discussing this overwhelming educational trend is that in one sense it is a good and necessary trend. It is the mark of a civilized country that it should be taken for granted that education is provided free, to everyone (even if there remain those who prefer to pay for their own). And so Government, which cannot and should not abandon this extremely expensive relic of the Welfare State, is absolutely entitled to demand value for money, and find ways of ensuring it. Thus the introduction into primary and secondary schools of a national curriculum, compulsory for all children, is a reasonable and defensible move, even if it may take longer to put in place than was at first hoped. To ensure that people do not leave school illiterate, scientifically or technically incompetent, unable to calculate, is a proper aim, one on which everyone could, in principle, agree. And if this is what is meant by ensuring educational 'standards', then we can be happy with it.

But there are two additions to this perfectly acceptable aim, both of them more dubious and both of them raising the question in the title of this chapter: the question 'Who Sets the Standards?' You will not, by now, be surprised to learn what I believe these additions to be: the first is the introduction into educational policy of the concept of the market; the second the supposition that, at all educational levels, it should be the market that should determine the *content* of education, and thus the definition of educational quality – that is, of standards.

It is necessary to examine the application of the market to education a bit further. In the context of broadcasting, we saw that the market meant the shareholders on the one hand and the advertisers on the other. Programme content and cost would be determined by these forces, working, as it is hoped, in harmony for the pleasure of the listeners and viewers. However, we saw reason to doubt whether the joint operation of these forces would in fact do anything to elevate broadcasting standards. In the case of education, the market means, first of all, potential employers and, then, students or, in the case of children, their parents. The hope here is that parents will demand what employers want and, increasingly, that employers will pay for what they want, either directly or indirectly, by financing schools and universities, sponsoring students, or paying their employees enough to enable them, in their turn, to pay educational fees. Increasingly, Government is beginning to think of free education (free to the consumer, that is) as a matter of last resort, a safety net to catch those too poor or too feckless to pay for it themselves.

The market here is a complex structure, but its working is supposed to subsidize schools, universities, students, and their parents in exchange for an educational outcome that will be of benefit to those who pay, ultimately industry and commerce. If all this worked, if industry (and thus, it is supposed, students) got what was required to make the whole industrial and commercial system operative, then this would entail that educational standards had risen. There is a shortage of skilled workers and good managers. Such a shortage would come to an end with the full operation of a free market. Such is the hope.

The question still to be raised is thus clear: Should we be content with such a market as the source and protector of educational standards? Should schools, and still more, universities, entrust themselves to such a system? I believe that the answer is that they should not. Just as in broadcasting it is necessary that in the end standards be set by those with vision and imagination, who may know, or find out, what people will enjoy and benefit from, rather than relying only on what it is thought that they want; so in education, standards must be set by those with the vision to see what will excite people, what will open their eyes – above all, what lies at the frontiers of knowledge and understanding. It is impossible to have a properly *educational* system that is inherently conservative, as a market-led system must be.

I am not arguing that innovation is impossible in industry. But in industry innovation generally comes about when there is a need, identified by the market, for a particular kind of product which subsequently comes into existence to fill that specific gap. Universities and polytechnics may sometimes have a part to play in such innovation. But it is not the primary role of educational institutions. Such innovation will mostly stem from the research and development department of the particular industry concerned, following upon market research. The R & D departments in industry badly need support; and they need well-educated graduates to work in them. But graduates ought not to be expected to come straight from university or polytechnic already knowing exactly what a particular industry demands. On the contrary, they are likely to be far more useful in the long term if they come with a *general* understanding of the science and technology involved, a readiness to learn, and, above all, an imaginative grasp of what is possible, and what may arise, technologically, out of what has gone before.

Universities and polytechnics ought not, that is to say, to concern themselves with the *immediate* needs of industry and commerce (or only occasionally, and if specifically commissioned to do so). They should devote themselves to *general* teaching and *pure* research, research which *may or may not* lead in the end to some industrial, saleable, spin-off. In the long run, society will benefit from the ongoing pursuit of pure research. But there can be no time-limit on such benefits. And it is too much to demand that particular industries, bent on their place and that of their shareholders among their competitors, should give lavishly to the support of research which may have no quick return, and may benefit their competitors as much as themselves.

A Government that believes in education and research, on the other hand, must in the end be prepared to pay for it, and to invest in the future. And it must at the same time manifest its trust in the universities, in such a way that the content of both teaching and research, in both the sciences and the humanities, be left to the academic communities themselves to determine.

I am not suggesting that education and research should not be 'useful'. All education and all research must ultimately be defended on grounds of its utility, its contribution to a civilized and advancing society, one which looks back to its own origins and also forward to possible innovations. All education looks ahead to what will be of benefit to the student after education is over (and thus will benefit society as a whole, of which the student is a part). All research must similarly be forward-looking, even if its nature is historical. It must aim to open up new ways of seeing the world and its history. But it cannot be for any government or any particular industry, still less the operation of the market, to determine what the content of such education and research will be.

If we enlarge the idea of the useful, we must recognize that it must be defined, in each particular area, by those involved in the subject, those with the imagination and foresight to see what may be potentially eye-opening, exciting, and new. It is these people, these experts, who must set the standards of the academically worthwhile. It cannot be done by the market, however enlightened. For people in the market-place do not, and cannot, know what it is that in the end will benefit them and, through them, society as a whole.

The present Government has shown itself extremely unwilling to trust either academics or professional broadcasters (for even if deregulation seemed like an expression of trust, it is really an expression of trust not in the experts, but in the advertisers, as I have tried to argue). With regard to education, a year or so ago I wrote as follows:

> The universities certainly stand at one end of a continuum of educational provision, starting at nursery school, which is organised and, to a large extent, provided, by Government. But they must not be seen only as the last of the institutions in which people may be educated. A National Curriculum at school is not objectionable, for Government may be entitled to demand that children should be brought up to a certain level of education as a minimum. But with universities it is different: they must be seen as a *source* of new knowledge, the *origin* of that critical, undogmatic imaginative examination of received wisdom without which a country cannot be expected to have its voice heard, and from which ultimately all intellectual standards flow.[2]

I stand by those words today. Equally, in the world of broadcasting, it must be from the committed and imaginative programme-makers and those who commission their works that standards must ultimately flow. In broadcasting, regulation, not deregulation, is the way to ensure that such programme-makers can be enabled to get on with their work, partly free from the demands of advertisers. In education, there is no help except for Government to give financial backing to the universities, in order to save them from total dependence on the demand of the market for instant results.

Allowing that broadcasters set, and must set, their own professional standards does not entail that they should not be accountable to Government and to the public. Indeed, regulation ensures that they will be. Equally, universities and polytechnics, if funded, as once they were, by Government grants, must be accountable to Government and the public for the way this money is spent. In both cases accountability should entail openness and readiness to accept the consequences if wrong decisions and worthless outcomes are exposed. But the more faith we, the public, have in those who set the standards, the more such accountability can be real and acceptable. We can ask for an account, and be certain that we are getting an honest one. We can learn from the manifestly high standards on display not to be cynical or suspicious of all promises.

Finally, it may be asked again whether such a notion of the origin of standards, whether in broadcasting or in education, is incurably élitist. The answer, I think, is 'Yes'. But we should believe in our own élite. And we have every reason, historically, to do so. The élite, after all, no longer come from a particular class or part of society. The opposite of 'élitist' is not 'classless'. An élite must carry authority: the authority of expertise, devotion, and the creative imagination, whose outcome can never be wholly foreseen. Only from such an authoritative source can we rely on the establishment of standards themselves worthy of respect.

# 9

## Philosophy in Education

Since the days of Plato there has existed a special relation between philosophy and education. In the *Republic*, Plato outlined an educational curriculum which was to be the salvation of society. It involved a rigid division of children into categories according to ability, the highest category being the future rulers, who, progressing through their long educational course until they reached the most lofty and abstract subject of all, philosophy, would ultimately become acquainted with the truth. They would then be the only people fit to legislate and to govern.

Centuries later, in a less grandiose style, John Stuart Mill argued that universal education was the most important means to the utilitarian end, the maximization of happiness. If people were educated, they would, he thought, inevitably come to prefer the higher to the lower pleasures, and would come to value freedom, intelligence, moral goodness, and the useful arts as they ought. So they, like Plato's elite class of rulers, would be fit to govern. Mill strongly believed that everyone should be given at least the chance to become educated; and, unusually for his time, he included women as well as men.

But philosophers cannot feel satisfied, at the present time, with what has come about. Everybody knows (or if they don't, they should, for we are told it often enough) that our educational system has failed. In 1977, James Callaghan instituted the so-called Great Debate, because it was generally held that young people were leaving school illiterate, innumerate, and ill-prepared for work. The situation is not thought to be much better today, in spite of the radical changes proposed and partly introduced by the 1988 Reform Act. I want in what follows to explore the question not addressed, as far as I know, by the authors of that Act: to what extent the injection of critical philosophy into education might help to improve it and to justify the importance of the role that philosophers have been accustomed to accord to it.

One of the most frequent, and in my view, best justified complaints about English education, especially as it affects the top, still small percentage who will go on to higher education in universities or polytechnics, is that it is too narrowly based. In the past pupils were often allowed to drop subjects on their way up the school, so that their total education was unbalanced. Though the introduction of the national curriculum may help in the early years, yet, when they are fourteen or fifteen they still have to make choices which narrow the number of subjects they study down to three often closely related subjects, such as pure mathematics, applied mathematics, and physics. Even if the national curriculum ensures that up to the age of sixteen children must carry a balanced range of subjects, including both English and science, yet the objections to their choosing just three subjects for their A-level specialization may in some ways become greater than they have been in the past. For the national curriculum promises to leave very little time for subjects other than English, mathematics, and science; so pupils will enter the sixth form with little in the way of general education or interests.

There is no doubt that in most English schools the sixth form (and its preparation for A-levels) is held sacrosanct. Politicians and those who work in universities tend to agree with this view. It is taken for granted that English universities could not do with anything less or different. Even those within universities and polytechnics who profess themselves anxious to comply with the demands of the Government for more students to enter higher education, nevertheless are demanding the very same A-level results as before, and are worrying that A-levels are changing their character to match the GCSE. The argument is that, so far, few students have dropped out from university but that, if the standard of knowledge when they entered declined, far more would find themselves unable to complete the courses and would leave. The thought that the courses themselves might have to change, or at least the teaching methods, is seldom entertained.

The result of this obsession with A-levels in English and Welsh schools (and increasingly a parallel movement is to be seen in Scotland) is that the pattern of sixth form work is determined by what the universities demand. Even those who do not go on to higher education are, many of them, forced down this specialist road. Yet it is well known that A-levels do not of themselves guarantee success at university or polytechnic, and that for many students they afford a narrow and frustrating kind of education. The alternative to A-levels is a bewildering variety of vocational courses. The gap between the academic and the non-academic becomes wider all the time. This in itself is an extraordinary paradox. For the very politicians and educationalists who are so anxious to retain the academic purity of A-levels are those who argue that universities and polytechnics themselves should be increasingly vocational.

There is thus a thorough confusion about the extent to which education should or should not be 'practical'. And so there are fundamental questions to be raised. How far should what is taught at school be regarded as a preparation for specific jobs or for particular courses in higher education? To what extent and for what purposes should we train people at school in technical skills? Is it right to insist that science take priority over the arts? Is a broadly 'humane' education at school justified?

In order to think about such questions, let us start again with the English sixth form. The objection to excessive specialization is twofold. In the first place, it is argued, rightly, that many pupils leave school, and even university, incredibly ignorant. There are enormous numbers of things of which they know nothing whatever, and about which they do not even have the concepts needed to enable them to learn. Secondly, because the examinations they take require such feats of memory, and are marked according to how much of what they have committed to memory they can get down in three hours, teaching in the sixth form has in the past too often been extremely boring, and there has been very little chance for pupils to exercise either their reason or their imagination. None of the remedies proposed to counteract excessive and excessively early specialization has so far had any success.

It is true that there has recently been introduced a system called the system of A/S-levels, whereby pupils could study for perhaps two A-levels and two examinations, each of which would occupy half the regular time allotted to an A-level and would be taken, it is hoped, in subjects not especially related to the A-level courses. Thus, whereas universities have in the past demanded three A-levels at specified grades, they may now accept instead two A-levels and two A/S-levels, or some other combination of passes. However, I do not think that this scheme will have a very long life. On the one hand, schools find it very difficult to lay on courses that are suitable and are not simply half the full A-level course. On the other hand, universities show little inclination to change their demands. Especially in the case of medicine and veterinary science, but in mathematics and the other sciences as well, it is in the highest degree unlikely that any but the old combinations of A-levels will be acceptable. I believe, therefore, that it is hardly worth considering A/S-levels as anything but another failure among the numerous attempts to loosen things up.

Indeed, I am not optimistic about the possibility of any new structure that will remedy the present ills of the English sixth form. Instead, I believe that we may have to change more radically the nature of the subject-matter that is studied. For when people complain about the failures of education, I believe they are not complaining that those who leave their educational institutions do not know enough. If that were the trouble, it might fairly easily be remedied. It is rather that they have no notion of their own ignorance; they do not adapt to the new demands that are made of them; and above all, they are conceptually impoverished. By this I mean that they do not understand enough to enable them to pick up new concepts or see new ways of applying old ones. It is this that is required of them when at last they stop being formally educated and take on the new role of producers or managers or educators of others.

It is essential, I believe, to change the content of the curriculum, both at school and at undergraduate level, so that it encourages those who follow it to become in this way adaptable or, to put the same thing in another way, encourages their imagination. In order to do this, it is necessary, while teaching pupils how things are, always also to teach them to raise the question of whether they might be, or might have been, otherwise; when teaching them within a specific subject area, say, biology or physics, always to teach them to relate this area to others; when teaching them about existing institutions, always to give them some idea of how these institutions arose and what alternative institutions there might have been. In short, it is essential that they should be encouraged to stand back from their subjects, even while studying them, in order to adopt a critical, analytic, and historical attitude to whatever they are taught. To do this is precisely the function of a critical philosophy.

To encourage such a philosophical attitude in pupils needs both confidence and courage; for it may be seen as likely to undermine authority and to force both teachers and pupils to adopt an unnervingly sceptical position, embracing nothing wholeheartedly, whether it be a matter of fact or of value. But it is a poor belief that rests solely on tradition and authority; a poor understanding that cannot examine its own foundations. Unless we undertake some such plan, I see no way to improve the effectiveness of education.

To stand back and criticize, to raise questions about the relation of one subject with another, to ask what counts as good evidence in this field or that, all these things constitute the proper function of philosophy. So what I am arguing is that philosophy should be introduced into education in the sixth forms of our schools, and should remain there throughout undergraduate education also.

It may be asked, then, whether what I am suggesting is that philosophy be taught as a separate subject at school, and perhaps as a compulsory subject to first-year undergraduates, in the old Scottish manner. There has been a considerable move in England for the introduction of philosophy as an optional A-level subject, and quite a lot of work has been done on a variety of syllabuses. But, whatever may be the case for undergradutes, I do not believe that philosophy is a suitable school subject if it is considered as a separate discipline. For one thing, whatever the dangers of specialization, we must continue to regard school as the time for laying foundations, and though I believe it to be crucial to introduce a philosophical *attitude* at school, I do not think that time should be taken away from the foundation-laying aspects of the curriculum, whether mathematical, scientific, broadly speaking historical, or linguistic.

Philosophy itself is a highly specialist subject, though it may overlap both with mathematics and with aspects of history. But being extremely abstract, it will, as a specialism, never be of great appeal except to a smallish minority of students. It is an academic discipline which in one sense lacks its own content, being always engaged in laying bare the foundations of other people's disciplines, mathematical, scientific, or historical. It is concerned all the time with presuppositions, whether of physics or of popular morality or the law.

Aristotle held that moral philosophy, unlike mathematics, was not a fit subject for the young; and to some extent he was right. For teachers of philosophy, especially if they are short of time, are exposed to two different dangers. On the one hand, the syllabus may demand that they treat the subject historically. And to some extent this is proper; for it is the mark of the amateur philosopher to suppose that his bright ideas are truly new, never entertained before; and it is an essential part of the discipline to read the works of earlier philosophers and come to understand their arguments. But at school, as the French baccalaureate shows, there is a temptation to teach what a philosopher, such as Descartes or Kant, said, to reduce the content to manageable or rememberable summary, and to omit all consideration of why he said it or what precisely he meant. Thus summarizing is a standing temptation.

On the other hand, if philosophy is regarded as simply a collection of interesting general questions, then the danger is that a different kind of superficiality will result, pupils being taught to put up and knock down different 'solutions', the smart and the trendy emerging as the almost inevitable victors in the contest. Pupils taught in either of these two ways find it very hard to engage in the subject later, in greater depth. And indeed, you may perhaps suspect that my objection to philosophy as a school subject is simply that it is so extremely difficult to teach philosophy at university to those who have been exposed to it earlier.

In any case, philosophy, being concerned with concepts which put in their appearance all over the place, such as the concept of causation or of the relation between mind and matter or of freedom, does not need the prop of a special slot in the timetable. It can, if we will allow it to, infiltrate all aspects of education, whether in the arts or the sciences. And to allow it to do so is the reform which I believe we have to bring about.

In the early years of this century there was a great educational dispute in Scotland. The chief protagonists were Alexander Darroch, the professor of education in Edinburgh, and John Burnet, professor of Greek at St Andrews for more than thirty years. Alexander Darroch was immediately concerned with the education on offer at the universities, though the chief purpose of his proposed reforms was to bring about a reform of school education. He aimed to change the direction of education away from those he referred to as the 'lads of parts' towards the whole population of school-age children, by replacing metaphysics, epistemology, and logic in the universities (and in teacher training) with the democratic philosophy of John Dewey, and by a greatly increased emphasis on the human sciences, especially psychology. Future teachers, educated in these disciplines, he thought, would radically change the whole nature of education in schools. John Burnet, on the other hand, was a passionate defender of classical studies and philosophy, with a view to creating what was, no doubt, an elite (and he did not deny this) but a broadly based elite.

Like the disputes we are engaged in today, this dispute was both strictly educational, concerned with what would be the content of the most effective curriculum, and also totally political: the two aspects of the argument could not and cannot be separated. For we may think of Darroch's schemes as reflected in the desire to open up higher education to far larger numbers of students; whereas John Burnet's elite may be conceived (in a way more fitting to the 1990s) as a group of people who, whatever their background and race, may be enabled to emerge from school as leaders and managers, prepared to win in what has to be acknowledged to be a highly competitive world.

Burnet drew a distinction between what he called 'interested' and 'disinterested' knowledge. He argued that 'interested' knowledge, which was knowledge acquired for a particular purpose, was the same as specialist knowledge. It was meant to be put to a special and specific use. 'Disinterested' knowledge, on the other hand, was essentially generalist. And he held that generalist knowledge must take priority over specialist. At the turn of the century, Scottish schools were still based on this principle. The belief was that, if he had been properly taught, a generalist could add specialist knowledge at a later time. That was, at a different level, the principle that lay behind the domination of the Civil Service in the first part of this century by people who had read Greats at Oxford; it was thought that after their education in the classics, and especially in ancient philosophy, they would be able to pick up whatever knowledge they needed, later, whether about the governing of India or the intricacies of trade treaties with Europe or the proper treatment of offenders at home.

Today, however, the word 'general' has a faintly suspect ring. A-level 'General Studies' has never been taken seriously, certainly not by universities. A 'general' degree is rated lower than any specialist degree, however dismal. I believe that we should try to reinstate the general, even if we have to call it something else (the disinterested or, indeed, the philosophical).

It will be said that what I am advocating will be the death of 'standards' in the sixth forms of schools. For if general issues concened with the nature of chemistry or mathematics or history are to take priority, what is to become of the content of these subjects? Will the curriculum not inevitably invite superficiality? We do not want, as our school-leavers, a lot of people who can talk about mathematics. We want competent mathematicians. There is nothing to be said for being able to discourse on the philosophy of history if you don't know the date of the Battle of Waterloo.

I concede that any curriculum aiming to introduce the general and philosophical aspects of a subject will have to be designed with great care. Disinterested critical consideration of a subject and of the relations between subjects must be seen to arise only out of a certain degree of specialist knowledge and out of an ability to grasp certain essential subject-specific concepts. Nevertheless, if we are to get away from the narrowness and inflexibility we now suffer from, we must introduce the general as an ideal. We must move away from the notion that academic standards will be kept up only by intense and detailed specialist knowledge, or that intellectual excellence consists in nothing but the ability to acquire detailed factual knowledge.

It has to be understood that the general, the disinterested, and the critical does not mean the vague or the watered down or the journalistic. I am not demanding that every subject which has a technical vocabulary or which employs concepts other than those employed by common sense should be rendered simple and fit for consumption by every man and woman in the street. I do not expect that every teacher and every pupil should adopt the role of the popularizing author or the television-style simplifier of the abstruse. If I, being ignorant, ask a mathematician about his work, I must expect, if I am to understand him, to be led into a realm of abstraction that I am unaccustomed to. I shall leave the world of concrete numerable objects, and follow him into a world of imagination where numbers themselves have discernible characteristics or may exist in hiding, waiting to be discovered. I may have to learn a notion of proof different from that to which I am accustomed. But one of the requirements of disinterested knowledge is that it should be capable of being shared; it is essentially a matter, as philosophy has always been, of dialogue and discussion. Therefore the mathematician must be taught to attempt to take me with him, so that I may have some appreciation of what he is up to and why he enjoys it.

For there is great danger concealed in the failures of communication consequent on the present specialist A-level curriculum. Concepts are introduced that are often barely understood by the pupils, let alone capable of being discussed by them. Processes are often mechanically and uncritically put into operation, unrealistic problems set and solved. The specialism of the knowledge makes it intrinsically free-floating, disconnected from the real world. A more critical approach would inevitably improve communication. Subject-matter has to be made more generally intelligible, both if it is to be discussed and if it is to be seen as no longer self-contained but as part of a wide and complex shared body of knowledge. We need an understanding of the principles that lie behind the selection of questions to be asked and the methods to be employed in answering them. Anyone who thoroughly understands a principle ought to be able to expound it so that other people, non-experts, should be able to understand it as well. And, of course, to enable people to expound principles in this way is a major part of the task of philosophy.

And so the general or 'philosophical' curriculum that I advocate would itself be based on a single principle: that the less narrowly a pupil's critical faculties are confined within the bounds of a single set of concepts or procedures, the more easily he will be able to adapt to life after school, whether at work or in higher education, and the more free his imagination will become; these two targets in fact being one and the same. Most of the detailed factual material learned in the sixth form is forgotten or superseded within a few years. What ought to remain is a technique for learning and a grasp of intellectual principles which may be applied, and reapplied, in different circumstances. It seems to me that, in this respect, we have a great deal to learn from the best American schools.

American students emerging from school are far more adept than our school-leavers, even the most academically able, at explaining their subjects, relating their interests to one another over a wide range, and demonstrating some notion of the unity of science. For years we in this country have been accustomed to say, 'American education is superficial', or 'The trouble with American students is that they have no idea of scholarship.' But such criticisms become increasingly unconvincing if one observes the enthusiasm with which such students throw themselves into new subjects and make themselves experts, within a short time, on topics they may never have studied before. Scholarship may come later to them; but when it comes, it has a surer foundation.

What we are essentially looking for in secondary education, then, is a curriculum and a method of pursuing it that will equip the student with transferable skills and transferable expertise. This is what the disinterested or philosophical should give us.

It is time now to turn to the question of how we could, in practical terms, get what we want.

The GCSE examination is innovatory in two ways. First, it is a single examination (or at least a single system) for all candidates. From the early 1960s, between 60 and 70 per cent of all children at school were divided into two groups, those who were to sit for GCE O-levels and those who would take the CSE examination (the remaining 40 or 30 per cent were regarded as 'unexaminable'). O-levels were examined externally by five different boards (between which schools could choose), the boards being largely dominated by university membership, though with increasing teacher participation. CSE, on the other hand, was examined regionally and by teachers themselves, with a considerable proportion of continuous assessment and course work included in the result. The new system is far more like the old CSE in the actual method of examining. Like the CSE, it has a marked emphasis on the practical and, in the case of languages, on the spoken as opposed to the written. Project work plays an important part in the overall result. The examination is organized regionally, and is conducted by teachers.

The second major innovation is perhaps even more important. The new examination is supposed to be marked, and grades given, according to criteria which include not merely the reproduction of knowledge acquired, but the demonstration of what a candidate 'understands, and can do'. Thus the aim is to reward the positive achievements of candidates in a newly realistic way, reflecting a newly pupil-centred project-orientated style of teaching. This style of teaching, it is generally held, has already had a marked effect on the motivation of pupils and their involvement in their own learning.

At the same time, the introduction of the national curriculum, with tests at fixed ages (including the age of 16), seems to suggest a different and more mechanical way of ensuring that students acquire a minimum standard of competence in numeracy and literary and scientific knowledge. It is not clear how such tests will fit in with the GCSE. We are left, then, with a good deal of uncertainty.

There are many questions that may be raised. Perhaps the most urgent are these: How vocational is school education meant to be? How much practical competence and how much conceptual understanding are we entitled to demand from those who leave school? How shall we know what standard in either they have reached? How much time will the new emphasis on science and technology leave for the study of other things at school?

To answer these questions, I believe that we need to look all over again at the differences between Plato and Dewey or, if you like, between John Burnet and Alexander Darroch. For here we may hope to find both some light to help us see through the present tangle and at the same time some manageable ways forward.

Darroch, like Dewey, believed that education was for everyone;

and it seems to me disgraceful that we have not done more to show that we genuinely share this belief. We have schools that are compulsory for all children, but a concept of education that is still to a large extent Platonic, the clever engaging in thought, the stupid in practical activity. But in rejecting the elitism and snobbishness of the Platonic ideal, we do not want to throw away the advantages of the kind of philosophical education advocated by Burnet; indeed, we cannot afford to do so.

The way forward, in my view, is to place at the centre of the curriculum, not the distinction between arts and sciences, but the distinction between the practical and the theoretical. We then need to make sure that all children have access to both sides of this division, whether in the arts or in science. It is proper that some children should have an education with a bias in one direction or the other; the important thing is to ensure that both aspects of any subject-matter are on offer and that both can be pursued with equal honour.

The theoretical aspects of a subject should be taught in the way I have already suggested: the aim should be for 'disinterested' knowledge of the subject, an understanding of the way the subject links with others, and the historical development of the subject, as well as the assumptions that lie behind it. This theoretical, or philosophical, treatment should make a pupil in one sense feel at home with the subject, feel able to pursue it with understanding wherever it may lead. In another sense, it should make the subject-matter seem unfamiliar, never to be taken for granted, always to be questioned and further explored.

· The practical aspects of a subject, on the other hand, should be taught so as to develop skills and actual uses; the knowledge so acquired would be 'interested'. It could always be demonstrated not verbally but in making, doing, or applying, to some specific end. Some of the skills taught in this 'interested' or practical way would be verbal skills: knowing how to speak and understand French or German, or indeed English, would count as a practical skill and would be to this extent 'interested'.

Let me take an example or two. In the case of the teaching of English, there is a clear distinction to be drawn between what pupils need to be able to do with their own language and what they need to understand about it. They need to be able to speak, write, and understand, to be able to communicate successfully and write in a conventionally acceptable way with fluency and competence. This is practical English, and whether it is to be taught by means of formal grammar or by other means, it is of the utmost importance to everyone, in a genuinely instrumental or 'interested' sense.

On the other hand, there is a different way of thinking of the teaching of English within which the possibilities of the language are understood partly historically, through the literature that has been written and the development of the language itself, and partly through the study of literature as a form of art, to be understood as living and infinitely worth pursuing for its own sake.

At present the teaching of English is ineffective, simply because these two aspects of the subject are not thought of separately. I am not saying that language and the development of literature are two totally unrelated things: I am arguing rather that pedagogically they should be treated separately. Literature is dispensable in a sense that language is not. Literature must be enjoyed for its own sake, disinterestedly, or not at all. Language, on the other hand, is a tool which everybody must learn to use. Obviously someone who comes to love literature may do so because he loves the language; but not everybody with a competence in, even a love and a taste for, language need necessarily have any particular interest in literature. If the actual teaching of these two aspects of English were different, the teaching of literature itself could be more adventurous and eye-opening than it is at present, when it is taught largely to people who have no liking for it at all.

A similar distinction could be drawn in other fields. For instance, there is a vast difference, often overlooked, between learning to use technology and learning to understand the theory or the science which makes the technology possible. It is one thing to be a competent mechanic, quite another to be a mechanical engineer; one thing to understand the uses of computers, make simple programs, and generally become at home with actual deployment of the hardware, quite another to be a computer-scientist, though of course the first may lead to the second. Technology, in the sense of the deployment of technology, is no more closely connected with the sciences than it is with the arts. We must learn to distinguish the ability to use from the ability to understand the theory. No one ever argues that only mechanical engineers should drive cars; no one attempts to confine the making and playing of tapes to those versed in electronics. We must extend this way of thinking to technology as a whole.

Because of the false assumption that technology and science must go together, with arts subjects somewhere over the other side of a great divide, there is an increasing assumption that science is 'useful' ('interested') and arts 'useless'. Thus politicians are prone to urge more and more people to pursue science subjects, creating the impression that those who pursue the arts are self-indulgent, aiming only for their own pleasure, while the virtuous scientists are aiming for the good of society as a whole. This is a misunderstanding; for much science is just as 'useless' (that is, 'disinterested') as literature or music or history. It is technology, not science, that is useful, in the sense of being immediately able to be deployed, immediately practical. And so it is that the balance to be sought in school education is less between the sciences and the arts than between the practical and the theoretical, the particular and the general or, we may say, the philosophical. For the particular is concerned with what lies immediately to hand; particular knowledge, as I have argued, may be shown by what someone can do rather than by what he can understand. General or philosophical knowledge is concerned with principles.

If we could learn to regard the school curriculum as divided in this way between the practical and the theoretical, then we would do best to allow the division to be reflected in a different system of examinations altogether, one that would be far more flexible than the present system, either in England and Wales, or in Scotland. We recognize now that everybody needs to be able to do things, and do them properly. And so we are ready to think of school examinations partly as tests of skills of a wholly practical kind. Such tests should be taken by all children at school, at whatever age they are ready for them (and could equally be taken by grown-ups). These should include tests in operational skills, ranging from the simple to the most complex use of computers and word processors; they should also include tests in communication, spoken and written, in English or in other languages; they should include tests in cooking or in car maintenance, sewing or the production of software. The tests should be part of a single examination system, and should be graded, with approximately a year's work presupposed for each grade. But the key would be that the tests should be taken by pupils of any age, according to readiness.

The other half of the examination system should consist in tests of understanding, in the philosophical or theoretical aspects of a subject, again ideally to be taken whenever a pupil is ready, but, failing that, in the sixth form. On such a scheme it would be quite possible for a pupil to leave school with a grade 8 in practical electronics, but only a grade 1 in the theory, or no grade at all; but it would be unlikely that a pupil would have grade 8 in, say, 'philosophical' physics without any passes at all in the practical tests.

Now is not the time to expand on the advantages I see in such a scheme (modelled as you will see on the familiar music examinations of the Associated Board and other music colleges); nor on the objections to it, most of which are organizational. My reason for outlining a system of examinations of this kind is that it would, if it were introduced, encapsulate the role of the philosophical in school education. For it would be impossible to work for a theory test without thinking about the subject-matter of the test. What would be tested would be the theory behind the practice; and this, after all, is the proper function of philosophy: to get behind the practical, the concrete, and the everyday, to the abstract and the speculative.

Such a system could also serve the purpose of broadening the curriculum in the sixth form at school. For alongside theoretical mathematics or physics, a pupil could take practical cooking or music, even if at quite a lowly grade. He could use his practical computer skills, perhaps, to make his own programs for his theoretical history or economics or geography. He could start a new language at the practical, or spoken, level.

There are two things needed to make such a scheme workable. First, the universities and polytechnics must accept it and, if possible, welcome it, as providing a profile of a pupil suitable for use as an entrance qualification. Secondly, teachers must become accustomed to a different approach to all their subjects. As to this last, I do not believe there would be much difficulty. Teachers have already had to change their style of teaching radically to accommodate themselves to the GCSE. The days of dictating notes to a class and hoping they will be able to reproduce them in continuous prose have gone for ever. The time is right for the philosophical and the practical, both, to be acknowledged as the twin pillars of teaching techniques. Moreover, teachers themselves have long been critical both of the lack of practical abilities in their pupils and of the enforced narrowness of what they have had to teach. They would, I am sure, be anxious to take on a system of graded tests which would gradually overtake the use of A-levels and GCSE, making it unnecessary to have great blocks of examinations at the ages of 16 and 18. As for the content of the theoretical curriculum, it seems to me certain that if we do not introduce into it an element of philosophy, of the general, the communicable, and the disinterested, then we shall continue to fail the children we hope to educate. For only by enabling them to see their subjects in relation to other subjects, only by training them to analyse the principles of the subject rather than merely absorbing the details, shall we put them in a position to turn their minds to other things when the time comes. As well as workers, we need leaders, managers, and communicators. All these will find a habit of analysis their most useful tool. Most important of all, however, it is only by an injection into the curriculum of this kind of philosophy that we shall enable those at school to exercise their imagination and become aware of their own freedom. For imagination is the power to see how things might be different, and thus to choose whether to try to preserve them or to change them. If we have any belief in democracy, this is the power we must foster, as a matter of duty.

# 10

# *Education for Pleasure*

When the Committee of Enquiry into the education of the handicapped was at last beginning to put together its report in 1975,
we found that, in order to try to introduce the all-important
concept of educational need, we had to formulate certain very
general principles of education. Specifically, we had to try to
define the goals of education, since it is only in terms of some
defined end that a need becomes clear. You need tools *if* you aim
to make a garden; you need an instrument *if* you aim to play in an
orchestra; you need food and air and water *if* you aim to keep
alive. So, in order to demonstrate the educational needs of handicapped children, the committee had to try to say what the
education of these children was *for*. It was a large task, and with a
committee of twenty-six very different people, each with his own
particular expertise and enthusiasm, one might have thought it
impossible that it should ever reach agreement. But it did. The
committee reached a reasonable consensus. Nevertheless, when I,
as chairman of the Committee, exercised privilege, and insisted
on including pleasure as one of the goals of education, indeed its
chief aim, there was some initial outrage among members.
Pleasure has a bad name, educationally speaking. It seemed to
some committee members little short of disgraceful to suppose
that the whole vast apparatus of the Department of Education
and Science, the millions of pounds committed annually, and the
millions of words written, should all be spent in the pursuit of
pleasure. I want, in what follows, to argue that pleasure *must*
necessarily be part of what we educators have in mind when we
go about our business.

First, however, I must say more about the need to establish

certain agreed goals or aims for education. In this connection it makes not the slightest difference whether the child to be educated is able or less able, where he comes in the continuum of ability. If he is to be educated, not just cared for or treated or disciplined, then his education must, by definition, be directed at certain common specifiable goals. For education must always look to the future. Teachers must always be prepared to answer the question 'Why should I learn this?' and to answer it by reference to life after education. We must be able to say, 'You are learning this because without it you would be worse off in the long run.' This is the justification we must be prepared to give for any item in a child's curriculum. To take the most obvious case: despite certain extremist views of the 1950s and 1960s, I doubt whether anyone now would seriously dispute the fact that a grown-up person, whatever his way of life, is worse off if he cannot read. And this agreement is the basis for what is generally agreed to be a necessary part of any curriculum for young children, and for older children if they have failed to learn to read at the ordinary time. I believe we should generalize from this obvious principle. The question must always be asked, 'Is the child getting from his education something without which he would, when education is over, be deprived?'

The difficulty in using such a criterion for justifying any particular curriculum content is that we are still so ignorant of the actual effects of learning various things, or having various experiences, at school. Are we better off all our lives for having learned Latin? Do the hours spent on the hockey field or in the gymnasium actually pay off in terms of physical or spiritual improvement? What books do we actually benefit from reading? The acute difficulty of answering such questions leads us for the most part to evade them. We fall back on the cliché of the good broad education of a roughly traditional pattern. Or, more usually, and with more excuse, we allow the curriculum content for our pupils to be determined by the examination syllabus. We can show that our pupils are better off after education than before it because they are better qualified; and qualifications are the doorway to a better life.

I am far from deprecating the pursuit of qualifications. I can think of no more harmful or ultimately silly educational rallying cry than that which speaks of certificates or degrees as 'mere bits of paper', the pursuit of success as mere 'grubbing for marks'. But of course, to accept the need for qualifications and, therefore, for examination syllabuses is not necessarily to accept uncritically the content of the syllabuses or the form and structure of the examinations. Everyone who is interested in education has a right and a duty to think about that content and, if it seems proper, to campaign to change it. We often say that education should teach children to think. We should not forget that their teachers ought also to think from time to time and even to act in accordance with their thoughts.

So I am not ashamed to enunciate certain rather banal thoughts about the *point* of education, and this should include the point of some of the subject-matter that by tradition, or the dictates of the examining boards, we are accustomed to see taught in our schools.

I believe that most parents, if asked what they most want for their children, might put at the top of their list the wish that they might enjoy their lives. When we think nostalgically of our own lives, when we long, perhaps mistakenly, to go back in time to some golden age, when we think about people we have admired or loved, there is common to these thoughts a sense of enjoyment – not merely that we now enjoy thinking them, enjoy the images they conjure up, but that they are images *of* enjoyment. There are few satisfactions so great for a parent as to be able to look at his child totally absorbed in what he is doing, wanting to go on with it, enjoying it; or to be able to say of him when he is older, 'He thoroughly enjoys his work.' If a parent believes that, in being educated, his child is being provided with a greater chance of enjoyment than he would have without education, then I believe this parent should be satisfied with the child's school. And to enjoy something is, of course, the same as to take pleasure in it. Can we as teachers, then, honestly say that we are teaching children to take pleasure in things they would not be able to take pleasure in without us?

There is one extremely important source of pleasure that I want to say something about first of all. We all of us take pleasure in power. I know that this sounds terrible; and particularly it sounds terrible from the lips of a one-time headmistress; for everyone is familiar with the image of the headmistress motivated only by, in Hobbes's words, the 'restless pursuit of power after power'. No amount of realistic talk about the constraints within which headmistresses operate will ever change this popular picture. But my contention is that not only headmistresses, but all of us, take pleasure in power. For power is not just a matter of bossing other people about. It is crucially the ability to control, understand, and act on our environment, whatever that may be, to order it and not be overwhelmed by it. To be powerful in this sense is the same as to be free. It is to be able to make choices, instead of being carried along as a passenger without will of one's own. It is to be active rather than passive, or, if passive, to be so from choice.

I want to illustrate the related concepts of power, pleasure, and freedom by an example drawn from the very lowest level of ability, from a child who up till ten years ago would have been deemed legally speaking ineducable. It is a case described in a study entitled *Teaching of Language and Communication to the Mentally Handicapped*.[1]

The pupil is called Ian. He is 14, and has been in a sub-normality hospital since he was a few months old. At the time his case was described, he had been at school for only a few months. He is in size and weight about like a boy of 4. He is quiet, vaguely discontented, often crying but motionless, occasionally reaching out to touch with his left hand a large yellow teddy bear if it is put close enough for him to reach. He has no means of communication except that he can pull at the clothing of a passing adult to attract attention. By means of a most precisely detailed programme, Ian is to be taught to point to things, first of all to the food and drink which he is given. The longer-term aim is to get him to generalize – that is, to understand what pointing is for; namely, to express a desire for something. At each stage of the programme, Ian's teacher has to be absolutely clear what she is doing and what the purpose of it is. When each exact aim has been achieved, then she can go on to the next. Each step is taken in order. The story of this teaching makes absorbing reading. Ian's progress is almost incredibly fast. At the end of six months he can point even to things on the other side of the room. He has learned that pointing expresses preference. It is as if, in learning to communicate, he learns actually to *feel* preference, to want some things rather than others and to realize that he can get them. He has learned to indicate that he prefers chocolate to raspberry angel delight. He has learned to move and to grasp the things he wants with both hands. He has learned to combine pointing with uttering sounds. He has begun to eat more, and at more regular times, so that inbetween meals he has begun to prefer to have things to do rather than things to eat or drink. He has learned to prefer and to express a preference for hearing music on the radio rather than hugging the teddy bear; he has learned to play by himself with a ball; and he has learned to interact with adults so that he can tease them, laugh at his own games, and, dare one say, enjoy himself. By acquiring a means of communication, simple as it is, he has, we are told, 'realised the power of being able to control situations'.

At this stage, Ian's teacher began to have to choose new things to teach him, working towards the development of general concepts and the labelling of items within each group. At this stage we shall leave him. But I hope it will be clear how greatly Ian's freedom has increased, even though his choices may be choices only between the chocolate and the raspberry instant-whip. He is no longer the totally passive recipient of whatever someone else decides for him. He is intervening, changing things, exercising power – hence his dawning experience of pleasure.

You may feel that this particular example is so totally remote from the educational experience of most of us as to be quite irrelevant. But I do not believe it is. For the purpose of education, wherever it occurs, is common. And just as Ian's education was directed to extending little by little his ability to do things, rather than have them done for him; to communicate what he wants, rather than withdraw and wait while the world goes on around him; so the education of other children must be directed, at their level, to an increase in their power to do things; and this equally includes an increase in their power to communicate the far more complex things they want to communicate and to interact at a far greater level of subtlety with the people around them.

They too, then, should be learning, step by step, new skills in controlling things and communicating with people. If a child is taught, step by step, day by day, to play the violin well, then this becomes a power that he has, to use if he so chooses. It becomes also in itself a means of communication and an extension of his possible pleasures. If he is taught to read a map, this increases his opportunity successfully to do things – to get from one place to another intelligently and knowing what he is about. The very best and the most satisfying form of teaching is the teaching of skills; and the reason for this satisfaction is that in teaching a child a new language, for example, or giving him the techniques to solve a particular kind of problem, we are giving him a new power, and making him, every moment, a more properly *free* person. Even if the acquisition of this power may be a slow, and even a painful, business, it is worth it if we can confidently say, 'You will enjoy being able to do this when you *can*.'

Of course, we have to recognize realistically that sometimes the obstacles to be overcome are too great, and the child, our pupil, will never be able to do *that*. Yet we must give the child such pleasurable increase of powers as is possible. This is the point of the educational programme.

I must turn now to another, related source of the pleasure to which education should, as I contend, be directed. This is the pleasure of the imagination. And I will start by explaining what I believe to be the connection between the pleasures of power and those of the imagination. It is that both pleasures are, in the end, the pleasures of freedom. The nature of the imagination is to concern itself with what is *not the case*. This is why it has sometimes seemed a frivolous human attribute, concerned with nothing but fictions and fancies, not contributing to the understanding of the real world. But to judge it thus would be totally mistaken. For, while it is true that the imagination deals in what is not, this very point can be put in another way: that it deals with the possible as well as the actual, the underlying as well as the superficial or the obvious. A person wholly without imagination, if such a person could exist, would be totally bound by the constraints of immediate experience. He would see no other way of interpreting his experience except the way in which it first presented itself. For a person with literally no imagination, a picture could not even be interpreted as a picture of something. It would simply be a number of colours and shapes on a two-dimensional ground. And if this person were taught to see the picture as representing something other than itself, it would still suggest nothing further to him. For such a hypothetical person, moreover, there would be no past and no future, no speculation, no anticipation – nothing but a blank present. When we say that the imagination deals with what is not, we mean that it is by means of this faculty that we think of things in their absence. And if we can do that, we can also think of them as they are not, or are not yet, but might be. We can plan, we can daydream, we can experiment; we can devise a future which is unlike the past, unlike anything that has ever been done or made or said before. And this, of course, is freedom. It is also the source of all the deepest and perhaps most mysterious of our pleasures.

The characteristic imaginative pleasure is that which makes us feel that there exists an infinity of possibilities. We feel that we shall never come to an end of that which we are interested in. The opposite of this pleasure is boredom, or *ennui*. Poor John Stuart Mill (to whom I shall return in a minute) records in his autobiography[2] that when he was depressed, his pleasure in music, hitherto always his solace, evaporated because he was haunted by the fear that, after all, music was finite. 'The octave', he wrote,

> consists only of five tones and two semitones, which can be put together in only a limited number of ways: most of these it seemed to me must already have been discovered, and there could not be room for a long succession of Mozarts and Webers to strike out entirely new and rich veins of musical beauty.

He goes on to record that it was the reading of Wordsworth which cured him. Speaking of the poems, he says:

> In them I seemed to draw from a source of inward joy, of sympathetic and imaginative pleasure which could be shared by all human beings; from them I seemed to learn what would be the perennial sources of happiness, when all the greater evils of life shall have been removed.[2]

We may be considerably less optimistic than Mill about the possibility of removing the major evils of life, but his concept of the *perennial* sources of happiness or pleasure remains central to education. If we want children to leave school full of interest in the world and understanding of other people, with a desire both to love the world and to change it, then, from the moment they are in their primary schools, we must be teaching them and helping them to use their imaginations.

One of the great aims of education must be in this way to enable a child to see that there is *more in* a subject than would appear to the superficial eye. And we can all tell from our own experience that this aspect of education is that which in fact gives pleasure, equal to, if not superior to, that pleasure I discussed just now, which arises from the ability to *do* things. Think of the joys of being taken for a walk when you were a child by someone who opened your eyes to things you had perhaps passed by every day of your life without noticing. Think of being taught by a teacher who, whatever the subject-matter, fired your imagination and made you see that something, grammar perhaps, or a part of history or some aspect of the physical sciences, was infinitely complex and in a sense unending. This eye-opening function of education is essential to it, whether in the arts or in the sciences.

Suppose, then, that my argument is accepted. Suppose it is agreed that it is the primary function of education to give a child these two kinds of pleasure, that of the increase of his power and that of the increase of his imaginative insight into the world, does this in any way dictate what he should be taught at school or how he should be taught? It is at this point that we come up against the difficulty of lack of evidence. For example, ever since the time of Plato and Aristotle, and probably before, people have disputed the effects, whether on children or on grown-ups, of literature and especially drama. Is it good, as Aristotle held, to feel the emotions induced by tragedy, the pity and terror evoked by the fall of the hero? Is witnessing or acting in plays a kind of therapy? Or is it, on the other hand, as Plato thought, a dangerous indulgence leading to uncontrolled and excessive emotion, to what we have learned to call 'copy-cat' behaviour, to delinquency and crime? All the same arguments are adduced in other terms with regard to the effects of television. In the end, for want of hard evidence (and hard evidence will, I suspect, always be wanting), one is obliged to follow one's hunch.

One thing is fairly clear. In so far as education is directed towards our first kind of pleasure, the pleasure derived from the acquisition of skills and powers which could not be had without education, then a child may permanently benefit from their acquisition. Either he will himself go on using the skill he has learned, perfecting and putting it to his own purposes, or, at the very least, he will understand the kinds of standards involved for those people who do excel in that particular skill. Either, for example, he will go on playing tennis, getting pleasure from his moderate or excellent control of the game, or, at least, if he doesn't play himself, he will have some idea of what playing tennis involves, and will be more prone to enjoy the performance of others, and admire it.

The difficulties of calculating the effects of pleasurable experiences at school are more acute, however, when we consider the second kind of pleasure, the imaginative pleasures so highly valued by Mill. What long-term benefit, if any, does the experience of such pleasures at school have on the pupil? One way of dealing with this question, and a perfectly respectable way, is to say that it doesn't matter whether there are any long-term effects or not. For one of the criteria by which we distinguish between a good school and a bad is whether the pupil actually enjoys school while he is there. (This was a tenet of the Plowden Committee.[3] Especially for deprived children, the point of school was that it should be fun at the time.) So, as long as he gets pleasure from learning at the time, it doesn't have to be shown that he gets any benefit in life after school, whether a pleasure-benefit or any other.

A different and, to my way of thinking, more attractive form of the same argument is to say that to get pleasure in learning is necessary if learning is to go on at all. If a child hates school, he will either truant or at any rate leave as soon as possible; and while there, he will learn very little. To get him to enjoy at least some of his learning is to give him an inducement to stay at school, not to reject it wholesale; it is thus to enable him to learn those skills which, as we have agreed, *are* of benefit to him later.

I should like, however, to be able to come up with a stronger argument still, and to show that if once a child has acquired a taste for what I have roughly called the pleasures of the imagination, he will not cease, on leaving school, to seek them out. Even if he stops being interested in the bit of history that excited him at school, still he will retain the general concept of history as fascinating and worth while pursuing. Even if he does not read the books he did or watch the television programmes which once gave him this pleasure, he will be ready to read and to watch programmes critically and with imaginative understanding for the rest of his life. And though, as I have said, there is no hard evidence that this is true, yet I am strongly inclined to believe it.

Nevertheless, though there may be such positive gains, probably the most important duty that a school has with regard to the pleasures of the imagination is *not to inhibit them.* It is a negative duty; but, after all, many commandments notoriously take this form of 'Thou shalt not'. I believe that this, then, is the first and most crucial of all commandments for schools and for teachers: Thou shalt not bore; thou shalt not turn off. It is quite a difficult commandment to obey. For school, after all, has an initial disadvantage here: it is compulsory. This feature alone makes school subjects *prima facie* boring, just as school food is *prima facie* disgusting (even if, secretly, you quite enjoy the chocolate puddings or macaroni cheese). Any teacher who manages to overcome this first obstacle deserves immense credit. The danger of turning off a child, of setting him against a certain subject-matter for ever and turning him, therefore, against 'school' subjects as a whole, is far greater in connection with those subjects which he might be expected to like and enjoy if it weren't for school than with subjects which are intrinsically school subjects. For the majority of children (though obviously not for all) things like chemistry, gymnastics, or the learning of a foreign language are quite specifically school-based subjects. There is little that school can spoil. But the case is quite different with most aesthetic subjects: with the visual arts, music, and literature.

Music, for example, is part of the lives of nearly all children unless they are deaf; but there is great danger that the huge gulf there tends to be between school music and 'home' music may entail a total absence of pleasure in the former. And this will not be put right by any attempt to incorporate 'home' music into school. Quite the reverse. On the whole, I believe that the best way to start to give a child pleasure in music at school is to increase his ability to play or sing. Then gradually it may be possible, and even easy, to increase his imaginative pleasure in a wide variety of music; but it has to be done with infinite tact.

It is even easier to cause a permanent absence of pleasure in literature. Most educated people believe that reading is one of the greatest of all sources of pleasure, of the perennial pleasure and happiness that Mill spoke of. Yet, for many children at school, even after they have acquired the basic skill of reading without difficulty, reading is a bore and a misery, and becomes more so as they move up the school. For such children I am sure that the only solution is to let them read anything that *does* give them pleasure, even if it is nothing but cookery books or *Exchange and Mart*, or even soft porn, just so that the peculiarly private, portable, and consoling pleasure of reading may continue to be available to them. Let us not worry about their taste, as long as the pleasure is there. Ultimately a teacher may be able to widen her pupils' taste. But if we fail to do that, then at least we haven't spoiled anything.

For many children the death of pleasure in reading is the awful fear they experience that they will have to analyse what they read. 'Write an essay about the plot, the characterization, the style, the choice of words, the imagery,' they may be told. All these things may make a child wonder why he ever thought he liked the book in the first place. I would make a plea for this kind of critical examination of what is read being carried out, if at all, by only a very few students, those who want to do it and who like that kind of thing (and there are some who are born critics). It is depressing how many, even of those relatively few who go on to study English at university or college, read only as a penance, who for pleasure revert to *Woman's Own*, and come to higher education having read nothing except those books which have been set them for critical examination. Such people have been, in my view, let down by their education. It has failed to give them the proper pleasures of literature. It has deprived them of that which should be the whole point of literature: namely, enjoyment. I would like to see examinations in English Literature as much a specialist concern as examinations in Classics or in Chinese – only for those who are real enthusiasts, in this case for the analysis of literature. Other people could, with much more profit, be examined rather in the skills they have acquired, including, of course, the skill of reading with understanding and writing with clarity and precision.

However, this is not the time to enter further into my ideal school curriculum. I must come back to the beginning, to the pleasure principle itself as the goal of education. I hope I have put a case for it. But it may still be objected that pleasure *cannot* be the sole aim of education. There must, it may be thought, be something higher, some specifically intellectual or moral good. J. S. Mill, that most high-minded of hedonists, distinguished different qualities of pleasure, and, putting moral feeling and conscience into the highest category, argued that simply on grounds of pleasure alone people will pursue morality.[4] He could thus have argued that morality was the point of education, but only because morality is pleasure. I would not care to go down this perilous and metaphysical path. But I do believe that pleasure is, roughly speaking, a *feeling*, and that to cultivate the feelings, to learn to 'feel as we ought' is not a trivial aim. I have tried to divide pleasures into two kinds: the pleasures of power, or control, and those of the imagination. Both are related to freedom, and I would argue that we *ought* to exercise the freedoms we have, and enable others to do so. We ought, in fact, to take both kinds of pleasure in our world.

There is one final point. We tend to expect a lot from education. We blame it for our failures. We hope that with its spread some, at least, of our ills will be diminished. But education will be ineffective in the role we assign to it unless people actually want to be educated, and unless they get out of education, not just qualifications, but new powers and new insights of the kind I have been trying to identify. It is not a mere exercise in academic analysis, then, to say that education should be for pleasure: we have a positive and serious duty to see to it that this is indeed its goal.

# 11

## Education with a Moral

Morality is, mercifully, not part of the national curriculum. If such a thing were to be suggested, there would be an outcry. No one would trust any teacher or syllabus-maker to get it right. We do not believe in moral experts, and we tend to hold that everyone must, in the end, be the arbiter of his own morals through his individual conscience. I can imagine, too, that it might be argued that if anyone were to be given the responsibility for teaching morality it should be the family. And yet many parents, in my view rightly, hope that by the time children leave school, they will have learned a bit about the difference between right and wrong, about how they should behave and what general attitudes they should adopt towards their neighbours; and that they will, it is widely hoped, have learned more about such things than they would have learned had they not been to school. Equally, society as a whole may hope, and should be entitled to expect, that in professional education – for example, in the education of doctors, nurses, lawyers, and estate agents – there will be an element of moral education, so that by the time these people emerge as fully qualified professionals, they may have not only professional but ethical expertise. So how is such moral instruction to be carried out?

I shall talk mainly about education at school, on the grounds that at school children are, most of them, being educated compulsorily. Since all children *have* to go to school, what they learn there has the widest possible effect on society as a whole. For all children are members of society. I shall, however, turn at the end of the chapter to the education of professionals; for here the effect of a morality acquired during training, though it may not be so widespread as whatever is derived from universal education, may yet be disproportionately influential, with significant consequences for the whole of society, because of the social influence of the professions themselves.

Before I embark, however, on the consideration of morality in education, at school or thereafter, there are some highly general points to be made.

I start with two propositions, both of them enunciated and elaborated in Isaiah Berlin's recent collection of essays *The Crooked Timber of Humanity*. The first is that *ultimate values conflict with one another*. There is, and can be, no Utopia in which all values are in harmony; nor can there be any final solution to all human ills. The concept of such an ideal world is not only difficult in practice, it is logically incoherent; for people *are* different, and value different traditions. To produce one world would *not* in fact be ideal at all. Thus, to quote Berlin, 'The best one can do is to try to promote some kind of equilibrium.'[1] This apparently modest best is, I believe, as important a goal in education as in politics.

The second general proposition is this (and I quote Isaiah Berlin again): 'Only barbarians are not curious about where they come from and how they come to be where they are, where they appear to be going, whether they wish to go there, and if so, why, and if not, why not.'[2] If education is, as I believe it is, the slow attempt to turn individual young barbarians into civilized persons, then it follows that, above all, this sort of curiosity-led reflection must be central to education. I want to explore both these general propositions a bit further.

I will start with the necessary conflict of values. It is often supposed that if you maintain that values must conflict or that there is no one single answer to the question of what goals should, above all others, be pursued, then you are an ethical relativist, regarding all goals as equally valid. This is not the case. Even within the life of one person it is easy to see how it is possible to understand and half-embrace more than one ideal (let us say the ideals of rural and of urban life, the ideals of the successful pioneering woman and of the angel in the house; the ideals of self-abnegation and of personal enrichment). But this does not entail that the person who understands and sees the point of these different images regards all as equally to be pursued. In the end, compromises, choices, decisions are made. What is left, after the conflict, is, so it is to be hoped, an understanding of what other people may have decided to pursue whole-heartedly.

Even in the world of aesthetics, it is not the case that simply because tastes differ, we can therefore assume that one taste is as valid, as likely to endure, as serious or well-founded, as another. Undoubtedly there are complicating factors in aesthetics, many of them snobbish, just as there are in matters of *literal* taste (a preference for Heinz salad dressing over home-made vinaigrette has to be maintained as a joke, an eccentricity, in smart circles, if it is to be maintained at all). There may be elements of snobbishness in a preference for one moral view over another (and this is something that historians and sociologists might investigate). But generally speaking, there are some human values that are fundamental, and are shared, or can at least be understood and respected, by all people of imagination. Moreover, when moral values change, it is generally on account of some *improvement* in human understanding, rather than the result of mere fashion or whim. Slavery was given up when people began to realize that *all* humans had attributes, at least potentially, which should allow them to have rights. The inclusion of women as full members of a democratic state was in the same way a result of a slow, but crucial, insight into the nature of the human species. We shall not go back to slavery or concentration camps or the incapacity of women to own property once they get married. It is therefore mistaken to suppose that it is simply a matter of accident: that it just so happens that what seemed good to the Victorians does not seem good to us, that what seemed all right to fifth-century Athenians does not seem right to us, and that it's all a matter of taste.

Such relativism is, in fact, incompatible with the way morality actually *works*. For morality must be capable of generating a passionate commitment. Enlarging human sympathy to include, say, servants, black people, or women is not something that is just a passing whim. Once it has been done (or is gradually being done), it cannot be undone, for there will be those who deeply believe that the new insight is a true one, and they will be ready to defend it. One of the tasks of education is to guard and protect such advances. We have moved on from the days of human sacrifice; indeed, from the non-enfranchisement and the non-education of women. We must teach people what *was once* the case, in order for them to value what they have got and to preserve it.

There are, then, shared values, as well as conflicts; and it is part of the task of education to show what these values are. But conflicts remain. One important example of such a conflict of values, within education itself, is that between the ideal of scholarly, élitist, 'pure' education, and the ideal of the buccaneer, the entrepreneur who will go out onto the high seas or into the boardroom and think nothing of the schoolroom or the library. Here, it seems to me, is a crucial case where an equilibrium must be sought both within schools and in higher education. Both ideals can be understood; both must be allowed as valid. We must try not to make things impossible for either the scholar or the pirate. And we must avoid type-casting those who embrace one or the other ideal, or regarding either as necessarily more valuable to society.

There is a related pair of conflicting ideals which I want to call to your attention, and that is the ideal of the market-place, within which people choose what they *want*, demand it, and pay for it if they can, and the ideal of *welfare*, in accordance with which everyone, whether they can pay or not, is given what they most *need*, by an essentially paternalistic State within which the satisfaction of needs is the main burden on taxation. I believe that, at any rate since 1945, most of us have been more or less committed to the latter ideal, and that the reversion to the former, known as Thatcherism, is the most fundamental change that many of us have experienced in our lives. I want to return to the educational consequences of this change in a moment.

But first I hope you will notice that everything I have said in the last few paragraphs has been thoroughly value-laden. I have spoken of or implied *advances in moral sensibility* to embrace the rights of women or of persons hitherto regarded as slaves. I have spoken of or implied a *preferable* world, in which there is no human sacrifice, no concentration camps. It is, I believe, of the utmost importance to realize that in a debate of the kind we as educators are engaged in there *is no such thing as neutrality*. And what is true of us, here, is true also of all teachers everywhere whether in school or institutions of higher education. No teaching can or should be value-free. A long time ago, fourteen years in fact, I wrote as follows (I was talking then about schools, but I would include all educational establishments under the same principle): 'You cannot teach morality without being committed to morality yourself, and you cannot be committed to morality yourself without holding that some things are right, others wrong. You cannot hold that, and at the same time sincerely maintain that someone else's view of the matter may be equally good.' I went on to say that it was fairly easy to maintain that our own view was right in contrast with another view (such as that it was all right or even right to expose weakly babies, or girls, at birth) if that view was separated from us by a wide distance in either space or time. It was less easy when the alternative morality was here and now, on our doorstep. But, I argued, the principle is the same. If members of the IRA believe sincerely that they are justified in planting bombs without warning in public places, then we must be prepared to condemn them if we think it wrong. No one needs much education to know that there are differing views as to what is right and wrong. They need to be educated, however, in the matter of defending their own position; and to this end, they need, from an early age, *examples* of people who are ready to do this with passion and integrity. They also need to see before their eyes people whose theoretical opinions actually make a difference to their own lives and practice.

In general, it is the values we hold which make up our culture. And among the most important values which go to make up a 'culture' are moral values. So, if education is the civilizing of people within a culture (or a mixture of cultures), we come up against the problem posed by Socrates: *Can virtue be taught?* (and we can add, along with virtue, the other values, tastes, preferences, loves and hates and habits that together make the culture, and ask whether these can be taught). It seems to me of the greatest possible importance that a teacher, any teacher, while demonstrating his understanding of other cultures, should nevertheless be brave enough to try to share with his pupils his own picture of a virtuous person or an original person or a person who has contributed and is contributing to the life of society or a person whose tastes and manners are attractive. And, of course, he must do this sincerely and as the outcome of his own genuinely held beliefs. Thus the education he gives his pupils will not be value-free. Far from it. It will be an education *in* values; and it is only in this way that it is possible for the central elements of his own culture to be passed on, or at least to come to be understood, and to make their proper impact.

In an article published in 1972, the philosopher Gilbert Ryle wrote, characteristically, as follows:

> Good examples had better not be set with an edifying purpose. For a would-be improving exhibition of, say, indignation would be an insincere exhibition. The vehemence of the denunciation would be a parent's, a pedagogue's or a pastor's histrionics. The example authentically set would be that of edifyingly shamming indignation...So it would be less hazardous to reword Socrates's original question and ask not 'can virtue be taught?' but 'can virtue be learned?'

Ryle goes on to distinguish learning by example from, on the one hand, mere copying or aping and, on the other hand, conditioning:

> It is certainly true that without conditioning a child will acquire neither conversational English nor manners nor morals nor a Yorkshire accent. But neither aping nor conditioning will get the child to the higher stage of making and following *new* remarks in English, of behaving politely in a *new* situation or making allowance in a competitive game for a handicapped newcomer. He now has to think like his elder brother or the hero of his adventure story...he now has to emulate their non-echoings.[3]

To speak thus of learning by example or teaching by example with a view to the *future* of the pupil places a heavy burden on a teacher. He must not just speak, but *do* and *be* what his pupils are to become. This is the consequence of the impossibility of value-free teaching, and it cannot be avoided.

If we take seriously the proposition that all teaching conveys *values*, not merely in respect of morality, but of aesthetic taste and historical perspective, as well as of simple enthusiasms and preferences, then it is beginning to be clear that in an important sense a culture is conveyed in school and university willy-nilly and, with culture, a consensus morality. A sincere, enthusiastic, honest teacher will inevitably pass on the culture and morality within which he lives his life, thinks his thoughts, and makes his choices. The kind of person who is needed as a teacher is someone who has the courage and confidence to say (or otherwise convey), 'There are other points of view, but this is what *I* believe (or love, or think worth doing).' This is where the equilibrium must be sought between dogmatism or fundamentalism, on the one hand, and non-judgemental relativism, on the other.

I turn now to Berlin's second proposition, that only barbarians are incurious about their past. This by itself constitutes an insight, a statement of fact which might serve to explain the importance of a thoroughly historical approach to education. I believe that it is of the greatest importance to make central such a historical dimension to education, not only for those studying the humanities, but for scientists and mathematicians as well. For it is only through the recognition of how the concepts we now take for granted have developed out of what went before that we can thoroughly understand and come to be able to delineate the framework of thought within which we currently operate. It was central to the philosophy of Kant that human beings impose a framework on the world of perception and that all our apparently necessary ideas, such as that of causation, constitute this framework. He sought to show that the framework we use is the only one possible for rational beings. It is perhaps more in conformity with our own notion of human beings (influenced by the study not only of history, but of anthropology and psychology) to recognize, as Kant did, that there is a conceptual framework within which we think and talk and act; but that this framework may change, albeit often slowly and imperceptibly. If this is true, then the understanding of past concepts is of crucial importance to us, for understanding how we think now, how we may possibly come to think in the future, and how people different from ourselves may think.

. And, in conformity with such an idea, Berlin goes on to say that non-barbarians will demand to know where they appear to be going, and, essentially, whether they wish to go there and 'if so, why, if not, why not'. This links an understanding of the past with the future, and a future which may be *changed*.

Without lapsing into the myths of a faculty psychology, it

seems to me that we may legitimately distinguish the human imagination from other attributes of animals, and that we may further, partly following Sartre, characterize the imagination as the power, which as far as we know only humans have, to think about and envisage things that are not the case. This means that humans can think about, and come to understand, what is *no longer* before their eyes, can reconstruct the past, and come to grasp what people who are no longer alive thought, felt, and intended. This power is, however, the very same as that which enables them to conceive of a future which does not *yet* exist and which may be as different from the present as the past was.

The present itself, though in principle the object of perception, is also the subject of imagination, in so far as it is not merely experienced, but seen to arise out of what is no loger present and lead to something not yet realized. Sir Keith Thomas once spoke of the need to deliver people from the 'shackles of present-mindedness'. I believe that this indeed constitutes a defence of historical and literary studies. But the need to avoid being locked into the present is just as important in understanding the sciences and mathematics as in the humanities. Children, and no doubt barbarians, are prone to believe that things simply are, and have always been, as they are now. And this is nowhere more so than in the case of scientific concepts. Vast revolutions in physics, mechanics, chemistry, biology, and medicine take place when people raise the question 'Need we think in this way?' (Does the notion of 'humours' or of 'force', for example, actually help us?) It is imagination which enables us to reclassify, change direction, see things in a new light, frame and test hypotheses. To exercise the imagination is the way, the only way, that we can exercise freedom; for if we could not envisage the new, we could not change what we have got. The exercise of freedom must arise out of the question 'How have we got where we are?' as well as the question 'Do we want to go on as we are going?'

Education ought to be directed to increasing people's freedom, helping them to rise out of the position in the present where, like all other animals, they just *are*, without thinking about where they are. If this is so, then education must have regard for the past, for the history and development of the institutions and social structures within which we find ourselves living, as well as for the concepts and classifications we use. The education of the imagination, then, whether in the sciences, the humanities, or the arts, essentially entails cultural education, and only this can increase the freedom of those who are educated. 'Freedom' of course is a *value*; thus education is, necessarily, value-laden.

This, you may say, is pretty high-flown stuff. I want now to say a little about how I believe the details of education should be affected by this kind of grand notion of its function. For it is impossible to separate general from particular thoughts about education. To talk about aims leads straight into considerations of the *curriculum*.

It will, I think, be clear to you from what I have said so far that by 'culture' I mean to refer to all the values that we thinkingly or unthinkingly embrace, including moral values, and all the institutions within the structure of which we thinkingly or unthinkingly live and whose history we need, as far as possible, to understand. In this sense our language and concepts are parts of our culture, as is the medicine we practise or have practised on us, the physics and biology we learn, the books and newspapers we read, the television we watch. Thus it is inevitable that if we educate people, we do so by unfolding for them and with them the numerous layers which go to make up their present life, so that they can look forward to the future and understand what they want to change, and so what they think they *ought* to change.

I want now, with this in mind, to return to the clash of ideals that I mentioned earlier, that between the ideals of welfare and of the market. It was one of the main assumptions of the Welfare State that, among other services, education should be provided by the State for everyone, regardless of income, up to the age of 15, and that thereafter those who wanted to, and could become qualified, should continue to be educated. The goal was not new, but the machinery put in place by the 1944 Act was.

Now we know that things did not work out exactly as was intended, and that in many ways the National Health Service and the pension provision were more successful than the Welfare State provision of education. Yet the aim was admirable, and I believe that we must go back to it. For the guiding principle was *equality*. There should be no one who could not have a proper and complete education. If the concept of education that I have outlined, or one like it, is something we believe in (roughly, the education of the imagination) and if that education is an exploration of *all* the culture of society, then it seems to follow that it should be accessible to everyone, and that only so can we move towards a society that is not divided by misunderstanding and dogmatism, but can exist in some sort of atmosphere of equilibrium or consensus (without which I believe that government is actually impossible).

Yet the philosophy of the market is strictly incompatible with that of welfare, or equality of provision. The market demands the workhouse, charity for the failures, and the acceptance of a *rump* of ineducable no-hopers. These people will of course, in the main, be children whose parents, for various social, economic, or psychological reasons, are least pushy and are resigned to something like ghetto schools, where both teachers and money will be in short supply.

Equality in education demands a common purpose and a common curriculum. So how are we to devise a curriculum which would, or could, be universally accessible? There is, I believe, one general principle that should be adopted, difficult and awkward though it would be. We ought to abandon the great gulf that at present separates the arts and humanities from the sciences and mathematics, and concentrate instead on a division between the practical and the theoretical.

The aim of the practical parts of the curriculum would be to ensure that no one left school with areas of incompetence in matters in which everyone needs to be competent if they are to be reasonably employable and independent. The practical would include spoken and written English, the use of word processors and computers; it could include practical music, spoken foreign languages, car maintenance, art and design in various media, photography, practical electronics, and so on. The theoretical would include the science that actually lay behind these skills and abilities, the relation of one science to another, the literature of England and other countries, literary criticism, history in all its manifestations, and so on.

The crucial thing would be to assess children at school in aspects of a given study separately, and not to insist that *both* the practical *and* the theoretical go together, and always at the same pace. Thus someone might leave school and go on to higher or further education or into employment with a list of subjects taken and a list of tests passed, at various levels in both the practical and the theoretical 'sides'. Each level of testing would represent an average year's work, and so a pupil, however unacademic, would be motivated to progress step by step, and leave school with proved competence in a variety of different areas. But even the most academic high-flyers would be able to acquire some practical competences as well as theoretical understanding.

The main obstacle to the adoption of some such scheme is, I believe, the obstinate conviction among some politicians that A-levels must at all costs be retained. I do not believe myself that a change to a new scheme of school education based on a distinction between practical competence and theoretical understanding would ultimately make for lower standards at university or polytechnic. On the contrary, I believe that standards overall would be higher. For there is no reason to suppose that, in the end, people are worse at physics because they have been required to think about the history and philosophy of physics and have subjected the concepts they have used and the calculations they have made to some sort of critical examination. Nor are they any the worse for being practically competent over a wide range. In fact, I suspect that potential university students would learn more, and more quickly, when they got to university if they had had a more critical, less passive education at school, and had acquired a variety of usable skills.

It might be that for those who wanted to go on to a doctorate, a further year after the first degree might be necessary. But a system of such an optional fourth year seems already to be gaining ground. And it is surely more rational to gear all education to those who do not intend to do Ph.D.s than to assume that everyone will do so, given the actual numbers involved. For my part, I simply do not see the need to have school leaving examinations in big blocks. I would like to see the end of examinations at 16 and 18, and in their place a whole series of tests, taken according to readiness. I do not think such a change, though revolutionary, is impossible from the school or university point of view. For already in certain subjects such as mathematics, the sciences, and foreign languages, such tests exist, and are increasingly used.

What is needed is that their scope and their availability should be increased.

In one way, to introduce such a scheme would be no more than to widen and extend the principle that lies behind the GCSE. For the GCSE was introduced to provide a single examination system available to all or almost all pupils in a school. Moreover, its aim was to try to test what candidates understand and can do, rather than what they can remember. These aims would be shared by a system of graded tests. And I believe that to have such aims at the centre of school education and to ensure that, as far as possible, they are carried out is essential if we are to overcome the divisions within society, the gaps between different 'cultures' that now seem to threaten us. We need an education system that is manifestly and visibly unified in its overall aims. For only a unified system would demonstrate our belief in the need to educate *everyone*, both for their sakes and for the sake of society, or the common good. We must not concentrate, as we are still prone to do, on one kind of person at the expense of all the others. We must neither elevate the scientist above the person who studies the arts, nor the other way round. We must bridge that gap, and at the same time demonstrate that, educationally, we believe there is no such thing as a no-hoper. We must provide something of value for everyone, and take pride in our ability to do so.

This, in my view, is the primary educational task. It is possible, but it will take time. Schools, universities, and, above all, Government, have to be persuaded that this, or something like it, is the most important reform. The introduction of the national curriculum may be a step in the right direction, provided the testing associated with it does not prove too rigid and constricting. For at least under the regulations of that curriculum the arts and the sciences will be studied side by side, and no one will be able to go through school with no scientific or technological education at all. So that is a start. But a more radical reform is needed if we are to be able to stop raising and re-raising the question of education and values. In a system in which a uniform purpose was clear, issues about one culture or many might gradually diminish in importance, and finally wither away. For school itself might begin to define the boundaries of a common culture, along with a common set of educational values. If all school-leavers emerged from school confident that there were things they could do (and could prove themselves able to do) and that therefore they were genuinely ready for the next stage, whether employment or more education, I believe that they would generate their own culture, which would properly arise out of the past and would contain within it moral imperatives learned at school and university.

It is impossible to exaggerate the extent to which our culture and our educational system are locked together. School and university are the crucial places where we can enable people to look both back and forward in the way that is essential if they are to understand where they are and where they want to go. What we essentially need is the confidence to create goals *common* to the whole of our educational system, a redirection towards the common good.

This, it seems to me, is the moral that education should teach; and we should regard education at school as especially bound to convey such a common set of goals, with the hope of an outcome advantageous to everyone who is educated. There is at present a gap in our educational policy at this point. We agonize about how to educate children in a 'multicultural society'. We tend to forget that it is only when we genuinely believe in education for everyone that we can properly teach everyone; and such faith in education demands a common purpose.

All this has application as much for higher and further education as for school. The co-existence within higher education of differing ideals is as important or even more important. For perhaps the more sophisticated education becomes, the more essential it is for it to embrace the virtue of non-dogmatism, a willingness to consider new ideas and new values, to be convinced by good evidence and arguments, and yet a readiness to hold onto what seems to be true. An imaginative grasp of other possibilities should go along with the greater complexity of education at university or polytechnic. The more a student realizes that no subject is simple, that there is far more to learn than he had any idea of at school, the more he should also be aware of the way concepts change, as well of the variety of different ways of thought that can co-exist.

Increasingly, too, for the student in higher education, values intrinsic to education itself become central. I mean the imperative to accuracy, the need always to produce evidence for one's statements, the need to argue, not merely assert, and the readiness to listen to critical appraisal of one's own results. Such values, if not the first we might think of as moral values, are nevertheless akin to moral values, and are a part of the culture of learning and research into which a student enters when he embarks on higher education, even if only for a time. They are, moreover, values not confined to higher education, but to be kept in mind in all professional life. So, though it would be regarded as monstrous presumption for a teacher in a polytechnic or a university to claim to be teaching morality to his pupils, yet within this particular institution of society, values are conveyed. Perhaps if this were more widely recognized, we should hear less of the so-called irrelevance of the universities. They might come to seem less remote, more closely connected to that professional morality which society does, on the whole, wish to see upheld.

Finally, I suggest that good teaching itself, whether at school or in further or higher education, must carry a central moral message: namely, the message of equality. The message is that everyone is equally worth teaching and is capable of being taught, and that being taught can improve a pupil's life-chances. If we think of education as a road along which everyone moves towards the goals of competence, understanding, and enhanced pleasure, and towards the distant horizons of the imagination, a road on which pupils will outstrip their teachers and teachers perhaps be unable to follow, then with this image in mind we may see that for some people there are fearful obstacles in the way of progress. They may suffer from physical, sensory, intellectual, or emotional disabilities, constituting difficulties that must be patiently overcome if they are to progress. And for some of them, progress will not take them very far along the road. But the teacher will recognize it as progress all the same. On the other hand, there are those for whom the road is pretty easy and who will streak along towards the distant horizon without hindrance. But the moral of education is that we are all on the same road. A real teacher is one who believes that for every eccentric, peculiar, unique individual, some progress is possible. A real teacher delights in progress when he sees it; nothing is so exciting as to be outstripped by his pupil; but there is equal satisfaction in the recognition that progress is possible for *all* pupils. To have such beliefs and to feel such pleasures is of course to adopt a moral attitude, and one in my view essential to education, and at its very heart.

# 12

# *Religious Imagination*

My topic must fall within the general heading of theology. But of course I have to say at once that I am no theologian. And I regard theology as a strange and paradoxical study. On the one hand, it admits its concern with a subject that is beyond human understanding; on the other, it claims to be a cognitive science, to do with knowing certain truths, even proving them. In this latter sense, to talk about the religious (or theological) imagination is to court disapproval. For there are those who say, 'That's all very well; but the imagination yields not truths but falsehoods, or at least fictions. It can have no place in the rigorous, truth-finding science of theology. Even if you can show that there is a specific kind of imagination to be characterized as "religious", this would do no more than show that religion, like history, has benefited from imaginative practitioners. They have been welcome and decorative additions to the mainstream of religion, itself a practical matter, but one which rests on a sound cognitive theological base.' This is the background against which those who think about the religious imagination tend to write. They are therefore prone to take up a rather defensive stance. However, this kind of argument in my view stems from the vestiges of a thoroughly old-fashioned faculty psychology, which demands that there should be a number of separate powers of the mind: the reason, the imagination, and the faculties of perception. Within this faculty tradition, perception and reason are generally held to be the faculties which give rise to truth or knowledge (which must rest on one or the other). Imagination is more or less whatever is left.

This is not quite fair. For both Hume and Kant were perfectly certain that imagination was a necessary addition to sensory perception if knowledge could be said to result from such perception. Hume deplored this dependence, regarding it as somehow unfortunate and low that what we think of as knowledge, especially of causal laws, should depend upon something so flighty and unreliable as the 'mere fancy'. Kant, on the other hand, welcomed imagination, but gave it a very special meaning. It meant the faculty that we necessarily exercise in seeing how general concepts apply to and modify the raw materials of sensory awareness. Kant, I believe, has the truth about imagination in his view, or at least a great deal of the truth about the acquisition of knowledge. For it must be the case that, if we are to claim knowledge and understanding of the phenomena of the world, whether scientific or 'common-sense' knowledge, we must be able to bundle these phenomena together under general concepts in order to frame laws about them (not necessarily the refined laws of science, but, just as much, the basic, assumed laws of our practical life). Neither words nor ideas on their own, nor mere perception (sensory experience by itself, if we can conceive such a thing), would be enough to enable us to see in what is in front of our eyes the exemplification of something common to that thing and others. It is this function, to relate sensory experience to concepts, that Kant ascribes to the imagination.

Whether we give a name to the power to go beyond our experience or not, we are bound to recognize that this is something we can do; and that if we could not, we could neither understand nor describe the world about us, or understand or describe ourselves. To say this is as much as to say that it is nearly impossible to separate from one another the various factors that go to make up our perception and interpretation of the world: sensory experience, sorting into kinds, projecting into past and future, reacting with pleasure or pain to what we perceive. I believe that we must await a major breakthrough in understanding the physiology of the brain before we can know whether such a separation is even in principle worth attempting. At any rate, faculty psychology, within which sense, reason, imagination, and emotion were all separate powers, has had its day.

Yet, even if this is so, it may still be useful from time to time to single out that part of our abilities which enables us to perceive the general and universal in the singular and particular. For this lies at the basis of language and of our human propensity to think about and discourse about things that are beyond what we can see and hear. Such a propensity, incorporated in language, is by far the most important thing that differentiates us from other animals (or, as far as we can understand them, it seems so). And so it is intelligible, though not inevitable, to give the name 'imagination' to this special power, which only humans have. Among other things, it is this power which gives to humans, alone among animals, the ability to conceive of religion.

Sartre, with his usual appealing mixture of the self-evident with the profound, defined imagination as the ability to think what is not.[1] In defining it thus, he was making a crucial distinction between the actual, our present situation and environment, and the possible; the non-present, even non-existent, and the existent here and now. This certainly fits in both with the role of imagination that I have just suggested (to see beyond the particular to the general) and with our ordinary definitions of imagination, always concerned in common parlance with the non-existent or fictitious or merely possible. Sartre went on, equally rightly in my view, though perhaps less obviously so, to identify the imagination with human freedom. For he argued that without the ability to envisage that which is not present (the absent, the unreal, the past, and, most important, the future), human endeavour would be at a standstill.

Sartre derived what he took to be the fact of human freedom from the power of humans to encompass and contemplate the possible, and so to project themselves forward, to change and surpass the limited present. This power is of the utmost importance to all of us. Everyone has always recognized that the creative imagination leaps on beyond what ordinary, non-creative, so-called earth-bound people can immediately grasp. Sartre held that anyone who could foresee a future that might be different from the present was to some extent possessed of this same creativity; and that without it humans would be no different from all other things in the universe, governed by laws, their development causally inevitable, given their past history.

If imagination, then, may be thought of as the ability to think of what is not, or not yet, the case, then certainly all language-users have it. Warnings, threats, promises, regrets, prognostication, as well as general principles, all turn on the ability we have to refer coherently to what is past, absent, or yet to be. In this sense of imagination, all language-users are imaginative. Using language commits us to a perception that goes beyond the immediate and the present.

Now there is another, related way of referring to things that are not present to us, and this is not by words but by symbols. An object that is present to our senses may be taken to stand for, or mean, one that is not so present. One material thing may become symbolic of something other than itself. Imagination can also be thought of as the faculty by which we use or interpret symbols. To do this is the mark of the essentially imaginative mind. And so if there is a function of the imagination that is particularly religious, we may start to search for it in this area. For as we have seen, theology in part demands that religion be concerned with that which cannot be perceived by the senses or understood in the way that natural objects are understood. It is always in search of truths, but truths which have application beyond the perceptible world. And so it is inevitable that in its search it should have recourse to symbols, visible signs of what lies beyond or behind the visible.

So if there *is* such a thing as the peculiarly religious imagination, its nature may perhaps be best understood through an understanding of the nature of symbols themselves. In the *Statesman's Manual*, Appendix B, Coleridge drew a famous distinction between allegory and symbol:

> An Allegory is nothing but a translation of abstract notions into picture language, which is in itself nothing but an abstraction from the objects of the senses. On the other hand a Symbol is characterised by a translucence of the special in the general, of the general in the special, of the universal in the general: above all by the translucence of the eternal through and in the temporary. It always partakes of the reality which it renders intelligible; and while it enunciates the whole, abides itself as a living part in that unity of which it is the representative.[2]

We may get some enlightenment from this distinction (though far from clear in detail) if we think of Coleridge's own use of symbol in, for example, the *Ancient Mariner*. The crucial point is that whereas in allegory we have to invent a picture or visible form or plot to convey an abstract meaning, in the case of symbol there is nothing invented. The symbolic object exists in its own right as a singular temporal object; but it is seen as significant of something other than itself. Thus to treat something as symbolic is a characteristic act of the imagination. The eternal is seen *in* the time-bound and particular. The albatross is a characteristically symbolic object.

To deal in symbols is an extension of language. All words, even the most familiar, are in a sense symbols; being particular objects, they stand for something other than themselves. But we are so familiar with words as physical sounds or black marks on a white page that they become to all intents and purposes transparent; we see straight through them, without stopping on their physical particularity, to the meaning that lies behind them. Yet they should be thought of as at one end of a continuum, at the other end of which lie symbols of the kind that Coleridge intended. A symbol in his sense, while it conveys a meaning, does so in a manner that divides our attention between the symbolic object and its sense; and that sense is always less than precise. Indeed, its function is provoke this divided attention and to convey something that cannot otherwise be expressed. It is a full-blown physical object with all its own characteristics through which can be read a non-physical idea. The interpretation of a symbol generally seems natural or inevitable.

In this respect a symbol is different from a sign. A sign is something precise in its meaning and, like words themselves, conventional in its signification; for example, the flag flying on the Houses of Parliament is, by convention, a sign that the House is in session; the college flag at half-mast is a sign that a member of the college has died. The sign may not tell us everything; but as far as it goes, it is precise, and can be read by the intellect, provided that the meaning has been taught. A symbol, on the other hand, has to be read by the eye of the imagination. And it is both because its significance cannot be stated precisely and because we often do not need to be taught to understand that we want to say that the imagination must be called into play, rather than the intellect.

Here, then, we have one central use of the imagination fairly obviously relevant to religion. Can this use be fitted with the demand of theology that its subject-matter, religion, should be the discovery of truth? Or does such a demand rule out the possibility of any genuine role for the imagination in the religious consciousness? There are two different ways of rebutting such a suggestion. First, as I have already suggested, we may answer that some element of interpretation lies at the heart of all our knowledge. If we could accommodate only the immediate, the present, the fluctuating and evanescent, without seeing in it any law-like regularity going beyond the present, then, as Plato argued in the *Theaetetus*, we could claim no knowledge at all, only instant present experience. We would not even be able to parcel up our experience into things likely to recur: no cats or dogs, no tables or chairs, with their expected continuities and regularities, no continuously flowing rivers. All would be Heracleitan flux. As I have suggested, our ability to claim and act upon knowledge is, according to a long and reputable philosophical tradition, derivative not from sense alone or from reason, but from imagination. Religious knowledge depends on the imagination, according to this argument, because all knowledge does so.

But this, it may be said, is a rather specialist and esoteric kind of reply. It does not deal with the objection that, even if imagination helps us interpret our experience, yet it is essentially a source not of truth but of fiction. Imagination deals primarily with what is not, with the unreal. After all, Hume, though he thought we relied on imagination to enable us to ascribe continuity and causal regularity to the world, nevertheless held that only reason or immediate sense could yield knowledge. What we get from the imagination is 'feigned', our supposed knowledge of the external world more a matter of probability, based on repetition and habit, than of certainty. And this kind of knowledge ought not to satisfy theologians who seek to prove the existence of God and to speak with authority about the nature of the Deity.

And so a more radical reply may seem to be called for. It seems necessary to embark on a defence of imagination as itself a source, not of fiction, but of truth. This is the path followed by Romanticism, by Keats, for example, and by Wordsworth and Blake. In his letter to Bailey, written in 1817, Keats said, 'I am certain of nothing but of the holiness of the heart's affections and the truth of imagination. What imagination seizes as beauty must be truth...The imagination may be compared to Adam's dream...he awoke and found it truth.'[3] Now this is an extreme claim, which bears the marks of poetic exaggeration. But a more sober account of the truthfulness of the imagination can perhaps be given.

In attempting this, I must try to say a little more about the tools that the imagination may use in its pursuit of truth. We have seen already that the imagination may fasten on a symbolic object; or rather, that it may come to treat an existing thing in the outside world as significant of something other than itself – that is, as a symbol. There is more to be said about this relation of 'meaning', or 'standing for' something else.

If we are not careful, we may think of meaning as a clear, two-term relation holding between one distinct object and another, more or less distinct. This is not the case, even when we are concerned with words and their meanings. And in thinking about the imagination and its proper object, the image, we have to be aware of a further difficulty, an inbuilt ambiguity. The image is sometimes an internal object, something in the mind; sometimes a physical object, a picture or a reflection, but outside, part of the world, and visible to the outer, not the inner, eye. Furthermore, sometimes, especially in the eighteenth century, the image was thought of as a prospect, something seen, but not reflecting anything other than itself. We could trace the history of this complexity of sense to the British empirical philosophers; but its influence was much more widely felt. In Wordsworth, for example, we find the most frequent and striking examples of such ambiguity, where the words 'image', 'shape', and 'form' are all of them used for both the outer appearance and the inner vision of what may be seen – seen both by the eye of perception and the inner eye. Indeed, both outer and inner work together, their object one. As C. C. Clarke wrote in his most illuminating book *Romantic Paradox*, 'Wordsworth's imagination in the sense of inner vision or inward eye seems to have been most active when the outward vision was also engaged.'[4]

The supreme example of the way in which present sense perception and mental image are mixed and transfused comes in *Tintern Abbey*; but there are innumerable other examples. In the last book of the *Prelude* the visible, real look of the mountains, of the mist and moonlight, are themselves a 'vision' and a type of emblem of the human mind itself. There can be no passage of poetry that more clearly shows the power of the imagination to read a timeless truth in a temporal 'image', a view or prospect, but not merely an object of sensation:

> When into air had partially dissolved
> That vision, given to spirits of the night
> And three chance human wanderers, in calm thought
> Reflected, it appeared to me the type
> Of a majestic intellect, its acts
> And its possessions, what it has and craves,
> What in itself it is, and would become.
> There I beheld the emblem of a mind
> That feeds upon infinity, that broods
> Over the dark abyss, intent to hear
> Its voices issuing forth to silent light
> In one continuous stream; a mind sustained
> By recognitions of transcendent power,
> In sense conducting to ideal form,
> In soul of more than mortal privilege.[5]

Now it may be argued that this, though impressive enough, is simply one poet's view of the imagination; and that there is no need for us to be unduly beguiled by a theory essentially Romantic and essentially belonging to the heady days of the late eighteenth century or early nineteenth century. But I believe that if we do not take seriously this aspect of the imagination and transfer it from its immediate historical context, we shall fail to understand the perennial excitement we may now experience when we enter into the world not just of Wordsworth, Keats, and Blake, but also of Kant and the post-Kantian philosophers; and this excitement is that of recognition.

We know this imaginative experience; we have had it ourselves. We know the sense of transcendence, if such a phrase can be used, which often goes along with a heightened awareness of the here and now, through which we dimly perceive a significance beyond the immediate. We nearly all have our 'spots of time'. In 1973 a study of such experiences in children and adolescents was published by Michael Paffard.[6] He followed this a few years later with another book consisting of accounts drawn from diaries and autobiographies.[7] Both books afford fascinating testimony to the nature of this kind of phenomenon, commoner perhaps in childhood, but by no means confined to it. It cannot be disputed that such experiences are the province of the imagination; and we would be missing an important aspect of imagination if we left them out of account. Moreover, it seems to me that it is precisely because there is a kind of truth-claim inherent in these experiences (they are visions or revelations that this is how things are) that they are relevant to the idea of religious imagination.

In his first book Michael Paffard discusses the question of whether these transcendental experiences are to be called aesthetic or religious (a question to which I shall return in a moment). He says:

> The difficulty, as always, lies in getting behind the words, behind beliefs, to the reality of the experience itself. If part of the experience itself is an unshakeable feeling of certainty that the phenomenal world is not the real world and that the 'something beyond' is all-powerful and the ultimate source of all value, then the experience would seem to contain a religious ingredient or dimension that carried it outside and distinguished it from the realm of the aesthetic.[8]

I would suggest that a test might be whether the word 'pleasure' was or was not adequate as a description of the effect of the experience on the person who had it.

I do not want to trivialize the concept of pleasure. Far from it. I think that some of the greatest moments of our lives can be characterized as the most intensely pleasurable. Nevertheless, there are clearly some experiences, some thoughts, about which it would seem inadequate to say that they gave pleasure. I will quote one passage which Paffard also quoted from the autobiographical writing of Willa Muir, the wife of the poet Edwin Muir.

> One evening when I was sixteen the feeling broke over me so strongly that I was awed into giving it a name. I was sitting alone in a boat beached at the back of the island. Except for a distant

curlew's call there was no living sound. The feeling came upon me like a tide floating me out and up into the wide greening sky...into the universe, I told myself. That was the secret name I gave it: Belonging to the Universe.[9]

She could not have called this experience one of 'pleasure'.

To return to Wordsworth himself: in his writing, the ambiguous object of imagination, part external, part internal, is mainly presented in visual terms. Indeed, 'visionary' is a word he uses to express the object of perception that carries a transcendent meaning. But the imagination can work in a precisely analogous way in dealing with the auditory. Indeed, in an investigation of the religious imagination, perhaps the auditory imagination is paramount. For there has never been a time when music has not been an 'emblem' or symbol in religious contexts, being used essentially to convey more than the mere sounds of which it is composed.

Ever since Plato wrote, on the whole disparagingly, about music in the *Republic*, it has been recognized that music affects, and can be deliberately used to affect, our spirits, our attitudes, our ways of behaving. It could be said that all music is mood music. And a mood is a disposition, if only temporary, to see the world in a certain light, to see meanings (in nature, in the weather, in other people's behaviour) which are peculiar to that mood. In a novel by Ivy Compton Burnett, the nurse said, 'Master Henry has one of his moods'; to which the child replied, 'Seeing the Truth about life is not a mood.'[10] But, if not, it is very near a mood; and to accept something as a truth may certainly be a mood, but also an attitude at the centre of religious consciousness. It is no wonder, then, that music has always been part of religion, but has also, by austere religious persons, been sometimes feared or mistrusted, as introducing frivolous distraction and a weakening of the cognitive. Where music has been used in religious worship, it has been because of its power to touch the imagination and carry the listener beyond the present into a sense of eternity and space that are to be heard in the sounds, though the sounds in themselves are nothing but physical vibrations. As Benedick says in *Much Ado*, 'Is it not strange that sheep's guts should hale souls out of men's bodies?' (Act II, scene 3, l. 58).

Without what Coleridge calls the 'shaping spirit'[11] of the imagination, music would remain mere sound.

It is time now to address the two strongest objections to the thesis that I have been indirectly putting forward. I have suggested ways in which the imagination is central to religion. But first, it may be said that I have totally failed to distinguish the religious from the aesthetic. Secondly, even if what I have said of the 'transcendental' imagination may be relevant to religious experience, even to religious belief, it cannot help to distinguish one religion from another. A theologian cannot really be a theologian in just any religious tradition. For if theology is concerned with truth claims, then it must be able to show that some religions are true, others false. My so-called religious imagination (if it exists) must exist for all religions. There is nothing in it specific to Christianity.

I shall once again defer a consideration of the difference between the aesthetic and the religious. But I must now say something about the imagination as it is relevant to Christianity. Any religion is concerned with a search for the truth about the relation between man and nature, about the permanent difference between the good and the bad (as distinct from the right and the wrong). It is concerned to explore and perhaps explain the contrast within human beings between their capacity for good and their capacity for evil, their sociability and their ultimate solitude, their longings for the unattainable and the awe they must feel from time to time in the face of an immense universe which must always remain partly beyond what they can either explain or control. It is because of these aspects of human life, presenting themselves differently at different stages of man's development, that religion exists. Religion depends on the fact that man is part of the universe; and, above all, it addresses itself to the facts of birth and death, the essentially temporal nature of life. Religion is a uniquely human phenomenon. Other animals, as far as we know, live from one moment to the next, and have no need to comprehend the whole of their lives as a unity, with a guiding principle, a particular value. As far as we know, they do not tell each other stories with a beginning, a middle and an end, and a moral. So far, then, it is obvious that religion arises out of the capacity which man, alone of the animals, has to exercise imagination: to interpret the universe and shape and mould it into something other than the immediate and the fragmentary. And central to this imaginative power is the ability to construct human history. Christianity is not unique in being an essentially historical religion, but those who are Christians, as opposed to Jews or Muslims, declare that the Christian version of history is the one they accept. This is the story they believe to encapsulate the truth about human nature.

The story of the life of Christ, culminating in his death and passion, tells a paradoxical and profound truth that no other story tells. The Christian religion turns essentially on a story, the story of a life and death. For any ordinary churchgoing Christian, who is familiar with the unfolding of the church year and who reads the gospels, the story aspect of his religion must be central. And it seems to me that in hearing and re-hearing a story, we begin to treat the whole story as symbolic, as revealing a truth beyond the actual events themselves. The story seems to be the inevitable and properly shaped clothing for the central truth. These is an important essay on stories by C. S. Lewis. It is concerned with children's stories, but what he says has a wider relevance. He argues in this essay that there are certain stories which appeal to the imagination because they embody a particular emotion, directed towards a particular kind of object. There is a peculiar fear, for example, which is directed towards the heaviness, monstrosity, uncouthness, and unpredictability of the gigantic (and this is a fear especially well known to children). 'Nature', he wrote, 'has that about it which compels us to invent giants, and only giants will do.'[12] The whole quality of the response to, for example, *Jack the Giant Killer*, lies in the fact that the enemy defeated in this story is a giant and the victor a small, ordinary human.

Now in the case of a story that embodies an idea, the reader will not be content to hear or read it just once. He will want to hear it over and over again. Simple anticipation, waiting and not knowing what will happen next, is not the same as the deep imaginative response that the story, when well known, may evoke. It is only when we know the plot, when in a straightforward way we know what happened, that we can grasp the story as a whole and contemplate its meaning, the idea it conveys. The purpose of a story, according to Lewis, is to catch an idea and convey it in terms of the concrete, the temporal – and, I would say, the historical. 'In life and in art, both,' he says, 'we are always trying to catch in our net of successive moments something that is not successive.' He is right, and in my view, it is imagination which grasps the story and reads it so that its successive moments yield a non-temporal truth. This is as true of the Christian story as of any other. The distinction between history, myth, and fiction begins to fade at this point.

C. S. Lewis himself would not apply his profound insight into the nature of story to the gospels. He was determined to separate the non-religious, aesthetic imagination from the religious knowledge of truth, the facts reported in the gospels from any kind of mythology. And yet he was entirely aware of the connection. Writing of his own conversion, in his autobiography, he said:

> I was by now too experienced in literary criticism to regard the gospels as myths. They had not the mythical taste. And yet the very matter which they set down was precisely the matter of great myths. If ever a myth had become fact, had been incarnated it would be like this. Myths were like it in one way. History was like it in another.[13]

It may be that the secret of Lewis's distrust of his friend Tolkien's elaborately constructed fiction *The Lord of the Rings* was that Tolkien claimed for it the status of 'true myth'. To Lewis this might have seemed near-blasphemy.

But I do not believe that we can draw so sharp a distinction between history and myth, or, to put it another way, between knowledge and imagination. There is no knowledge without imagination; and this is nowhere more true than in our knowledge of history. In attempting to understand history, any history, we have to exercise imagination in the interpretation of evidence – that is, of the present fact out of which we have to extract the meaning of the past. The history of the life of Christ is hardly different. The early Christians and the writers of the gospels saw the life of Christ as the culmination of the Messianic tradition; we cannot understand how the events appeared to them unless we know something of that tradition (hence the binding up of the Old Testament with the New). The crucial fact that we have to go on is that, for the first Christians, the prophecy had been fulfilled. Kierkegaard put it thus: 'If the contemporary generation had left nothing behind them but these words: "we have believed that in such and such a year the God appeared among us in the humble figure of a servant, that he lived and taught in our community and finally died," it would be more than enough.'[14] We have to take the gospels and extract from them what happened historically, and this has always been the role of the Christian Church.

What we bring to this interpretation, what the shaping power of imagination makes of it, will necessarily change from time to time. For we have standards of historical evidence, as well as of scientific understanding, quite different from those of the early Christians. The shaping power of our historical imagination will therefore be different from theirs, and different from that of those who lived, say, in the fifteenth century. Yet the truth encapsulated in the story may remain. Denis Nineham in his *Explorations in Theology* put it thus:

> If you suspect that the Virgin-Birth stories are not wholly authentic, you can still see how they grew up in order to express the conviction of Jesus's followers that his fully human activity had been of more than natural origin, that God's initiative had lain behind it and God had been uniquely active in it. It is the character of these stories as part of the earliest disciples' response to what had happened that we need to grasp; and I believe that if we could look at them from that perspective we could be more relaxed about them and they would reveal profound truth we are at present missing.[15]

The religious imagination, then, is in part identical with the historical imagination. But the symbols of religion are interpreted as speaking not only of the past, but also of the present and the future. Christianity arises out of the continuity and the continued interpretation of a tradition starting long before the birth of Christ and continuing until now. I suggest that the specifically religious imagination is peculiarly dependent on apprehended continuity. Since religion itself, any religion, is so centrally concerned with the contrast between time and eternity, between the transitory and the abiding, anything that can be fastened on by the imagination as a symbol of endurance is likely to be central to religion and to religious belief. This is the crucial role of the Christian Church. It is the rock, the unmoved centre, the vehicle of belief from one generation to another. An apprehension of continuity, whether geological, biological, or, in terms of human artefacts, archaeological, is itself accompanied by awe and sometimes by a passionate interest akin to love, the very emotion central to the imagination itself and to religion. The continuity of the liturgy, for example, has a double importance. It is that which conveys the repeated Christian story, and it is itself a signal of the continuity of the Church since its foundation.

To speak of the liturgy leads me at last to my final point. If religious imagination is, as I have suggested, connected in one aspect with historical imagination, it is also connected in another aspect equally closely with the aesthetic. The Church has always had an ambiguous attitude towards aesthetics. It has always tended, and still tends, to write off the aesthetic as productive not of truth but of pleasure, as frivolous, therefore, and a distraction from the hard, supposedly clear question whether what the Church teaches is true or not. It has often seemed that the pleasures of the imagination, however deep, must be set in contrast with the different, more practical response demanded by the proper reading of the gospel story, which, rightly understood, is supposed to change people's lives. No one's life was ever changed, except perhaps superficially, and for the worse, by the beautiful. Poetry, music, and the visual arts are all of them dispensable frills compared with the harsh realities of the moral. And so there have been repeated efforts to cut out the aesthetic from the centre of worship and return to the facts. Christianity must be rendered intelligible and plain; poetry and music must be banished unless they can somehow be shown to be the necessary vehicle for the historic truth.

Such movements in Christianity (and they are very strong at the present time) seem to me to stem from two sources. One is a kind of egalitarianism. The Church must not seem to exist for the elite, the finer spirits, the Wordsworthian few. Access to Christian doctrine must not depend on the cultivation of a particular kind of refined sensibility. It must be available for all – hence the many attempts we are all familiar with to render Christian doctrine homely, obvious, and generally down-market. Now this might be a respectable motive if it could be shown that only a few could experience the joy or come to grasp the truth in the interpretation of symbols. But I do not believe that this could be shown. On the contrary, I believe that the imagination, the way of thinking of one thing as signifying something beyond it, is common to all human beings, though some may think more reflectively in this mode than others. Everyone, to a greater or lesser extent, seeks an imaginative response to the immediate and the present in terms of that which is neither immediate nor present and which cannot be precisely stated in plain terms. And indeed, if this were not so, there could be no religion. For no one has seen God face to face. As Kant held, all religious language is symbolic.[16] To think otherwise is anthropomorphism.

The second source of the anti-aesthetic movement is the exaggerated dichotomy of which I have spoken already within the category of story, between the fictional and the historical, between myth and fact. There is the insistent demand to be told whether someone believes the gospel story to be true or not, yes or no. Does he believe in the virgin birth, the resurrection of the body, the miracles? This seems to me to show a failure to understand the dominant part that the shaping and interpreting imagination plays not only in religion but in history and in life itself, lived as it is through time, yet demanding a constant effort to make sense of time, to turn events into stories, in order that their significance may be understood. To quote Denis Nineham again:

> The characteristic religious difficulty today is a metaphysical difficulty, at any rate in this sense; where men seem to need help above all is at the level of the imagination; they need some means of envisaging realities such as God, creation and providence imaginatively in a way which does no violence to the rest of what they know to be true. They need to be able to mesh in their religious symbols with the rest of their sensibility.[17]

This seems to me to be profoundly true. And such meshing will not come about as long as the religious imagination is held to be totally different, because of its different subject-matter, from the imagination we use in our understanding of nature and of history, on the one hand, and our aesthetic imagination on the other.

Within the aesthetic philosophy of Kant there are to be found two elements. When we perceive what we judge to be a beautiful object, we apprehend it as having a kind of finality, a design, the form of which we can present to ourselves in an image. Understanding and imagination work together in our apprehension of design, and this is the source of our pleasure in beauty. But, paradoxically, Kant also holds that we get an entirely different kind of aesthetic experience from that which is apprehended as so vast or infinite or numinous or powerful that we can find no design in it. When this happens, 'the object before us lends itself to the presentation of a sublimity discoverable in the mind.' Here we have Kant's version of what was then the fashionable doctrine in England, the distinction in taste between the beautiful and the sublime.

The presentation of sublimity cannot, in Kant's view, be in the form of a sensuous image, simply because there is no form or design in the object to be grasped, and therefore reproduced. But it is, he says, the very impossibility of our forming an image of the idea suggested by the object which constitutes our notion of the sublime. We see ourselves in two lights: in the first place as feeble because we cannot comprehend the idea, in the second place as grand because, unlike other animals, we have a glimmering of this ineffable idea. Now in Kant's vocabulary an 'idea' is precisely not an image. In some ways it is akin to a platonic 'Form'. In his words, it is 'what the highest power of the mind can produce but what can never in any circumstances be exemplified in the world nor brought before the sense to be observed'. An idea is like a goal or an ideal, never to be completely realized. The sense of the sublime, according to Kant, excites in us not pleasure (as beauty does) but awe. We are in awe of the mysterious ability of the human mind to frame ideas which cannot be either intuitive (like the notions of space and time) or comprehended by sense or understanding. Imaginatively we stretch out towards that which even imagination itself cannot encompass.

In the *Critique of Pure Reason*, a distinction is drawn between concepts of the understanding and ideas of reason. We see concepts of the understanding exemplified in nature; indeed, we ourselves impose them upon nature, and understand nature through their network. Such concepts are those of substance or of cause.

The great ideas of reason, on the other hand, are necessary to us, but cannot ever be perceived in nature. Such are the ideas of God, freedom, and immortality. In that part of Kant's aesthetic theory that deals not with the beautiful but with the sublime, he introduces the expression 'aesthetic idea', which is a kind of counterpart to an idea of reason. A great artistic genius may introduce us to an aesthetic idea; or we may have such an idea suggested to us by nature itself. An aesthetic idea is, Kant says, 'a representation of the imagination which induces much thought; yet without the possibility of any definite thought (that is, concept) whatever being adequate to it, and which consequently language can never get quite on level terms with or render it completely intelligible'. The imagination, Kant says, is 'a powerful agent for creating as it were a second nature of the material supplied to it by actual nature'. In this way the imagination 'strains after something lying out beyond the confines of experience'.[18] The materials of actual nature employed by imagination in this creative role are what we call symbols.

Now we have seen already that Kant regards the whole of the language of religion as necessarily symbolic, rather than literal. It therefore follows that, for him, there can be no sharp distinction between the aesthetic idea and the idea of reason. The aesthetic idea will be presented in a form that is symbolic; but the idea of reason, in so far as it is anything but a vague inkling or aspiration (or an inner sense of our own moral freedom), will necessarily be presented in the same symbolic form. For language will be as inadequate in the one case as in the other.

If we take the central concerns of religion seriously, it seems to me that we must take Kant's argument seriously as well. There can be no language, whether it is moral, historical, or more narrowly theological, that can possibly do justice to the ideas of religion. We therefore have to allow that such language as we accept as religious is suggestive and symbolic in the way which we are prepared to allow is characteristic of the aesthetic. And we should allow, too, that 'language' in this context will include not merely words but the 'language' of painting, architecture, and music as well.

I hope to have suggested that we cannot get on without the imagination in our ordinary life; nor can we claim to know things in the most ordinary and practical manner possible without the exercise of imagination. But imagination is also essential to us whenever we try to go beyond sense and experience into a world more dimly perceived, wherein we see 'through a glass, darkly' (1 Cor. 13: 12). If the language of religion is taken to be absolutely literal, then that must be the end of religion. This is a possibility we need to take very seriously, and many would claim that religion is already dead. But if, on the other hand, the language of religion is not literal, then no sharp distinction can be drawn between the religious and the aesthetic. Imagination, in both religious and aesthetic contexts, must be allowed, to the same degree, to be a source of truth; but not a truth which can be translated into a medium from which the imagination is excluded.

# 13

# *Personal Continuity*

At the very centre of the idea of personal continuity lie two other ideas. The first is that of the identity of an object – any object – over time. The second is that of memory. I want to explore, though only superficially, the links between these two in order to show how, together, they contribute to – perhaps constitute – the notion of personal continuity.

Let us start, then, with the notion of identity. If we raise the question of the identity of an object, we must be referring to what are, or rather could be, two or more objects, at least in some sense. To ask 'Is it one?' entails 'or more than one' (that is, a *different* one). Thus, if we ask whether a particular table is the *same*, we must mean the same *as* something; for instance, the same as the one I wrote at last year or the same as the one my sister bought at an auction ten years ago. Of course, we use the words 'the same' in other ways as well. It often means 'the same kind' or 'the same make'. So I may properly ask if you have the same rose as I have in your garden or the same car in your garage. But, on the other hand, we may want, as in the first example, to raise the question of whether this thing before us is the very same identical object as another. As what other, then? For if the table is one and the same, there is no *other* for it to be the same as. There is only one thing, as our affirmative answer makes clear. Yet the original question makes sense.

Nevertheless there *are*, even when there is an affirmative answer to our question, in one sense two things involved, a past thing and a present thing; a table we remember and a table at which we now sit and write. What we are identifying is the past table, the table I can remember writing at last year, with the present table, before which my chair is now drawn up. There is thus no sense in the identity question, asked with regard to an individual object, unless we can think of persistence through time, the past and the present being separated.

This is the common-sense and, I believe, the only possible or intelligible view. There have been philosophers, however – notably Bergson – who have denied it. Bergson held that we properly answer questions about identity not in terms of persistence through time but in terms of the occupancy of space.[1] Two things occupy two different spaces, one thing occupies one space. He held that we identify temporal items (the bird I saw yesterday with the bird I can see today) only by a kind of metaphor, by making them spatial, that is to say, and laying them out end to end before our inner view and counting them. He believed that the true and non-metaphorical view of time is that which avoids the spatial metaphor and refuses to treat things (birds or tables) as if they had hard identifiable edges such that they could be laid out end to end. Although he concedes that in our ordinary practical life we need to think of things as separable and singly identifiable, forming a kind of series, yet our notion of time itself is in fact one of pure duration, a fluid continuum with no separable parts. What we think of as having duration in this pure sense cannot be distinguished into a series. Bergson speaks of 'interpenetration' as being like the beginning, middle, and end of a melody. A melody must be thought of not as separable notes, but as a whole. Matter and the nature of the physical world and of our own organs of perception impose upon us the spatial concepts in terms of which, superficially, we think of persistence and change through time. But spirit acquaints us with the fluidity and permanence of pure duration, and at this level our memory brings us into contact with the spontaneous, the free, and the eternal. At this level, to remember would be to have a pure intuition into how things are and were without the restrictions of space or of the ordinary concept of time which is assimilated to that of space. At this level, too, we could know ourselves. For we are acquainted with spirit.

The drawback to this theory, apart from its intrinsic unintelligibility, is that knowledge of our own personal and timeless identity, our continuity in pure duration, such as Bergson supposes that we may have, must, if it exists, lie for ever below the level of consciousness – or at the very least be incapable of being expressed or shared. For as soon as we start to use words to say *what* we are acquainted with, what our intuition was actually *of*, we will have reduced these things once again to the boundaried, the speakable, and the spatial. We would be back again with the everyday notion of the identity of things over time (what we normally and actually mean by 'time'). For it is on this that language (within which we identify and re-identify things in real life) is founded. So, from the viewpoint of a language-user, one who may want to ask and answer the question 'Is this the same table as I used last year?', the notion of identity is meaningless unless it means identity (or possible multiplicity) over a period of time. For it is of the essence of material objects that they can many of them be moved about in space. One single object can be in many places, but not at the same time. And so we cannot identify a table as the same merely because it is in the same place as it was. We have to have a notion of temporal duration which can survive many changes of place.

I labour this point because it is, I believe, of the greatest importance in our notion of personal continuity. It may be objected that, by taking the example of a table, I have prejudged the issue. For tables are, notoriously, physical objects, able to be moved about from one place to another. It might indeed require the notion of temporal continuity through spatial change to speak of their identity. But what of less spatially determined objects? Could there not be a concept of identity for them that was not spatial at all, but purely qualitative? Suppose, for example, that you and I have the same thought. The sameness in such a case must surely be determined by the content of the thought, and by this alone.

I do not believe that this is so. If we both think at the same time of the same object, say a heron which we both saw this morning as we had our breakfast, then the thoughts certainly have an identical content, and may therefore be called the 'same thought'. But the sameness of the content is itself determined by the identity of the spatial object, the heron, upon which our thoughts have fastened. It is only in virtue of *this* identity that our two thoughts are the same.

If, on the other hand, the 'same thought' which you and I both have is a thought about something abstract or general, let us say the origin of the species or the logic of counter-factual conditionals, then perhaps at first it may seem that the thought has qualitative identity, an identity in no way spatial. But suppose that the two people who share the same thought are, let us say, musicologists or logicians or other academics anxious for their own reputations. Is it not extremely likely that they might fall into dispute about whose thought the same thought really was? Each might wish to lay claim to the thought as his own. If it could be established that each had the thought entirely separately, then in one sense they would have to admit that there were after all two thoughts, strikingly like each other in content but spatially and temporally different. In other words, it becomes clear that the term 'same thought' is ambiguous just as 'same rose' is. In one sense, it may mean thoughts with (more or less) the same content, to be expressed in the same words. In another sense, thoughts are simply not the same if you had one of them and I had the other, even if we had them at the same time. This ambiguity could be illustrated equally by the concept of 'pain'. In one sense, I cannot feel your pain or have your thought, even if we are both suffering from sinusitis or both contemplating the origin of the species. In another sense, our pain or our thoughts can be said to be the same if they can be articulated in the same words. If there is a dispute about the authorship of a thought, personal identity over-rides identity of content. Qualitative similarity, however striking, is not enough by itself to allow us to identify two thoughts as one and the same.

To return, then, to the question of the identity of physical objects. It seems that continuity over time is the crucial criterion of identity; and when we tried to widen the examples to take in thoughts as well as things, it was the identity of either things or persons which in the end determined the identity of thoughts. And so we come to the question of what leads us to say that a *person* is the same as he was. Note that, just as in the case of a table, a statement of identity with regard to a person contains the implication of tense: 'He is the same as he *was*.' There is a necessary reference to time past. Continuity of *history* is the central notion, just as it is with tables and chairs. But people have other attributes besides the obviously physical. If we think of *their* past histories, we are led inevitably to consider their memory of their own histories. So we must ask: Is the continuity of my history dependent on my recollection of it?

At first sight this looks an extremely implausible suggestion, for we are all perfectly well aware that there are many aspects of our lives which we would not try to disavow but of which we have no recollection whatsoever. The only reason why the suggestion that personal identity is dependent on memory should ever have been taken seriously at all is that the philosopher Locke, and other philosophers since, argued so strongly in its favour. To find wherein personal identity consists', he wrote, 'we must consider what *person* stands for; which I think is a thinking intelligent being that has reason and reflection and can consider itself as itself, the same thinking thing in different times and places.'[2] Locke insists that the concept of personal identity consists wholly in this continuity of consciousness. As far as the idea of 'same person' goes, he is not interested in any question about whether a man's body was composed of exactly the same physical particles in the past as it is composed of now; nor is he even interested in whether there is or is not some continuing 'thinking substance' in the body, but distinct from it. 'For', he writes,

> it is by the consciousness it has of its present thoughts and actions that it is *self to itself* now and so will be the same self as far as the same consciousness can extend to actions past or to come; and would be by distance of time or change of substance no more two persons than a man be two men by wearing other clothes today than he did yesterday.

In order to make his definition plausible, Locke has to distinguish between 'same person' and 'same man', the former dependent wholly upon the extension of consciousness or self-consciousness, the latter on bodily continuity. 'Same man', in Locke's usage, is no different, as far as criteria of identity go, from 'same butterfly' or 'same table'. 'Person' is, according to Locke, a forensic term, 'man' a term of natural history. Thus, for Locke, the two concepts which, at the beginning, I said were central to the idea of personal continuity are split apart. A man may be identical with the man he was last year, just as a table may be identical with that which it was last year and according to the same criteria. But memory is a different criterion of identity altogether, and can ensure the continuity of a person, but not of a table, which has no memory. There is thus an enormous gulf between the external criteria of identity that we may apply when seeking to identify the table and the internal criteria which each person must apply to himself. So if a man has changed radically in his appearance and his habits between the time when he was 8 and the time when he is 80, he may still say of himself that he is the same person now as he was in 1908. But other people, who have no access to his memories, may be inclined to say that he is a different man. Locke says: 'If the soul of a prince, carrying with it the consciousness of the prince's past life should enter and inform the body of a cobbler as soon as deserted by his own soul, everyone sees he would be the same person as the prince, accountable only for the prince's actions. But who would say it was the same man?' It is this split, insisted on by Locke, that I wish to question. And I am not by any means the first to do so. For example, Bishop Butler, in the *First Dissertation to the Analogy of Religion*, complained, first, that Locke's theory would entail that 'a person has not existed a single moment nor done one action but what he can remember'; and, more fundamentally, that 'One should really think it self-evident that consciousness of personal identity presupposes and therefore cannot constitute personal identity, any more than knowledge in any other case can constitute truth, which it presupposes.'[3] Without wishing to follow Bishop Butler into the intricacies of general epistemology, I must say that, prima facie, his claim about the primacy of the concept of identity over that of memory is to be accepted.

In order to substantiate this intuition, it is necessary to look a little further into the notion of memory, or consciousness of past actions and experiences. William James argued in his *Principles of Psychology* that there is a crucial distinction to be drawn between memory and other thoughts about the past.[4] After all, I am quite capable of imagining the Battle of Waterloo, even of imagining myself in the role of the Duke of Wellington, if I so please. But plainly this is not memory. In order to identify the thought as a memory, not only must it be dated as belonging to the past, but it must be clearly thought to be part of *my* past. It must, he says, possess that certain 'warmth and intimacy' which characterizes any experience appropriated by someone as *his own*. Indeed, he suggests that this appropriation of experience never happens while we are actually experiencing something and cannot happen until after the event. He says: 'All the intellectual value to us of a state of mind depends on our after-memory of it. Only then is it combined in a system and knowingly made to contribute to a result. Only then does it count for us.' Thus, what happens to me can be turned into one of my possessions; but it is the concept of myself as the possessor, the systematic organizer, of experience that is central. Memory could neither exist nor be valued if this centre of experience, the continuing person, did not exist.

Sartre in *Being and Nothingness* goes even further. He argues that the very notion of the past depends on the existence of people who have experiences. 'The past', he writes, 'is characterised as the past of someone or something. One *has* a past. There is not first a universal past which is later particularised into concrete pasts. On the contrary, it is particular pasts that we discover first.'[5] Sartre held that the notion of myself as a recipient of experience is itself given in the immediate awareness I have of any experience whatsoever. In this, he might be thought to be following Descartes, who held that in the *Cogito* we become aware of ourselves as thinking, experiencing beings, and that this is what we essentially are. But the great, and enormously important, difference between Sartre's so-called pre-reflective cogito and Descartes' original consciousness is that for Sartre this consciousness is of our bodies as much as of our mental experiences. We are unreflectively aware of ourselves as objects in the world of other objects.

And thus we come to the crux of the problem of personal continuity. Memory would generally be thought of as a 'mental' phenomenon, something essentially 'in the mind'. Are we to believe, then, that personal continuity, interwoven as it is with memory, is itself a 'mental' phenomenon? Is it the case that if someone is the same person as he was five years ago, he must primarily display 'mental continuity'?

Now it must be noticed that in asking this question I am not raising the question of *responsibility* for past actions. When

Locke distinguished between 'same person' and 'same man', referring to 'person' as a forensic term, he did so because he was
concerned with questions of responsibility. It is indeed true that,
as far as the law goes, there might well be a case for saying that
actions performed by the 8-year-old could not be laid at the door
of the 80-year-old, any more than in the case where the prince's
mind entered the cobbler's body, the resulting person should
be held responsible for what the cobbler did. But it is for the
courts to decide in particular cases what they will hold a man
responsible for and what they will let him off. Legal decisions
cannot entitle us, in general, to draw a distinction between
'person' and 'man' if that distinction has no other utility or
coherence than in the distinction between different degrees of
responsibility. What we are concerned with at the moment is not
legal liability, but our own sense of continuity; and in this field it
seems to me that there is no case at all to be made for distinguishing 'man' from 'person' – or, if you prefer it, 'body' from
'mind'.

I have already suggested that Bishop Butler was right when he
stated that we can perform, and later have ascribed to us, actions
of which we now have no recollection. So what does it mean to
say that I can be known to be the person who did something,
even if I do not remember it? The answer is very simple. The
person who did the thing in question must be shown to be
identical with me in the sense that if someone else had had their
eye on that agent from the moment when she was doing the thing
until now there would have been no different person involved.
There was only one agent, who is I. The hypothetical observer,
watching me then and confronting me now, would be able to fill
up all the temporal gaps between now and then; he would be able
to tell the story, and say, 'No one else came along. No one took
her place. There was no one *else* involved.'

The continuity thus established is the continuity of a spatial
object, which can move and change and yet be said to be the
same. Suppose I find a box of christening clothes in the attic and
say, 'Those were my christening robes. I wore them.' In this case,
identifying me with the baby who wore the robes all those years
ago is no different in principle from identifying the clothes
themselves, when we find them yellowing in their box, with the

clothes worn at my christening. In the history of the clothes, however much their appearance has changed over time, there was no time when someone actually destroyed them and substituted new ones. We are perfectly accustomed to this kind of identification, even though we have not in fact had our eye on the object all the time. All that is necessary is that we should be able to fill in the gaps. Looking at a big fat elderly cat, I can say, 'That is the cat my daughter brought home from Devonshire in a basket twelve years ago.' It does not surprise me that he could then fit into a small basket and could not do so now. I know how cats grow. I have not watched the cat unremittingly for twelve years. But I have been aware of his comings and goings. And at no time have I given him up for lost and got a new cat.

Notoriously, gradual replacement of parts of an object (whether a bicycle or a human) does not lead us to say that the objects is no longer the same over a period of time. Normally we think that there are two objects in question only when a *whole new* object has been introduced to take the place of an old one; and this is true equally of bicycles and of butlers. If I identify someone as the person who, years ago, pulled my hair, even though he has no recollection of doing so, I identify him by my access to his history as a physical object, however much he has changed over the years. It is more difficult, no doubt, to make such identifications than it is to identify the table at which I now write as that which I wrote at on an earlier occasion. But this is because people move about more than tables, and change in more complex ways. Yet the principle is no different. Locke would say that this is to identify a man, not a person. I am arguing that this distinction is confusing and mistaken.

Of course, it seems to make sense to raise the question, 'Am I the same person as I was forty years ago?' – and this despite the fact that in one way the question contains its own answer. For if 'I' is intelligibly used twice in this question, then obviously the referent *must* be the same. Yet, if between different phases of a person's life that person changes radically, not just in the predictable physiological ways, but in tastes, habits, and abilities, we may say of him that he is a 'different person'. Proust, profoundly concerned as he was with questions of identity and change, was aware that in one sense people's lives are fragmentary.

There is a sense in which Marcel in love is different from Marcel not in love; nor can he seriously think of himself as the precursor of the Marcel who will one day be able to write the loved one's name without emotion. For to be obsessed simply is to be in the state of feeling that there could never be a world that did not contain me in the grip of the feeling I now have (even if, by long experience, I know that in the past I have got over such things). On the other hand, Proust also knew that my past self in some sense exists for me, even if I cannot at the moment remember exactly what that past self did or felt. The past self can be revived. There is always the possibility of feeling the identity of myself now with myself then. And for Proust, of course, this felt identity is the source of a deep and overwhelming joy.

I want to emphasize here simply that there would be no point in re-experiencing past experiences if we could not show conclusively, and know, that the same physical object which is me had had the experience in the first place. Just as one may say of a child who has come back from hospital cured, 'He is a different child', yet may know and rejoice in the fact that he is the same child, only better; so one may say, reflecting on one's own past follies (or glories), 'I am a different person now.' But the whole point is that one knows it is not so. After all, if a genuinely different child had come back from hospital (which is perfectly possible), one would be frantic. And if the person so different from myself were not in fact myself, then the fascination and the astonishment would be gone. There would be no incentive, as there is, to make sense of the changes, to tell a coherent story of my life. We all know ourselves to be physical creatures, body and mind together. We know that if our brain were damaged, our mind would be changed too; that our memory is a function of our brain, which is a part of the body like, though more complex than, any other. It is impossible to conceive of our experiences detached from our bodies, and so our continuity is bodily continuity, first and foremost.

Inanimate objects and animals other than humans are identified by us through their histories. My table left the carpenter's hand one day, and has changed hands on and off until the day when it came into my room, where it still is. More interestingly, (because more like our own case) an animal, any animal, is born and dies.

It has a life that it leads, and is identified by that continuous life. Of course, for humans there is, as well, an extra dimension. They, probably uniquely among animals, not only have a life to lead, but can reflect on it and make it into a story. They can remember – that is, recall – at least some of the events of their lives, but they are not on that account totally different from other animals. And so, like the rest, they are identified by being the individual creatures they are, born of the parents they are born of at a particular time and place and dying at an equally specifiable time and place.

But this is not all. For, in reflecting on his own life, a man (or a person – I don't mind which I say) may perceive his life, or try to do so, as a whole, as a plot with himself as the central character. And it is at this point that memory and imagination overlap and intertwine. For imagination must not be thought of as the faculty that gives rise merely to fiction or fancy, though it may do that. Its central function, as both Hume and Kant understood, is to bring coherence and universality to what would otherwise be a random and unintelligible sequence of impressions appearing before the mind like the shadow puppets in Plato's cave. It is the primary function of the imagination to find the general and universal in the particular, to find significance in an otherwise incoherent world. Imagination, which other animals do not have in the same way as men do, enables men, as Wordsworth puts it, 'to see into the life of things'.

So, being imagining, reflecting, remembering creatures (although, like all other animals, tautologically, we live in the present), we are not bound totally to the here and now. In reflecting on past experience and bringing the past to bear on the present, we recognize the fact of personal continuity through time, and can bridge the gap between the past and the present (and indeed, between the present and the future), and thus overcome the drawbacks of the ephemeral and the immediate.

The experienced continuity of our own lives, then, is the vehicle of significance for us of the world as a whole. This has often enough been demonstrated in the art of those like Wordsworth and Proust who have quite deliberately attempted to show the role of memory in the creative process. For both of them, and for many others too, especially for explicitly autobiographical writers, memory is an essential part of the aesthetic imagination. The theory that lies behind such works of art is this: the aesthetically significant, however much it may be rooted in particular experience, is of universal and unlimited value, not just for now, but for always. If a man, through his memory, can reconstruct a scene, then he must also know that he was the man who figured in that scene, and that there is a causal continuity between him (his body) then and him (his body) now, however changed that body may be. To understand this continuity, to grasp his own duration, may give him personally intense joy, such as Proust felt when the past flooded over him on tasting the madeleine. But more generally, to grasp this continuity is in some measure to defeat time. The past is not after all finished and done with. It, with the present and perhaps the future, together make up a pattern which is universally intelligible.

Personal continuity, then, is the continuity of a human being as a biological entity, a member of a unique species. The uniqueness lies in the ability each man has to grasp and assert his individual continuity, through memory. Within this felt and experienced continuity, it is impossible to separate the mind from the body as though they were different ingredients. To try to do so is to misunderstand the nature of memory, itself a function – though an infinitely astonishing one – of the human brain.

# 14

# *The Concept of Inner Experience*

The subject of this chapter is the relation between studies in child development and the extraneous discipline of philosophy. I will try to describe an area within which, as I believe, philosophers could benefit from the empirical findings of experts in child psychology and child development. In order to explain myself more fully, I must start with some very general remarks. I hope I will be forgiven if they seem rather elementary. It is a characteristic feature of philosophy that it deals in the obvious.

At the very most general level, philosophy is concerned with *what there is*. Yet, if a natural historian discovered a new species of beetle or a car manufacturer turned out a new make of car, neither would be contributing anything of relevance to philosophy, though each had changed the list of what exists. So philosophers must be represented as concerning themselves with a more general question: What *kinds* of things exist, perhaps; to which the answer will not be in terms of species or classes, but of such entities as 'minds' or 'material objects', entities which are simply assumed to exist by non-philosophers, though they may never put general names to them. Such philosophical questions overlap with, and lead into, others about, for example, the nature of our *knowledge* of things, the nature of the *causal connections* between things, and the nature of the *meaning of words*.

Here, once again, the philosopher is concerned with what seems self-evident to normal people. We all assume that we know, for example, that other people exist, and that they have experiences, such as the experience of pain or of dreams, that are roughly like our own. But philosophers are bound to ask, *how* do we know? Equally, as far as meaning goes, we assume that we know the meaning of words like 'pain' or 'nightmare'; but the philosopher will ask what *precisely* we mean by such words, and how we *come to know* what their meaning is. In all such cases it must be understood that the philosopher will be raising his questions in highly general terms. The question about knowledge could not be answered simply and solely by asking a doctor or a vet whether an animal was or wasn't in pain; nor could the question about meaning be answered by consulting a dictionary. Have philosophers, then, merely to sit and think, without consulting anyone? This is certainly very often the picture presented. But it is misleading. Philosophers, after all, however general their preoccupations, have to reflect on the world as they find it: both on the familiar world itself and, especially, on the language commonly used to talk about that world. They are therefore perfectly entitled, if they want to, to consult experts on animal behaviour or to consult chemists or physicists or anyone else they choose. But, above all, they must consult language-users, including themselves, on the meaning of words.

Since it is only through language that we can discuss, categorize, or even think about what there is, it is the primary concern of philosophy to raise the question how our language relates to what there is. It is here that we begin to enter the territory within which philosophers may want to learn from children. For children are engaged in learning language; and as they learn, they are, like philosophers but with more practical intent, exploring the relation between words and experience. Philosophers theorize about this connection; children may sometimes unwittingly demonstrate in their explorations what the connection is and what it is not.

Within this broad framework there is a group of questions, roughly classified as the philosophy of mind, where the relation between words and things is especially tantalizing and where the question *what there is* seems peculiarly obscure. These are questions concerned with inner experience. It is my contention that in pursuing this branch of philosophy practitioners have a great deal to learn from experts in the language acquisition of children. Perhaps empirical scientists may themselves come to clarify their findings a little with the help of philosophers; but that outcome seems to me at present more dubious.

I shall take two examples to illustrate the difficulties philosophers find in discussing inner experience: that of pain and that of dreaming. In the course of a single chapter I shall be able to give no more than a taste of the concepts traditionally deployed in their treatment, but I shall conclude by bringing them together under a wider concept where I believe that philosophers can above all learn from their psychologist colleagues.

Let us begin, then, with pain. There is a long tradition in modern philosophy, starting with Descartes and continuing in this country with the empiricists, Locke and Hume among others, but also Russell and Ayer, which emphasizes the essential privacy of all our experiences. The thought that you do not see what I see – not, that is, from behind my eyes – is probably one of the first philosophical thoughts that most people have. How do I know that when you call something 'red', it looks to you as my red looks to me? When you complain of pain, how do I know that it hurts like my pain?

According to Descartes, this essential privacy of experience is unique to man. For he held that men were divided into two parts: the mind and the body, *res cogitans* and *res extensa*. A thinking being is conscious of his own thoughts, perceptions, feelings, and dreams; and those items, which make up the content of his consciousness, are called 'ideas'. Animals other than men are not, he held, conscious in this crucial way. They cannot have any concept of an 'I' who thinks or, therefore, of the ideas an 'I' has. And so, though alive and active, not being conscious they are automata, activated entirely by causes operating on their bodies, reacting continuously to their environment. In the case of humans also, the environment acts on the body and so, through the medium of the senses, gives rise to some of our conscious ideas. Other ideas of which we are conscious are innate, among them the idea of God and the idea of the thinking 'I' itself. So men are self-knowing and self-motivating and, in exact proportion, free. In Descartes' view it followed that animals, though they react to stimuli in regular and predictable ways, cannot be properly said to feel. For to feel means to be conscious – that is, to have ideas and know that you have them.

Not surprisingly, Descartes got into terrible difficulties when he tried to explain how the body acted causally on the mind to produce ideas, given that he had distinguished body and mind into two totally distinct substances. Luckily, we need not concern ourselves with his attempts to extricate himself from this problem. What matters to us is that according to the Cartesian picture of man, the content of his consciousness was a collection of ideas, a mixture of thoughts, perceptions and emotions all related in the same way to himself. All were the 'property' of the man, who 'had' them in his mind.

Locke, an avowed empiricist, was critical of some aspects of Descartes' theory, especially that which held that we are born with innate ideas in the mind. But he took over without criticism the assumption that, for each of us, experience comes in the form of ideas which enter our consciousness and are available to each alone. Our primary knowledge is knowledge of our own experience. Locke and subsequent empiricists (like Descartes before them) believed that our knowledge of other people is essentially a matter of inference. We see and hear them, and this gives us ideas of them. But there is no guarantee that our ideas are true representations of how they really are. As for what goes on, if anything, in their minds, we can never know this. We infer that they feel pleasure and pain, that they think, calculate, love and hate, because they behave in ways similar to the way we behave when we do these things. We watch their outsides and guess what goes on within, by analogy with ourselves. But analogy can yield no more than probable conclusions. It remains logically possible that I am the only person who feels pain.

Pain has no special status in this kind of theory. Whether I say 'I see a red glow in the sky' or 'I dreamed last night that there was a camel in the garden' or 'I have toothache,' I am simply reporting an experience of my own. I am telling you my idea. It is more likely that you will report a private experience of a red glow at the same time as I do than that you will report a dream of the same kind or a parallel experience of toothache when I do, but there is no other difference between perceptions, remembered dreams, and pain sensations.

It eventually became clear that there was something wrong with such theories as Descartes' and Locke's, difficult though it is wholly to give them up (for there is almost no philosophical theory that does not reflect something that we are strongly inclined non-philosophically to believe). The wrongness can be seen in various ways.

In the first place, the concept of undifferentiated mental content, or ideas, proved incapable of standing up to investigation. What I 'have' when I look at a red glow is not the same sort of thing that I 'have' when I report my remembered dream or when I have toothache. Indeed, as we shall see, the notion that I 'have' anything, in the case of ordinary perception, is suspect.

Secondly, and more important, the nature of language has gradually come to be taken much more seriously by philosophers than it was in the seventeenth and eighteenth centuries. Descartes paid practically no attention to language at all. Locke believed that the words out of which language is made up are names for ideas. He recognized that this view gave rise to some difficulties, but did not realize quite how fatal the difficulties were.

In the first place, ideas are very numerous. Ideas were supposed, by both Descartes and Locke, to be the raw materials out of which all our experience is built. Now Locke suggests that it is because we would not be able to remember names for all our ideas that we lump them together. 'If it be looked on as an instance of a prodigious memory', he wrote, 'that some generals have been able to call every soldier in their army by his proper name, we may easily find a reason why men have never attempted to give a name to each sheep in their flock...much less to call every grain of sand that came their way by a peculiar name.'[1] And he goes on to tell us what he believes actually happens: in the case of young children,

> the ideas of the nurse and the mother are well framed in their minds; and, like pictures of them, there represent only those individuals, and the names 'nurse' and 'mama' the child uses determine themselves to those persons. Afterwards when time and a larger acquaintance has made them observe that there are a great many other things in the world that...resemble their father and mother...they frame an idea which they find those many particulars partake in, and to that they give...the name 'man'.

Well, whatever you may think of this as a bit of observation, as an explanation of the beginnings of language, it simply won't do.

And there is a still more serious difficulty. Ideas, as we have seen, are not only *numerous*, but *private*; and thus it is totally mysterious how the name I give my idea, which I call 'toothache', can become intelligible to you, equipped as you are only with *your* private store of ideas. If I have in the toy cupboard a doll called Biddy whom you have never seen and you have one called Charlie whom I have never seen, we may refer as long as we like to Biddy and Charlie, but if that is our whole vocabulary, we shall fail to inform each other of anything, even that it is our dolls we are talking about.

Locke partly realizes this. He says:

> Though words as they are used by men can properly...signify nothing but the ideas that are in the mind of the speaker, yet they in their thoughts give them secret reference to two other things. First, they suppose their words to be marks of the ideas in the minds also of other men with whom they communicate. Secondly, because men would not be thought to talk barely of their own imaginations but of things as really they are, therefore they... suppose their words to stand also for the reality of things.[2]

Secretly, then, people make language work by referring it to shared experiences and referring it to the outside world. But Locke does not tell us whether men are entitled to make these hidden hypotheses or why they make them except to avoid seeming too egocentric and fanciful. But of course, language-users are entitled so to refer their words outside themselves; nor need they make any secret of it. Increasingly, philosophers have become able to recognize that language is *first and foremost* a means of communication with other people; that it is *primarily* concerned not with private experiences but with public objects; that it is *originally* general and classificatory, enabling us to talk about things not in their presence, but in their absence. Only later, and with difficulty, do we attempt to get this public language to cover our unique and private experiences. A wholly private language is logically impossible.

We have come to understand, then, that Locke got things the wrong way round. Moreover, we have learned that language is used not only to inform but also to express. It may therefore be viewed as a part of the general pattern of expressive behaviour. If I stub my toe, I may jump about and swear. The swear-words do not name my private feelings. They call attention to them in a totally different way.

Considerations such as these led philosophers to try to think of consciousness without reference to private content, or 'ideas'. A variety of forms of behaviourism came into being.

In this country, Gilbert Ryle in the *Concept of Mind* (1949) and Ludwig Wittgenstein in the *Philosophical Investigations* (1953) tried to turn our attention away from 'inner experience', the private content of consciousness for ever inaccessible to anyone except its 'owner'.

Our concept of pain, for example, must, so Wittgenstein argued, derive from pain behaviour, our own and other people's equally. For only in this way could we ever have learned to understand the language of pain. As a child, you fall over and cut your knee and cry, and someone comforts you and says it will soon stop hurting and soon be better. This is how you learn what 'hurting' means, how it relates to the graze on your knee, and that it is universally thought to be nasty – something from which you must and will *recover*. When someone else is in pain, you see him, and simply understand him as someone in pain. All our perception involves interpretation. You don't, as Locke seemed to suppose, see a lot of green and brown things (have a lot of green and brown ideas) and, being too lazy or forgetful to name them all separately, roughly lump them together under the heading 'tree'. On the contrary, you see them immediately *as a tree*; or perhaps as an arbutus tree or as a good place to hide from your enemies. When you look at someone's face, you see his expression as happy or sad or agonized. You don't see that it has certain lines, and then infer the mood from the lines. We can, according to Wittgenstein, dispense with the argument from analogy. We see *directly* the pain of another. Pain means pain behaviour, and certain behaviour means pain. You can know that someone is in pain. He is groaning. You also know that you are in pain. You are groaning.

There is great attraction in this theory. It seems to eliminate what Ayer calls the 'egocentric predicament'. The word 'hurt', the word 'pain', and so on are shown to apply in the same sense to everyone. The word 'pain' means exactly the same whether I say 'You are in pain,' 'I am in pain', or 'Pussy is in pain.' And this is what we demand. The *teaching* of pain language suddenly presents no difficulty.

Yet there are obvious objections. Just as we want to be allowed to say that someone can see something without his necessarily reporting that he sees, so we also want to be allowed to say that someone may feel pain without reacting to it overtly. Suppose he is stoical and conceals his feelings? Suppose he has been injected with curare? And when we teach children the words 'pain', 'ache', 'hurt', even though we may take the opportunity offered by pain behaviour or visible damage to give the lesson, are we not manifestly teaching them to talk about their personal experiences? Are we not getting them to realize their inner life? We may agree with Wittgenstein that we can *know* that another person is in pain, and not merely guess or infer that he is; but when we have this knowledge, we know *what it is like for him*, within himself.

Thus, although all language is public language devised for communication and we can learn to use this public language about pain, yet there remains an irreducibly 'inner' element in pain. And this inner element is *what pain is like* (or, to use a less clear, jargon phrase, 'the affective aspect' of pain). There is no such thing as pain without the thought, however inarticulately expressed, that if things go on like this (or, in the case of sharp pains, if this happens again), it will be unbearable. And emotional reactions, however clearly they may be expressed in our faces or by our words, are inevitably *felt by the individual person*. Indeed, that people are treated as individuals, worthy to be considered separately, is largely to be explained by our knowledge that each is capable of feeling. Moreover, we know that feelings are 'private', because of the great difficulty we experience in expressing them articulately or describing them intelligibly.

It is because of the privacy of emotional experiences that there seems an element of mystery about how children learn words to express it. Since there is an emotional content in the experience of pain, the mystery seems not to be completely dissolved by the idea of teaching through external pain experiences.

It is not easy to disentangle the emotional content or concomitant of pain from pain itself (and the difficulty is compounded if we think of pain not only in humans but in, for example, laboratory mice or lobsters boiled alive). What is 'physical', what 'mental' or 'psychological', about pain? Sorting out the issues here is made more complicated by the habitual pairing of 'pain' with 'pleasure' as its supposed opposite. They do not in fact fit exactly together, in that pleasure seems more centrally a psychological, or 'mental', phenomenon than pain. It is far easier to construct cases where what would normally give you pleasure does not do so, for vaious psychological reasons such as embarrassment or guilt, than it is to construct parallel cases for pain (though doubtless some exist). Moreover, saying that some purely 'mental' activity (such as solving a puzzle) gave me pleasure conveys no sense of metaphor. On the other hand, to say that failing to solve the puzzle was painful does appear to be metaphorical. In any case I propose to leave the question of distinguishing the 'mental' from the 'physical' element in pain, and proceed on the assumption that pain is an inner experience having a certain emotional quality. What are the implications of such an assumption?

We know that if an animal or an infant displays pain behaviour (*ex hypothesi* non-verbal), we can say truly 'He is in pain.' More than that, we know that the evidence on which our statement is based is not only the evidence of overt behaviour, but of certain neurophysiological happenings which, if we knew enough, we could describe in detail. This neurophysiological story is one that we believe *could* be told even if we can't tell it (and even if no one has yet got it quite right). What we can add to the story is that if the creature is a normal animal, he will be disliking what is happening to him. We may say, if we choose, that he is perceiving what is happening to him, but perceiving it in a particular way, *as nasty*. And what is happening is not simply nasty, but nasty *for him*. To put it another way, the pain is irreducibly his pain. He 'has' it.

If we want to teach a child the word 'camel', we may lead him to the place in the zoo where the camel is in his visual field and point and utter the word. That he can see the camel helps him to learn the word. Especially if we use, as we probably will, the indefinite article to introduce the word, saying 'That's a camel' the first time he sees it, he will grasp at once – whatever Locke may have suggested to the contrary – that the word 'camel' can be used for creatures other than the one immediately in front of him (it can even, he realizes, be used for pictures of camels). He understands, that is, now for the first time, that there is that kind of thing in the world. The camel in no sense has become his. It is irreducibly out there in the world for all to behold.

If, on the other hand, we are bent on teaching the infant who has a pain to speak and to use the peculiar language of pain, as well as the natural expression of it such as crying, we introduce words like 'hurt' or 'agony' and ascribe them to him, or, more likely and more significantly, to parts of his body. The sense in which he 'has' a knee or a finger becomes, then, the very same sense in which he 'has' the pain. The pain thus becomes something that is not simply nasty, but is nasty for him, because the injured knee or finger is his, and no one else's. And so, I suggest, he learns that just as his body is not my body, so the pain in his body is not mine or anyone else's, but his very own. And so it is horrible *for him*. It is remarkable how quickly children learn that things may in this way be nasty for other individuals (including, incorrectly, their own toys). If, in seeing, we were conscious of our eyes as, in falling over, we are conscious of our knees, I suppose there would be more temptation to think of the seen camel as 'our' camel. But this is not how the nervous system works. The eyes and ears are not themselves normally objects of perception when we see and hear. They are, as it were, transparent media *through* which we receive impressions from objects other than themselves. The injured knee is not in this sense transparent. We feel pain not *through* our knee but *in* it.

And so it seems to me that we experience pain essentially as something that cannot be described as either wholly physical or wholly mental. We think of it as a physical phenomenon because it is *in* our bodies; and so it is our own. But because of its emotional content, as well as its happening in our bodies, it belongs to us in another way, just as our anger or fear or excitement do. It is part of our psychic experience, as well.

I turn now to my second example, which is in some ways more complex. Children can, as we have seen, learn the language of pain from situations in which we (non-children) know that they are (must be) in pain. They can learn it, that is, from their own circumstances and behaviour. We, the grown-ups, can help them translate their crying into words, which become the language in which they learn to talk about pain. They learn to communicate specifically about where the pain is (and with more sophistication what it is like), rather than relying simply on non-verbal communication that something horrible is happening.

If we consider my second example, dreams, on the other hand, we may be equally certain that there is, here, an inner experience as well as a frequent attempt to communicate it. But to attempt to analyse how communication is possible is more perplexing. The difficulty lies in the fact that, leaving aside any experimental or scientific observations of rapid eye movements in sleep (or any other records that may become available of sleep behaviour apparently correlated with dreaming), the only way we know that someone has had a dream is that they tell us. But they do not, obviously, tell us at the time, as they may learn to tell us at the time that they are in pain. They tell us afterwards.

Daniel Dennett in his essay entitled 'Are Dreams Experiences?' discusses this problem in detail.[3] His essay is in part a critique of a book by Norman Malcolm, who attempts a thoroughgoing behaviourist analysis of dreaming (an analysis even more bizarre than the behaviourist demolition of pain as an inner experience).[4] Malcolm asserts that it is the very same thing for a dreamer to be under the impression that he had a dream and to have had a dream. There is no criterion, that is to say, by which one can judge the truthfulness of a dreamer (or rather a waker) asserting that he dreamed such and such. To try to find such a criterion would be to introduce a wholly new way of distinguishing truth from falsehood. What the subject of the supposed experience says about his experience has therefore no special status as revealing the truth. He may be convinced that he did dream, but all we know is that he has such a conviction. Apart from the vague correlations of eye movements to dreams, we have nothing else to go on ourselves. So, as Dennett puts it, 'The subjective realm floats out of ken altogether.'[5]

Arguments such as those of Malcolm, themselves derived directly from Wittgenstein (cf. *Philosophical Investigations*, paras 222–3), seem to gain credibility from the use of dream confessions by psychoanalysis. Malcolm quotes with approval the words of Freud in *A General Introduction to Psychoanalysis*: 'Any disadvantage resulting from the uncertain recollection of dreams may be remedied by deciding that exactly what the dreamer tells us is to count as the dream.'⁶ 'Uncertainty of recollection' is in fact a misnomer. In ordinary life we may, in attempting to recall an incident, doubt whether a man's tie was red or green. It was *either* red *or* green – or indeed some other colour, in point of fact. We cannot remember which it was. In the case of dreams, however, we are told to act on the presumption that there was no point of fact. When I tell my dream, I am not recalling well or ill; I am asserting only that it is as if I recall, and that my quasi-recollection sometimes falters.

It is my contention that one must defend, and reassert, the common-sense view of dreaming as an inner experience; otherwise the whole language of the dream will become hopelessly confused. If there is anything of which we would in common-sense terms be prepared to assert that it is an experience which is private, mental, and not easily communicated to others, it is the dream. But this does not, in my view, make dreams totally mysterious or totally without parallel in our experience. We should try to place dreaming in a continuum of mental experiences. We may start from perfectly ordinary thoughts that we may have, but may not express at the time, about some object in the past (or at any rate an object not immediately within our sensory field). Let us take the case where I think about one of my children, that I promised to ring him up this evening. Then let us suppose that I do more than just recall this promise, but begin to speculate on what he might want to tell me, what advice I should give him, what my reaction will be if the news is bad (that one of his children is ill, or that he has been declared bankrupt), what it will be if the news is good (that his wife is going to have another child, or that he has won the football pools). Now let us suppose that running over my hypothetical conversations with him in my mind, I become a bit sleepy and stop noticing my immediate surroundings (that the light is getting dim, the fire burning low), and my imagined conversations become more real to me than my own increasing cold or inability to see. Finally, let us suppose that I go completely to sleep, and become altogether unaware of my immediate surroundings. Now my thoughts, if they continue, will become dreams rather than day-dreams. And if I recall them when I wake up, I will say that I dreamed; but I may be quite unsure where the thought ended and the day-dream began or where the day-dream ended and the dream began. This continuum seems to be absolutely internally coherent, without any major discontinuities. There is no immense gulf between thinking and day-dreaming or between day-dreaming and dreaming.

If this is the case, then, if we are prepared to say that thinking about something in its absence is part of our inner experience, then we may say the same about dreaming. Dreaming is a kind of thinking in absence, with the aid of images. Whether we say that both are 'experiences' or that neither are seems to me not to be a matter of great importance. The important fact is that both are inner, in the sense that in order to communicate them to someone else we cannot simply point to a public object; nor can we even point to a part of the body where the experience is located (as I may point to my head if I have a headache). We simply have to ascribe to ourselves the image or the thought and try to find words to explain what the thought was about.

And this leads to the crucial difference between the kind of inner experience, if so we wish to designate it, that has as examples thinking, wondering, worrying, asking, picturing, and dreaming, and the inner experience of pain. The former group of mental goings-on are all necessarily directed to an object (not necessarily an *external* object: I may worry about my own thoughts or feelings, wonder whether the emotion I am experiencing is jealousy, wonder why I am obsessed with a particular melody or the tones of someone's voice and so forth). Nevertheless, my thoughts, wonderings, and imaginings are of their very nature thoughts, wonderings, and imaginings about something: they are directed towards an object. That being so, in attempting to communicate them to someone else, it is necessary to refer to that object in telling him what I am thinking about. To take a simple case: I think about a chair I have just bought at an auction. I have not yet collected the chair from the auction room, so I cannot show it to you. All I can do is describe it. We have, being language-users, developed a vocabulary and a syntax by means of which we can talk to people intelligibly about things which neither of us can see or feel at the present moment. If we move along the continuum (which we could call the 'continuum of imagination'), I can tell you my image of the chair. I can describe my day-dreams about the chair (that one day I shall get it covered in cloth of gold and have it in my study) or, finally, my dream about the chair, the dream I had as I slept in the train on the way back from the auction. In all these cases I must use the words to describe the chair which I would use if I had to describe it when it was before my eyes (let us say, I am still looking at it and I ring you up to ask whether you would advise me to buy it). But that I use the words which fit the chair as a physical object present to me when it is not present to me does not entail that somehow, mysteriously, the chair *is* present to me when I merely think about it. Indeed, as I have suggested, the whole point of language is that it should be capable of being applied (the very same language) to things whether they are present or absent. There is, in my view, nothing more mysterious in my describing the chair as I dreamed it than in my describing it as I now see it (but you don't) or as it now fills my thoughts when neither I nor anyone else can see it. We can say that dreams are experiences if we want to; but if we do, we shall also have to say that day-dreams are experiences and that silent thoughts are experiences. What we *must* say is that these thoughts, day-dreams, and dreams are 'inner'. They are mine. I 'have' them. It always requires an effort (the effort of choosing the appropriate words) to convey them to, or share them with, someone else.

The difference – and it is an important one – between 'my' pain and 'my' thought or imaging or dream is that I may feel more confident in the case of the latter of 'my' possessions that I have succeeded in sharing them with you. I may be content to say that you now have the same thought as I do about my chair. In the case of 'my' pain, since it is mine partly in virtue of its being in my body not yours, I may be more inclined to say that you *sympathize* with me in my pain than that you *share* it (note that when pain is used metaphorically, to mean 'sorrow' or 'distress', I may say that you share it when I have explained to you what caused it).

Wittgenstein remarked that an inner process always needed an outward criterion. Those who took this remark too seriously were inclined to say that pain was nothing but, or no different from, pain behaviour, the outward criterion. But since in the case of dreaming there was no related dream behaviour, dreams tended to drop out of existence altogether. If rapid eye movements were supposed to be the criterion of dreaming, then it became quite mysterious how one dream could be different from another. The outward criterion seemed incredibly schematic and crude compared with the infinite variety, subtlety, humour, or romance of a series of dreams which could be told. Yet, to identify the dream with the telling of the dream was to leave out of account the undoubted fact that the teller of the dream believed himself to be recalling something from his, albeit immediate, past. The language of dreams and the convention of telling them make no sense at all except in the wider context of talking about our thoughts or feelings, none of which can be ascertained except through the language we choose to use about them.

The concept common to my examples, of pain and of dreaming, is the concept of the person who 'has' the experiences, that is, of 'I'. It is here, I think, that, above all, philosophers have something to learn from child psychologists who have long studied the growing sense of identity that a child acquires, and acquires exactly alongside, and as part of, his acquisition of language. Competent language-users deploy the first-person singular pronoun of themselves as a way of referring to their own bodies. For example, if an undergraduate whom I do not know comes into my room and says, 'I'm James Smith,' he means to indicate to me that the tall person in jeans and a sweater is the bearer of the proper name 'James Smith'. I can see him (and he knows this) as a physical object, and he goes on to identify that physical object for my benefit so that on another occasion I can re-identify it. He then goes on to fill me in about some of James Smith's needs or aspirations. The use of 'I' for a physical object in the course of identifying it is central to its use. Each grown-up, competent physical human body has a unique knowledge of his body, how it is disposed, whether it is hot or cold, hungry or thirsty, whether a bit of it is in pain or uncomfortable, where roughly its feet and hands are in relation to its head. Each gets to know without thinking how tall or wide it is, whether it needs to duck to go under the beams or turn sideways to get past the chair (this is why swiftly growing adolescents are so clumsy: their knowledge keeps going out of date). This kind of knowledge is not articulated, but is possessed by the body itself through experience. The body may acquire similar knowledge about tools it habitually uses, which become virtually extensions of the body, such as crutches, cars, or violin bows. Other aspects of this collection of knowledge are of likes and dislikes, fears, wishes, projects, and capacities (though since these last refer to both the past and the future, the unspoken claims may be falsified, either because capacities change, or because circumstances in which the capacity could be exemplified are variable. I may feel confident that I can hole a twelve-inch putt, but have overlooked the borrow). Now James Smith, the undergraduate, carries all this knowledge about with him wherever he goes. He does not think about it most of the time, but he 'has' it, none the less. So when he introduces himself to me as James Smith, he introduces me to the body I can see (so that I will know what to call it next time), and, in so far as he wants to, he introduces me to the knowledge he has of himself, the baggage he carries around with him. As I share some of this knowledge, so I 'get to know' him. But I do not know what it is like to be him. He knows what it is like to be himself.

The notion of 'what it is like to be' such and such is important in the 'placing' of the concept of inner experience in our general beliefs about persons. It is also what seems to be the ultimate barrier against holding that a computer could be constructed to be exactly like a person, or to be a person. It is connected both with the idea of being alive and with finding things nice or nasty, and finally with using language.[7]

Daniel Dennett in his paper 'Toward a Cognitive Theory of Consciousness' wrote as follows:

Philosophers of mind have much to learn from cognitive psychology, but one of philosophy's favourite facets of mentality has received scant attention from cognitive psychologists, and that is consciousness itself: full-blown, inner-world, phenomenological consciousness. In fact if one looks in the obvious places...one finds not so much a lack of interest as a deliberate and adroit avoidance of the issue. I think I know why. Consciousness seems to be the last bastion of occult properties, epiphenomena, immeasurable subjective states – in short the one area of mind best left to philosophers who are welcome to it. Let them make fools of themselves trying to corral the quicksilver of 'phenomenology' into a respectable theory.[8]

The concept of inner experience is a crucial aspect, as Dennett suggests, of the idea of consciousness itself; and consciousness, in turn, is central to the notion of an individual 'I' (as Descartes discerned long ago). I do not believe that things have progressed much since Dennett wrote. But I do believe that psychologists and philosophers could co-operate to shed light if, together, they explored the origins of language in individual beginners in language-using. It is for this reason that I have been glad to talk to child psychologists, and look forward to hearing their side of the story.

# 15

# The Nature of Choice

Philosophers, since philosophy began, have concerned themselves with questions about human choice. In particular, they have been concerned with the question of free will. Do we make any real choices? Are we ever free to choose? Or is everything we do, however apparently freely chosen, really determined, either by the will of God (who knows what we will do before we do it, and therefore we *cannot* have any choice) or by the laws which govern the natural world (every event has a cause, and our choices are events like any other and are therefore caused, and inevitably follow from what went before)? Or are our choices determined specifically by our genetic or psychological make-up? Could we ever have done anything except what we did? Such were the questions which Milton's angels sat discussing in heaven and which philosophers have discussed from time immemorial.

We need not, here, concern ourselves with such lofty themes. Whatever the metaphysics of the matter, we all know more or less what counts as a choice. I want, it is true, to start with philosophy, but at a more lowly level. Philosophy indeed is not so pure and abstract as people used to think. Nowadays it is expected to have a practical side to it. I want to try to say something, first, about the nature of choice and those things which in quite everyday terms tend to inhibit our freedom, and then, to show how such inhibitions bear especially on the aged.

Let us start in proper philosophical style with Aristotle. Aristotle defined choice as a deliberative stretching out towards something that it is within our power to have or to do. This is, it seems to me, a very accurate definition. Nobody, as he says, deliberates about, and therefore nobody *chooses*, things that are completely beyond their control: no one could be said to choose to be immortal, much as they might wish to be so. Nobody chooses the weather, though they may choose different ways of protecting themselves from it. We do not choose to be human; this is just the way we were born. But we do choose our manner of being human. Equally important in his definition is the conjunction of deliberation and action, that 'stretching out' which is the first step towards *doing* something. Just acting by itself, without deliberation or thought, is not choice. If I clean my teeth before I go to bed every night, without thinking, I can hardly be said to choose each night to do so. It is just something I do, from habit. Once I may have made choices in this area, but no longer. Again, if I sit at home fantasizing about a holiday in the Bahamas, but know in my heart that I shall never go, and don't get as far as reaching for the telephone to book a ticket, or even walking to the travel agent to get some brochures, then I am not in the process of *choosing* so much as dreaming or pretending.

These distinctions, all of them implied in Aristotle's definition, are important. They distinguish real choice from other, related concepts. And Aristotle is quite right to be interested in the idea of choice. He is concerned, in the *Nicomachean Ethics*, with *goodness*.[1] And human goodness, he thinks, is a matter of having a particular kind of character, a disposition which determines choice. So what you are like, what sort of a person you are, shows in what you deliberately decide and choose to do. If you are a brave person, you will make brave choices which will result in brave actions. A coward may utter brave words and have brave longings, but these will not be brave choices. His actions will betray him.

Aristotle holds, then, that *what a person is like* is reflected in his choices; and he thinks that children do not, in the full sense, make choices at all, because their characters are only just forming and their deliberations are usually, or often, not their own, but somebody else's. As they grow up, so, more and more, they make choices for themselves – true choices. He does not say anything about the other end of the age scale. On the whole, the Greeks assumed that the older you were, the more worthy of respect, and the more deliberate and firm and well based would be your choices. You choose, as you get older, in a manner that is consistent with your fixed and settled character; and your deliberations are now based on experience, and therefore are more sensible and better fitted to serve as a model for the young. It is a rosy picture of old age. And it is a picture to which I believe we would do well to attend. I shall return to it in due course.

But it is easy to see that one of the problems about using Aristotle's concept of choice, when we are thinking about the old, is that it raises the question of *power*. To choose is to go for something that *it is within your power to do*. When I am 20, I can choose to walk with all my luggage the two miles from the station and save my money. For it is well within my power to carry my luggage so far. When I am 60, with luck, I can still do this, but it may be a struggle. When I am 90, I probably can't do it at all. I *have* to take a bus or a taxi.

From this single example we can see that what 'it is within our power to have or to do' cannot be taken in any absolute sense. It is relative to us. Everyone knows that money means power (even if it is thought not to mean happiness). If I am rich, I can choose to take a taxi rather than a bus, and my choices are thereby extended. Someone who is 90 and rich can make more true choices than someone who is 90 and poor. Though Aristotle doesn't say so, it is obvious that someone who is both old and poor makes *fewer* choices than other men, however admirable and however consistent with his character these choices may be, because there are fewer things that it is within that person's power to do or have.

But before we pursue this point, I want to call your attention to some of the other things, besides age and poverty, which may inhibit choices. And I shall turn for help to a different philosopher, Jean-Paul Sartre, for my examples. For the first years of his philosophical life Sartre, as everyone knows, was an existentialist. His great existentialist work *Being and Nothingness* was written in 1943 during World War II. Its central theme was that man is free. Whatever people do or become, they have chosen to do or become this. Even if circumstances seem to force a man to do certain specific things or to endure them, he still chooses *how* to do or endure these things, how to 'live them' as Sartre rather oddly puts it. We do not start with fixed characters; we create ourselves by our choices as we go along.

It is easy to see why existentialism was so extremely popular in Paris under the occupation. Like Christianity in the days of the Roman Empire, its message was one of hope and self-confidence; even a slave was free to serve God. In Paris in the 1940s, even a prisoner of war was all the time making choices. He was the hero of his own story; he was making up his own character as he went along. The most uneventful and restricted life could be seen, with the eyes of an existentialist, as full of significance. You spend your life propping up the bar, talking to your friends; this is the character you have decided to be. And if, tomorrow, you choose to be different, that too would be open to you.

But Sartre held that, though the existence of such freedom is a fundamental fact about the world, it is not a fact which people much relish. They are afraid of total freedom. They prefer to feel themselves bound. It gives them security. If you are free to choose, and do choose, there is no one but yourself to blame if you choose badly. The existentialist hero is entirely on his own. So just as, according to Aristotle, children do not make real choices and are therefore not held wholly responsible for what they do, so in Sartre's view most people prefer for themselves the childhood condition. They like to be able to say that they *had* to do this or that, they *couldn't help it*, that the situation *demanded* it, or that it was a matter of duty. The favourite existentialist example here is of Abraham preparing to sacrifice Isaac, his only son, saying that it was the command of God that he was obeying. But, Sartre argues, it was Abraham, and he alone, who decided that the command came from God and had to be obeyed. It was his own interpretation of the voice. He cannot shuffle off responsibility, even onto God. The pretence that you are bound when you are really free is what Sartre calls 'bad faith'; and we are most of us in bad faith much of the time.

One kind of bad faith, then, is that in which, in a conventional or ordinary situation, someone says that he is obliged to do this or that – that the path of duty lies clear before him. To believe that such felt obligations are real forces which truly bind a man is to succumb, in Sartre's view, to what he calls 'the spirit of seriousness', the belief that there are absolute values in the world, things which are in themselves to be described as right or wrong, indisputably. In fact, Sartre argues, values are simply imposed on the world by humans themselves. They are not part of it. Such a view is, of course, by no means peculiar to existentialism, and it need not concern us further.

A more interesting source of bad faith for us to consider is that which is wished onto us from outside: the consequence, that is, not of our own theories about the world, but of other people's beliefs about us. We have seen how the existentialist hero, in part at least, is supposed to create his own character, to be responsible for his own role in life. But Sartre was well aware that most people are not clear-headed or self-confident enough to do any such thing. Most people, instead of choosing a role for themselves and acting it out, have a role imposed on them by others, and play the part assigned not by themselves but by the world at large. 'The Other' for Sartre is the enemy; it is the other, other people, who try to enclose each of us in chains, chains which we are all too ready to accept. The best-known example that Sartre gives of such role-playing in *Being and Nothingness* is the example of the waiter. Here is his description:

> Let us consider this waiter in the café. His movement is quick and forward, a little too precise, a little too rapid…. He bends forward a little too eagerly; his voice, his eyes, express an interest a little too solicitous for the order of his customer…. There he returns trying to imitate in his walk the inflexible stiffness of an auto-maton, while carrying his tray with the recklessness of a tightrope walker, putting it in a perpetual unstable equilibrium which he perpetually re-establishes by a light movement of the arm and hand…. But what is he playing? We need not watch long before we can explain it. He is playing at being a waiter in a café…. The waiter in the café plays with his condition in order to realise it. This obligation is not different from that which is imposed on all tradesmen. Their condition is wholly one of ceremony. The public demands of them that they realise it as a ceremony. There is the dance of the grocer, the tailor, the auctioneer, by which they try to persuade their clientele that they are nothing but a grocer, a tailor, an auctioneer. A grocer who dreams is offensive to the buyer because such a grocer is not wholly a grocer. Society demands that he limit himself to his function as a grocer, just as a soldier at attention makes himself into a soldier-thing with a direct regard which does not see at all, which is no longer meant to see, since it is the rule and not the interest of the moment which

determines the point he must fix his eyes on. There are indeed many precautions to imprison a man in what he is, as if we lived in perpetual fear that he might escape from it, that he might break away, and suddenly elude his condition.[2]

Here, Sartre is mostly thinking of what is demanded of a man by those who see him from the outside, and who see him in only one dimension, fulfilling a specific and quite precise role in someone else's life. It is extremely familiar that we make such demands on people. Who would want a dentist who complains about his health while filling their teeth or a marriage guidance counsellor who is known to have problems of his own? Even children prefer that their teachers just *teach* (and often presume that they think about their pupils day and night) rather than worry about their mortgages or the problems of their aged parents.

However, as Sartre goes on to suggest, parallel with these demands from the outside, there may be internal perceptions of role which may lead a man into bad faith or be the expression of it. He says:

> From within, the waiter in the café cannot be immediately a café waiter in the sense that this inkwell *is* an inkwell or the glass is a glass.... He knows well what his condition means. The obligation of getting up at five o'clock, of sweeping the floor of the shop before the restaurant opens, of starting the coffee pot going. He knows, equally, the rights which it allows. But all these concepts, all these judgments refer to the transcendent. It is a matter of abstract possibilities, of rights and duties conferred on 'a person with rights'. And it is precisely this person who I have to be and am not.... He is a representation for others and for myself. If I only represent him, I *am* not he. I *am* not he; I can only play at being he.

And so, when there is pressure from outside that someone should fulfil a certain function, play a role which society assigns to him, there is also pressure from within, Sartre argues, that this role should be the whole of life. The role-player, therefore, pretends to himself that it is inevitable that he should do the things belonging to his role. He *must*, if he is Sartre's waiter, get up at five and perform his other duties. He forgets – and indeed may deliberately push to the back of his consciousness – the fact that he *need not* be a waiter, and that it is he himself who confers value on being punctual and doing his job well. The waiter, once again, gives in to what Sartre calls the 'spirit of seriousness'. He forgets that values are not features of the world, but are imposed on it, given to it, by us.

The thought of someone else's total freedom, however, is obviously disconcerting. If we go to a restaurant, we want to be able to rely on the waiter to serve us. If we have a wife, we want to be able to rely on her still being there when we come home in the evening. Our doctor *must* treat us...and so on.

Obligations, as the very word tells us, tie things up, bind them, make them predictable and reliable. In casting other people in roles, then, with functions, duties, kinds of behaviour attached, we render these people and the world predictable. It is as if we are turning people into objects which obey natural laws. It would disconcert us hopelessly if stones began to float or eggs had shells so hard that we couldn't crack them to make omelettes. We need things to obey laws, because we want to *use* them. So we need other people to be as like things as possible, for our own uses. A truly free 'other' person is a threat to the orderliness of life. The more another person is seen to have the power to choose, the more *my* power is diminished.

On this existentialist theory of personal relations, there is a perpetual conflict between your view of yourself from within and my view of you from without. You think that you are late for work today because of a particular set of accidents: there was a power cut that delayed the train; your watch stopped; the telephone went just as you were leaving the house. You know that you *would* have been on time if all these things hadn't happened. I, on the other hand, simply know that you are an unpunctual person. It is your character, a fixed immutable fact about you. Sartre presents us with just such a chilling little dialogue. One person says, 'I will be on time tomorrow. I swear it.' The other says, 'It may be so. I should like to believe you.' But he knows that you won't, just as he knows that sparks fly upwards.[3]

It is clear, then, that one of the major factors which can inhibit our freedom and diminish our power to choose is not age or poverty, but simply the role bestowed on us by other people who wish us, puppet-like, to play the scene their way. You have got married and had a child. Very well, you are a wife and mother. You know the lines. You have to say them. You are a grand-mother. You are a pensioner. Again, you know the lines. Other people have said them before you; now it is your turn. It would be outrageous if you refused to play. You cannot choose. You *must* do the things that old people do. Your duty is plain. Where would we all be if old people became unpredictable, if they refused to conform to type?

I believe that the old very often feel that they are subject to this kind of manipulation, being given a role which has nothing to do with them as they really are, being seen as something quite alien from themselves – still, as they would like to believe, real people in the real world.

Ronald Blythe in *The View in Winter* writes thus:

> One of the fearful developments in the consciousness of old people is that in the eyes of society they have become another species. Ironically an intensive caring and concern for their welfare is frequently more likely to suggest this relegation than indifference and neglect. The growing bureaucracy, amateur and professional, voluntary and state, for dealing with geriatrics makes some old folks feel that they no longer belong to the human race. They want to tell these efficient planners who appear to be corralling them off from other generations who they really are, they are people not things.[4]

Ronald Blythe quotes an old schoolmaster of 84 who uses some entirely Sartrean expressions: 'Old age doesn't mean that one is entirely old, *all old*. It is complicated by the retention of a lot of one's youth in an old body. I tend to look upon other old men as *old men* and not include myself.... What is generally assumed to have happened to a man in his eighties has not happened to me. The generalisations that go with my age don't apply.'[5] And this highly articulate old man goes on to regret that, though the young are always going on about being young, it is, as he says 'not permissible' for the old to talk about the reality of old age, what it is actually like. They are relegated, and have to conform. We are disconcerted if we are not allowed to be sorry for them. Their situation is very much like that of the physically or mentally handicapped, who are regarded as essentially either brave or tragic, characteristics which can so dominate our perception of them that we cease to remember that they may also be funny, clever, boring, vindictive, generous, mean – that a vast range of characters may be theirs. In taking away their characters, we take away their true choices, the Aristotelian choice which arises out of character and expresses it. We smooth them off so that they fit the categories we have prepared for them. They become the puppet victims of our clichés.

If I may, I would like at this stage to make a somewhat feminist point. It is this: I believe that the ossification in a role, which I have tried to describe, the fixing by what Sartre calls the 'look of the other', starts earlier and is more destructive for women than for men. The reason is easy to see. It is because women are more frequently relegated to a uniform, functional role early in their lives, from the very beginning of their lives even, than men are. Their role is to be 'attractive'. Being attractive is supposed to entail being young, and so once they are no longer young, they have no function left. You may think this is a gross exaggeration, and of course I am not saying that everyone feels this way about women, or that all women think their own role must be to attract. Nevertheless, where there is a stereotype which is totally accepted commercially and in romantic fiction and is even embedded in language as this stereotype is, it is hard for anyone to stand completely outside its influence.

This sort of attitude to women is part of the framework of ordinary society: the whole concept of the pin-up; the fact that the expression 'old woman' has a pejorative sense, when used metaphorically (there is, as far as I know, no such metaphorical use of 'old man'); the insistence in literature, as well as in advertisements, that when a woman 'loses her looks' she is a pitiable object – such things may not bear much relation to reality if we look at reality analytically, but they are all around us, and very hard to reject. And if women themselves do not reject such a stereotype, as they for the most part do not, it necessarily leads them to have a gloomy and negative picture of themselves, not merely in old age, but in middle age as well. They may try to look younger than they are, may try to conceal their age (all the jokes about age-concealment refer to women, not men); and when such things are no longer possible or are too much trouble, they may simply give up, and regard themselves self-pityingly as out of the competition, left behind, uninteresting, and without value.

To put it at its most practical, it seems to me a *commercial* waste to treat women in this way. There is probably a larger number of women over fifty than any other class of persons alive in the Western world. It would make good sense to treat them as an intelligent critical *market* and to present them with choices, not as a despised subclass, 'the elderly', but simply as people who have had time to develop mature tastes and can make informed decisions. Middle-aged – even old – men are not so down-graded by advertisers and sales people. It is assumed that middle-aged men are successful, powerful, rich, able to buy better cars, better shaving brushes, better shoes and luggage and shirts, than when they were in their twenties. Not so women. If there are ever women with these dashing older men in the advertisements, they are young things. For elderly women, nothing is on offer except cosmetics to hide the wrinkles and chair-lifts to help them up to their solitary bedrooms.

However, it could be argued that, in the past, though women were relegated to nothingness in middle age, men followed them quite soon, when it came to retirement. The stereotype woman, after all, didn't retire; she just kept on doing the housework as before. The nothing-man of retirement was depicted a long time ago by Charles Lamb in the 'Superannuated Man': 'I am no longer clerk to the Firm of etc. I am retired Leisure. I am to be met with in trim gardens. I am already come to be known by my vacant face and tireless gesture, perambulating at no fixed pace nor with any settled purpose. I walk about, not to and from.'[6] The image of the retired man with time and ability enough to make choices, but incapable of real choosing in the Aristotelian sense because he has nothing to deliberate *about*, nothing that he actually wants to stretch out towards, is familiar enough.

But perhaps here lies the greatest hope for the future. For if old age is to improve, we have got to try to change the stereotypes, remake the moulds into which we are accustomed to force people. The increase in general unemployment should turn our minds not to lamentations about the plight of the young (or for that matter, of the old) who cannot get work, but to a much more radical rethinking of working hours and working conditions. We should think far harder about part-time or shared work and about the intermingling of work at home with work outside the home. This, incidentally, would have a radical effect on family life itself. If it ceases to be presumed that the young, and especially young men, would be working outside the home; if it was just as likely that women and the old would be working partly at home and partly outside; it would follow necessarily that a new range of choices of activity would arise.

If this happened, the great gulf between pre-60 and post-60, the non-old and the old, would perhaps begin to be bridged. It would be a matter of long habit to decide how to fill your life, what useful or satisfying things to make or do, how literally or metaphorically best and most economically to cultivate your garden. The transition to old age would thus be eased, and communication between young and old thereby made more satisfactory. There would be less temptation to treat the old as a race apart, as manipulable objects, since everyone would to a certain extent be in the self-same boat.

Of course, there will be times when old people are genuinely unable to choose; when either they can no longer deliberate or there is nothing that they want or there is nothing that lies within their power to have or do. But I suspect that, if we did not relegate the old to powerlessness in order the better to manage them; if we thought of them in a new role, as among the daily useful contributors to a new pattern of life, as much able to do some things for us as we are able to do some things for them; if we didn't freeze them into immobility and the acceptance of the image of helplessness, we might find, not only that the cases where we had to choose *for* them were fewer, but that the choices they made for themselves were more worthy of respect. We might come at last to something more like the Greek view of the old. It is *sad* to be old, not young, it is true; but the compensation of old age is the respect you have earned. And the choices the old could make, though they might not always be altogether convenient to the non-old or exactly what would have been chosen *for* them, might turn out to be more sensible than we are now inclined to suppose. We cannot, of course, overlook the effects of weakness or poverty in restricting choices. But we can do something about those other inhibitors of choice, the roles we arrange for people to fill. Let us at least try to change the stereotypes, and see what happens.

# Notes

## Chapter 1 Man and Other Animals

1 All quotations from the Bible are from the Authorized Version.
2 Peter Singer (ed.), *In Defence of Animals* (Blackwell, Oxford, 1985), pp. 6–10.
3 Jeremy Bentham, *Introduction to the Principles of Morals and Legislation*, ed. J. H. Burns and H. L. A. Hart (London, 1970), ch. 17, sec. 1, note, p. 282.
4 Singer, *In Defence of Animals*, p. 8.
5 John Locke, *Essay Concerning Human Understanding* (1688), ed. P. Middich (Oxford University Press, Oxford, 1975), Bk II, ch. 11.
6 R. G. Frey, *Rights, Killing, and Suffering* (Blackwell, Oxford, 1983), p. 31.
7 Peter Singer, *Practical Ethics* (Cambridge University Press, Cambridge, 1979).
8 G. J. Warnock, *The Object of Morality* (Methuen, London, 1971), p. 151.

## Chapter 2 Man's Duty to his Own Species

1 Mary Midgley, *Beast and Man: The Roots of Human Nature* (Harvester Press, Brighton, 1978), pp. 222–3.
2 J. S. Mill, *A System of Logic*, ed. J. M. Robson (Routledge and Kegan Paul, Toronto, 1973), Bk III, ch. 5, n. 51.
3 Helga Kuhse and Peter Singer, *Should the Baby Live* (Oxford University Press, Oxford, 1985), p. 190.
4 Ibid., p. 189.
5 Jeff Lyons, *Playing God in the Nursery* (W. W. Norton & Co., New York, 1985), p. 210.

## Chapter 3    The Human and his World

1    Immanuel Kant, *Fundamental Principles of the Metaphysics of Ethics* (1785), trans. T. Abbott (Longman Green, London, 1929), *passim.*
2    William Wordsworth, *The Prelude*, Bk XIV, Conclusion, in *The Poetical Works of William Wordsworth*, ed. L. de Selincourt (Oxford University Press, Oxford, 1952).
3    William Blake, *The Book of Thel*, pp. 69–70, 72–4, 88–96, in *The Poetical Works of William Blake*, ed. John Simpson (Oxford University Press, Oxford, 1913).
4    D. Parfit, *Reasons and Persons* (Oxford University Press, Oxford, 1984), p. 357.

## Chapter 4    The Human Genome Project: Ethics and the Law

1    Human Genetic Information, Science, Law & Ethics. Ciba Foundation Symposium (John Wiley & Sons, New York, 1990), p. 167.

## Chapter 5    The Good of the Child

1    *Convention on the Rights of the Child.* Adopted by the United Nations General Assembly, 20 November 1989; opened for signature 26 January 1990; entered into force September 1990.
2    H. L. A. Hart, 'Are there any Natural Rights?' *Philosophical Review*, 64 (1955), pp. 175–91.
3    *Children First*, July 1989.
4    R. Snowden and G. D. Mitchell, *The Artificial Family* (George Allen and Unwin, London, 1981).
5    *Children First*, March 1989.

## Chapter 6    Towards a Moral Consensus

1    *Report of the Committee on Homosexual Offences and Prostitution*, Cmd. 247 (HMSO, London, 1957).
2    P. Devlin, *The Enforcement of Morals* (Oxford University Press, Oxford, 1965).
3    H. L. A. Hart, *Law, Liberty and Morality* (Oxford University Press, Oxford, 1963).

4   Jeremy Bentham, *An Introduction to the Principles of Morals and Legislation*, ed. J. H. Burns and H. L. A. Hart (London, 1970), ch. 1, para. 7, p. 13.
5   Immanuel Kant, *The Fundamental Principles of the Metaphysics of Ethics*, tr. T. Abbott (Longman Green, London, 1929), *passim*.
6   J. S. Mill, *Utilitarianism*. Fontana Philosophy Series. (Collins, London, 1962), pp. 276–7.
7   David Hume, *Treatise of Human Nature*, ed. L. A. Selby-Bigge (Oxford University Press, Oxford, 1969), Bk III, Pt 1, sec. 2.
8   See e.g. Jane Austen, *Mansfield Park*, ch. 20 and 23.
9   S. Hampshire, *Morality and Conflict* (Blackwell, Oxford, 1983), pp. 140ff.

## Chapter 7   Honesty and Cynicism

1   *The Times*, 26 April 1988, p. 1.
2   *The Times*, 31 July 1988, p. 16.
3   *The Times*, 7 August 1988, p. 3.

## Chapter 8   Who Sets the Standards?

1   Asa Briggs, in Richard Hoggart (ed.), *The Future of Broadcasting* (Macmillan, London, 1982), p. 21; emphasis original.
2   Mary Warnock, *Universities: Knowing our Minds* (Chatto and Windus, London, 1989), p. 41.

## Chapter 10   Education for Pleasure

1   *Teaching Language and Communication to the Mentally Handicapped*. Schools Council Curriculum Bulletin no. 8, by Ken Leeming, Will Swann, Judith Loupe, and Peter Mittler (Methuen, London, 1979).
2   J. S. Mill, *Autobiography* (Longman, London, 1873), pp. 145 and 148.
3   *Children and their Primary Schools*. The Plowden Report (HMSO, London, 1967).
4   J. S. Mill, *Utilitarianism*. Fontana Philosophy Series (Collins, London, 1962), p. 259.

## *Chapter 11   Education with a Moral*

1  Isaiah Berlin, *The Crooked Timber of Humanity* (John Murray, London, 1990), p. 19.
2  Ibid., p. 49.
3  Gilbert Ryle, 'Can Virtue be Taught?', in *Education and the Development of Reason*, ed. R. F. Dearden, P. H. Hirst, and R. H. Peters (Routledge and Kegan Paul, London, 1972).

## *Chapter 12   Religious Imagination*

1  J.-P. Sartre, *The Psychology of the Imagination* (Methuen, London, 1977), pp. 207–20.
2  S. T. Coleridge, *The Statesman's Manual* (1816), in *The Collected Works of S. T. Coleridge*, vol. 6, ed. R. J. White (Bollingen Series, Routledge and Kegan Paul and Princeton University Press, 1972), p. 69.
3  *The Letters of John Keats*, ed. M. Forman (Oxford University Press, Oxford, 1935), p. 68.
4  C. C. Clarke, *The Romantic Paradox: An Essay on the Poetry of Wordsworth* (Routledge and Kegan Paul, London, 1962), pp. 40–1.
5  Wordsworth, *The Prelude*, Bk XIV, in *The Poetical Works of William Wordsworth*, ed. L. de Selincourt (Oxford University Press, Oxford, 1952).
6  Michael Paffard, *Inglorious Wordsworths* (Hodder & Stoughton, London, 1973).
7  Michael Paffard, *The Unattended Moment* (SCM Press, London, 1976).
8  Paffard, *Inglorious Wordsworths*, p. 135.
9  Paffard, *Unattended Moment*, p. 38.
10  Ivy Compton Burnett, *The Present and the Past* (Gollancz, London, 1953), p. 9.
11  Coleridge, *Dejection: An Ode*, in *Coleridge's Poems*, ed. E. H. Coleridge (Oxford University Press, Oxford, 1912), p. 362.
12  C. S. Lewis, 'On Stories', in *Of This and Other Worlds* (Collins, London, 1984), p. 31.
13  C. S. Lewis, *Surprised by Joy* (Fontana, London, 1958), p. 188.
14  Søren Kierkegaard, *Philosophical Fragments* (Princeton University Press, Princeton, 1936), p. 130.
15  D. E. Nineham, *Explorations in Theology* (SCM Press, London, 1977), p. 85.

16  Immanuel Kant, *Critique of Judgement*, tr. J. Meredith (Oxford University Press, Oxford, 1952), Pt II, p. 130.
17  Nineham, *Explorations in Theology*, p. 4.
18  Kant, *Critique of Judgement*, Pt I, p. 221.

## Chapter 13   Personal Continuity

1  H. Bergson, *Matter and Memory*, tr. N. M. Paul and W. S. Palmer (Sonnenschein, London, 1911).
2  John Locke, *Essay Concerning Human Understanding* (1688), ed. P. Middich (Oxford University Press, Oxford, 1975), Bk II, ch. 27.
3  J. Butler, *First Dissertation to the Analogy of Religion* (W. Gladstone, London, 1921).
4  William James, *Principles of Psychology* (Henry Holt, New York, 1890), vol. 1, ch. 3.
5  J.-P. Sartre, *Being and Nothingness. An Essay on Phenomenological Ontology*, tr. Hazel Barnes (Hutchinson, London, 1969), pp. 112, 134.

## Chapter 14   The Concept of Inner Experience

1  John Locke, *Essay Concerning Human Understanding* (1688), ed. P. Middich (Oxford University Press, Oxford, 1975), Bk III, ch. 3.
2  Ibid., ch. 2.
3  Daniel Dennett, 'Are Dreams Experiences?', in *Brainstorms: Philosophical Essays in Mind and Psychology* (Harvester Press, Brighton, 1978), pp. 130ff.
4  Norman Malcolm, *Dreaming* (Routledge and Kagan Paul, London, 1959).
5  Dennett, 'Are Dreams Experiences?', p. 143.
6  Sigmund Freud, *A General Introduction to Psychoanalysis* (Norton, Garden City, N.Y., 1943), p. 76.
7  See Thomas Nagel, 'What is it like to be a Bat?', *Philosophical Review*, 83 (1974), pp. 435–51.
8  Dennett, *Brainstorms*, p. 149.

## Chapter 15   The Nature of Choice

1  Aristotle, *Nicomachean Ethics*, Bk II. *Aristotle's Ethics*, trans. J. Ackrill (Faber, London, 1973).

2  Sartre, *Being and Nothingness. An Essay on Phenomenological ontology*, tr. Hazel Barnes (Philosophical Library Inc., N.Y., 1956), pp. 59–61.
3  Ibid., p. 293.
4  Ronald Blythe, *The View in Winter* (Allen Lane, London, 1979), p. 37.
5  Ibid., p. 227.
6  Charles Lamb, 'The Superannuated Man', in *Selected English Essays*, ed. W. Peacock. World's Classics (Oxford University Press, Oxford, 1903), p. 93.

# Index

Note: capital roman numerals denote chapter references